The All-American Crew

A True Story of a World War II Bomber and the Men Who Flew It

RUSSELL N. LOW

Bob Livingstone, technical advisor

CRAVEN STREET BOOKS

Fresno, California

The All-American Crew
Copyright © 2022 by Russell N. Low
All rights reserved.

Published by Craven Street Books
An imprint of Linden Publishing®
2006 South Mary Street, Fresno, California 93721
(559) 233-6633 / (800) 345-4447
CravenStreetBooks.com

Craven Street Books and Colophon are trademarks of
Linden Publishing, Inc.

ISBN 978-0-941936-13-2

135798642
Printed in the United States of America
on acid-free paper.

Library of Congress Cataloging-in-Publication Data

Names: Low, Russell N., author. | Livingstone, Bob, 1948- technical
    advisor.
Title: The All-American crew : a true story of a World War II bomber and
    the men who flew it / Russell N. Low ; Bob Livingstone, technical
    advisor.
Description: Fresno, California : Craven Street Books, [2022] | Includes
    bibliographical references and index.
Identifiers: LCCN 2021046600 (print) | LCCN 2021046601 (ebook) | ISBN
    9780941936132 (paperback) | ISBN 9781610353885 (epub)
Subjects: LCSH: United States. Army Air Forces. Bombardment Group,
    90th--Biography. | Flight crews--United States--Biography. | B-24
    bomber. | World War, 1939-1945--Campaigns--Pacific Area. | World War,
    1939-1945--Aerial operations, American. | World War,
    1939-1945--Participation, Chinese American. | World War,
    1939-1945--Regimental histories--United States.
Classification: LCC D790.253 90th .L69 2022 (print) | LCC D790.253 90th
    (ebook) | DDC 940.54/49730922 [B]--dc23
LC record available at https://lccn.loc.gov/2021046600
LC ebook record available at https://lccn.loc.gov/2021046601

PRAISE FOR *THE ALL-AMERICAN CREW*

"*The All-American Crew* is not just a great read. It is an experience. Russell Low's talent as a writer and storyteller and his description of aerial gunners allow the reader to feel the hard G pullouts and the recoil of the machine guns, smell the burned powder, and feel the hot cartridge cases falling on his feet. It brought back memories and the feelings and smells of catapulting off the ship heading for Saipan, the distinctive odor when we were over land, and the powerful nostalgia."
—Andy Winnegar, former ARM2/C, Composite Squadron Four (VC-4), *USS White Plains* (CVE 66), and recipient of the Distinguished Flying Cross and seven Air Medals for his service over Saipan in World War II

"So awesomely real, from conveying family conversations and interactions to describing flying and gunnery training situations and aerial combat engagements. This is a book for young and old and a book for families. The incidents and stories within the book are well documented and substantiated with real postcards, letters, and photos of the time. What stands out for us today is the full blending, integration, and assimilation of the crew, whether on the town, in training, or in combat—truly an all-American crew. And it's heartwarming to learn in the epilogue about the postwar life of these all-American heroes."
—William S. Chen, major general, US Army, retired

"Russell Low's *The All-American Crew* is remarkable from many perspectives. Low is a talented storyteller who has woven engaging family tales into a greater American story of ten men from different lives and backgrounds who went to war and bonded into a tight crew, symbolic of an America that is uniquely able to forge strength from diversity."
—Ted Gong, executive director and founder, 1882 Foundation

"Russell N. Low captures the essence of diversity that defines what it means to be an American. He skillfully brings the crew together and brings to life the effects of the war on their families before, during, and after the war."
—Bob Tupa, 90th Bomb Group Association

"*The All-American Crew* is a remarkable, well-researched invitation into the fascinating lives of World War II heroes. Russell Low blends historical events with intriguing family history to spin a fresh story that will appeal to history buffs as well as readers who simply enjoy good literature."
—Zohreh Ghahremani, author of *Sky of Red Poppies*

"Like a sculptor, Russ Low brilliantly connects the reader to a past that is raw, powerfully impressive, and unforgettable. No doubt Russ Low is an exceptional storyteller. In this well-researched book, some of the characters who served the nation in World War II will remain etched in memory and heart. This story belongs to the movie theaters!"
—Tererai Trent, author of *The Awakened Woman*, speaker, scholar, and humanitarian

"Russell N. Low's *The All-American Crew* is an achievement in intimate storytelling. The narrative brings the reader along as a diverse group of Americans form a fighting unit. We sense the great range of emotion only conflict can evoke, from triumph to tragedy. *The All-American Crew* is deeply personal, yet as epic as its World War II context. It is a family history not only of young men who fought together as a bomber crew but of America."
—Phil Scearce, author of *Finish Forty and Home: The Untold World War II Story of B-24s in the Pacific*

CONTENTS

PART II: Saipan:
Aviation Engineers and Flying Leathernecks

PART III: The Aftermath

*B-24 Liberator, Maxwell Field, Alabama. Green
camouflage paint has been stripped.
Public domain. Wikimedia Commons.*

*Jungle python in the Southwest Pacific.
Courtesy of Bob J. Tupa.*

In Memoriam

Corky Lee, 1947–2021

A photojournalist who used his camera as a "sword to combat indifference, injustice and discrimination while trying to get rid of stereotypes."[1]

✳✳✳

Joseph Rotenberg, 1949–2021

Author, scholar, storyteller, and one full of life and joy. Joe shared my fascination with the World War II stories of our parents' generation.

1 Raymond Chong, "Corky Lee—In Pursuit of Photographic Justice," AsAmNews.com, October 10, 2020.

DEDICATION

The All-American Crew is dedicated to the sixteen million American men and women who served our nation in World War II, and most especially to the 407,000 Americans who gave their lives protecting our freedoms and to the 72,000 Americans who to this day remain missing in action.

PREFACE

They did not intend to be heroes and would not welcome the description. They came from every walk of American life. Many came from some of the oldest families in America, who first set foot on the soil of colonial Virginia and Massachusetts in the 1600s. Others came from families that migrated to America in the 1800s from Ireland, Scotland, Germany, Austria, and China during the tremendous wave of immigration that built this country. They were the sons of farmers, oil company engineers, cotton brokers, garment industry workers, and Chinese laundrymen. These ten young men were a mix of college graduates and those who did not have time to finish high school before the war called them. They were the privileged and the downtrodden poor. They all had dreams that were put on hold. Each was driven by a patriotic fervor that was only matched by his love of flying. In truth, this group of young men could only have been formed in America. They were the best that America had to offer, and each was willing to sacrifice everything for the country he loved. This type of all-consuming patriotism inspired America then, just as it inspires us today.

Here is a toast to the all-American crew and to the hundreds of thousands of other young men and women who put their lives on the line for our freedom. We are their legacy.

PART I

THE ALL-AMERICAN CREW: LIBERATORS AND PYTHONS IN THE NEW GUINEA JUNGLE

CHAPTER 1

A PILGRIMAGE TO THE MISSION HOME

1942

The cold, damp breeze blew across Stanley's face as he trudged up Nob Hill. He felt the crumpled paper in his right coat pocket with the address his mother had made him memorize: 920 Sacramento Street, San Francisco. It was a typical June afternoon, with hazy sunshine failing to warm the fog-shrouded City by the Bay.

Why am I doing this? I have better things . . . His thoughts were interrupted by two boys who saluted Stanley as he passed.

"Hello, boys! Do you know where Cameron House is?"

"Yes, sir! We can take you there. Are you going to fight in the war?" they asked, wide-eyed, admiring Stanley's crisply pressed olive uniform, garrison cap, and perfectly polished regulation brown shoes.

The boys were the same, yet different. Both had straight jet-black hair, wide cheekbones, almond-shaped eyes, and the dark-brown skin of their ancestors and Stanley's. One was dressed in an army helmet and fatigues, and smartly carried a miniature rifle over his right shoulder as he stood at attention. The other was dressed in jeans and a red-and-white-checkered shirt, looking at his friend with envy and then at Stanley in awe.

Clifford Stanley Low (1922–1943) and his mother, Kay Low, in Los Angeles prior to Stanley going overseas (1942). Courtesy of the Low family.

"At ease, men. What are your names and ranks?" Stanley inquired with a slight smile.

"I'm Willie, and I'm a sergeant," the boy with the rifle replied promptly.

The other boy looked up at Stanley, quietly sizing him up before announcing, "I have a gun, too. It's big, but I don't have any real bullets."

"What's your name?"

"I'm Rusty, and I don't have a rank. You wait here. I'll be right back." Turning to his friend, Rusty continued, "You guard him, Willie. Don't let him go! Promise!"

Willie stood in front of Stanley with his rifle ready. "You stay right there, mister!"

Rusty ran across the street, up a flight of wooden stairs leading to a second-floor apartment. The screen door flew open and slammed shut as Rusty disappeared into the building.

"Where's your friend going, Willie?"

"You wait right there and don't talk! You're my prisoner!"

"I can't wait too long. My unit is shipping out soon. I'm going to miss the war if we don't get a move on."

Willie looked nervously at Rusty's apartment, trying to will his friend to appear. Just then, Rusty came bursting through the screen door and jumped down the flight of stairs in two strides. He was dressed in fatigues and an oversize army helmet, with an ammunition belt draped over his right shoulder. A revolver completed Rusty's transformation from civilian boy to fighting GI.

"OK, now march!" Willie ordered as he and Rusty followed Stanley up Sacramento Street with their guns drawn.

"It's not far," Rusty reassured his prisoner.

The odd trio continued up Nob Hill, passing the First Chinese Baptist Church. Stanley paused and looked down Waverly Place, wondering if he could find the barbershop where his grandparents had met. It was all legend to him, but he had grown up hearing the stories of his grandmother, Ah Ying, and how she had outrun and outwitted the Tong highbinders who kidnapped her from her honeymoon apartment. She had died the year before Stanley was born in 1922, but the stories about Grandma Ah Ying kept her alive. Still, he always felt a bit cheated that his four sisters and five brothers knew Grandma, while all he had were the stories about a Chinatown legend.

No time for stories now. *The war is calling, but first, I have to do this thing at Cameron House for Mother,* Stanley mused.

Just before Joice Street, the boys stopped in front of a brick building on the right side of Sacramento, originally the Occidental Mission Home for Girls, now known as Cameron House. Stanley inspected the odd, deformed, and discolored bricks jutting out from the walls at angles.

His sisters had told him about these clinker bricks, reused from

San Francisco's Presbyterian Occidental Mission Home. Photograph courtesy of Karen Barnett.

buildings destroyed by the 1906 earthquake.[1]

"We Chinese don't ever waste anything," his father had lectured the family before he passed away in 1925 in Salem, Oregon, leaving his young wife to care for nine children.[2]

I doubt Father was talking about bricks, Stanley said to himself, *but who knows.*

Willie rapped on the large oak door. *Rap! Rap! Rap!*

The door creaked open, and a young Chinese girl peered out. "Oh,

---

1   Over many decades, the Presbyterian Occidental Mission Home, founded in 1874, rescued thousands of young Chinese women and girls from human traffickers.
2   The second son, Arthur, died in 1915 when he was four years old.

*Robert C. Chinn.
Courtesy of the
Chinn family.*

another soldier, I see. Come in, but you'll have to wait in the parlor. There is a lineup of soldiers waiting to visit Lo Mo."

She opened the door wide, allowing them to enter. "Willie, Rusty, leave your guns outside! You know Lo Mo's rules."

The boys hid their weapons on the porch behind a stack of crates. "No one better steal these. We'll need them to patrol the streets."

"Who is Lo Mo?" Stanley inquired. "I'm supposed to meet Miss Cameron."

The girl smiled. "She is one and the same. Lo Mo is our mother, Miss Cameron. Now, take a seat with the other soldiers."

Stanley sat down next to another Chinese boy dressed in a khaki Army uniform, holding his cap in his hand and reading. The wooden chair creaked under Stanley's 145 pounds. Stanley was tall and slender, but the old chair had seen better days in decades of use at the Mission Home.

The soldier looked up, greeting Stanley. "Hi. I'm Robert Chinn," he said as he extended a hand.

"I'm Stanley Low." He took Robert's hand. "Who are all these guys?"

"Beats me. They're pretty quiet, but I guess we're all here for the pilgrimage," Robert replied with a smile. "What's your story?"

"I'm headed for basic training at Sheppard Field in Texas."

"No. I mean, what's your connection to this place?"

"My grandmother stayed here for a few years."

"Your grandmother! Wow! Mine too! She must be really old. When was that, anyway? My grandma, Alice Louie Lamb, stayed here around 1900. I thought that was old. When was your grandmother here?"

"Not really sure, but it must have been even earlier, a really long time ago, like before they had lights and indoor plumbing, maybe."

For a moment, the room of soldiers fell quiet. Stanley looked down at his cap, crumpled by his hands. He smoothed it out on his lap, hoping the others hadn't noticed. Stanley felt something brush his cheek. He turned to greet the new arrival, but the seat next to him was empty. The soft footsteps running up the stairs and young girls' giggles

The stairway of Cameron House, at 920 Sacramento Street in San Francisco. Photograph by Cindy Yee.

coming from the landing drew his attention away from the empty chair. He looked up. The landing was silent and still.

"Did you hear that, Robert?"

"What?"

"Those girls running up the stairs laughing."

"Nope! You must be losing it, Stan."

Stanley sank in his chair but couldn't stop looking back up the stairs. "Maybe I am losing it," he muttered to himself. Stanley's musings were interrupted.

"Here, have a look at my girl," Robert said, holding out his wallet. "Her name is Janet. We got engaged last December."

"Wow! She's a swell-looking girl," Stanley said. "It must have been your uniform she fell for, Robert," he added with a smile. "When's the wedding?"

"Middle of August. If you're still stateside, you are definitely invited!"

Donaldina Cameron (1869–1968). Public domain.

"I'll probably be learning how to shoot a .50-caliber Browning machine gun around then at Harlingen Air Force Base, but I'll be thinking about you and Janet."

Suddenly, a young Chinese girl came down the oak staircase from the second floor. "You two can come up now," she said, pointing at Stanley and Robert.

Stanley and Robert rose and followed the girl up the curved staircase to the second-floor office of Donaldina Cameron. As they entered the office, a tall, white-haired woman rose and extended her hand, greeting both boys with a mother's warmth and compassion.

"Stanley and Robert. Thank you for coming to visit me. Both of you are part of our Mission Home family and God's family." Her handshake was firm, and her smile filled the room. "Now, sit and tell me about your families."

Donaldina listened intently, glad to hear the details of the lives of two women who had found a new life at the Presbyterian Occidental Mission Home for Girls. Robert told the story of his grandmother's life in Butte, Montana, with her husband, Dr. Wah Jen Lamb, and their ten children. Robert brought out a framed photo that he presented to Donaldina.

"This small gift is a token of my family's deep appreciation of the new life and home you gave my grandmother, Alice Louie Lamb."

Holding the photo like a precious jewel, Donaldina exclaimed, "Ah Oie and her children are exquisite. God clearly had a plan for this young woman. I will treasure this photograph always, Robert."

Stanley next recounted the memorized details of his grandmother Ah Ying's life after her time at the Mission Home. He listed her five children, including Mother and his aunts and uncles. Stanley described in more detail his nine siblings in Salem, Oregon, the children of Ah Ying's eldest daughter, Kay.

"My goodness, ten children in both families!" Donaldina exclaimed. "Each of your families is another one of God's miracles. Stanley, your grandmother, Ah Ying, was our sewing teacher at the Home for several years before the earthquake in 1906. The girls always said that she

Alice Louie Lamb and her children in Butte, Montana. Courtesy of Valerie Tawa, Chinn family collection.

was the best with the needle and thread. It was part of God's plan that Ah Ying returned to us."

"What do you mean?" Stanley asked quietly.

"Well, my predecessor, Maggie Culbertson, used to call her Little Runaway Ah Ying!" Donaldina laughed. "Here, let me show you the logbook. It tells your grandmother's story."

She pulled out an old logbook and opened it to page 100. The handwritten entries were written in cursive.

"See, on September 6, 1886, Mr. Nathaniel Hunter and Reverend Daniel Vrooman brought Sun Choie to the Home. She was so small that Maggie thought she was only twelve years old. I think she was really about fifteen years old. She had been held captive at 611 Jackson Street as a child slave by cruel owners who mistreated her. She wanted to take the name Ah Gew but later changed her name to Ah Ying."

Stanley read the handwritten entries one by one. They told the story of his grandmother's rescue, elopement, kidnapping, habeas corpus court trial, and eventual marriage by Justice of the Peace Hebbard in May 1889.

"So, all those stories about my grandmother are true?"

"I am not sure what they told you, but your grandmother was a very determined young woman. She knew her own mind and never let anyone get in her way. I think that her spirit and God's grace eventually brought her back to our Mission Home."

Turning to Robert, Donaldina continued, "Your grandmother, Ah Oie, was every bit as determined. I was here the day she ran away from her cruel owners on Prospect Place and came to the Home on her own, seeking protection. Here's the entry on page 218. It was in the afternoon of April 22, 1895, when little eleven-year-old Ah Oie showed up at our doorstep. Her owners came to retrieve her that evening, demanding that she be returned, but she refused to go with them. It actually says she stoutly refused! Several years later, Ah Oie

Presbyterian Mission Home registry of inmates entry of Ah Ying, aka Ah Gew.
September 1886. Courtesy of Cameron House.

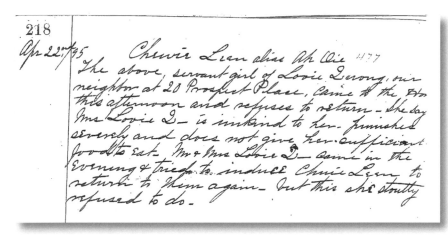

Presbyterian Mission Home registry of inmates entry for Ah Oie. April 1895. Courtesy of Cameron House.

was married to your grandfather right here in the Presbyterian Mission Home."

Remembering the purpose of his visit, Stanley reached into his jacket pocket and pulled out the small gift his mother had prepared for Miss Cameron.

"This is a small token of our family's undying gratitude to you and the Mission Home. You gave my grandmother and our family a new life in America," Stanley recited, just as his mother and sisters had instructed.

Jade and pearl earrings. Courtesy of the Low family.

Donaldina accepted the gift, opening the package to reveal a small pair of jade and pearl earrings. They were identical replicas of the pair that Ah Ying's mother had given her in 1880, and that she later passed on to her daughter, Kay, on her wedding day in 1903.

"These are so precious, Stanley. Please tell your mother that I will always treasure these earrings, and I will always remember how you boys took time to visit me before your trip overseas."

Beaming, Stanley and Robert stood and turned to leave. "Thank you, Miss Culbertson, I mean Miss Cameron," Stanley stammered.

"Maggie and I both wish you boys well. May you find peace and safety in God's hands, now and forever."

Donaldina looked out the window and watched the two young men in uniform walking back down Sacramento Street with Willie and Rusty trailing behind.

There were tears in her eyes and a foreboding sadness in her heart that only a mother sending her sons off to war can fully understand.

CHAPTER 2

GUNNERY SCHOOL AND WEDDINGS

JULY–AUGUST 1942

The three-year-old Union Station in downtown Los Angeles was packed with recruits headed to points unknown. Up to a hundred troop trains departed every day, taking young men from every walk of life on a journey from which some would not return. For many, it was their first trip away from home. The mission revival and art deco building on North Alameda Street was an architectural masterpiece that was hardly noticed by the thousands of young soldiers, whose upbeat, save-the-world bravado masked the butterflies and loneliness each felt.

Remembering the day, Stanley could still taste the dim sum. His friends from the produce market in Woodland had insisted on driving him down from Northern California. The trip in Bill Gong's 1932 Ford roadster with a flat-top V-8 engine had been an adventure. With a top speed of sixty-five miles per hour, the roadster ate up the 380 miles in no time. Wally Gee and George Din had insisted on treating Stan to a "last meal" in LA's Chinatown.

"Oops! I didn't mean the last meal. I meant your last Chinese meal!" George corrected.

Union Station, Los Angeles, California. Courtesy of Security Pacific National Bank Collection / Los Angeles Public Library.

Stan laughed. "No matter. Chinese food is always good. It's probably safer there anyway. No one will mistake us for Japanese guys and try to start a fight."

"We're not afraid of some white boys," Bill said, puffing out his chest. "Besides, we can outrun them in this jalopy."

The meal was surprisingly quiet. The boys were famished, but their silence was born from the knowledge of where their friend was going. Each silently knew that they might never see Stan again on this side.

The waiter at the five-story, neon-encrusted Golden Pagoda restaurant approached the boys at the end of their meal.

Looking directly at Stanley in his wrinkled, olive-drab Army uniform, he proclaimed, "This one's on the house. You go over there and fight good for all of us!"

"Thanks, mister," Stanley replied sheepishly.

Bill, George, and Wally rose and crowded around Stan, clapping him on the back.

"See, Stan, you're already being treated like a war hero!"

"Leave me alone, guys."

"This is your life, Stan. Get used to it. Free food and dames draped all over you," Wally gushed enviously.

"That uniform just kills the girls," Bill said. "Make the most of it, Stan, my man!"

"No! No free girls here! You go now before I get in trouble," the waiter shouted, shoving the boys toward the door.

A few minutes later, Bill pulled up to Union Station.

Golden Pagoda Restaurant, Los Angeles Chinatown. Postcard. Courtesy of the Low family.

"Give 'em hell, Stan!"

"Yeah! Show 'em how real men fight!"

"You'll have this whole mess straightened out in no time and be back for Christmas!"

Stan, quiet as always, embraced his three best friends. "Sure thing, guys. See you at Christmas."

Walking toward the station, Stan did not turn around but held the image of his three friends in his mind as he entered his new world of Army-issued olive drab.

Stanley Low and friends in Ford roadster with rumble seat. Courtesy of the Low family.

* * *

The 480-mile train trip from Los Angeles to Tucson took Stanley the farthest he had ever been from home. Each of the seventeen hours took him farther and farther from Salem, Oregon, and his mother. After a sleepless night, Stanley stared out the window as the train rolled on through the Sonoran Desert with its reds and greens and magnificent saguaro cacti. It was the first of many new worlds that Stanley was to experience.

Remembering his promise to write his mother every day, Stan pulled out the postcards he'd purchased at the last stop, picked up a pencil, and pondered how to begin. He addressed the card to Mrs. Kay Low, Rt 2 Box 258, Salem, Oregon. Just then, the train started to slow as it approached the station. Stan quickly dashed out his first card home.

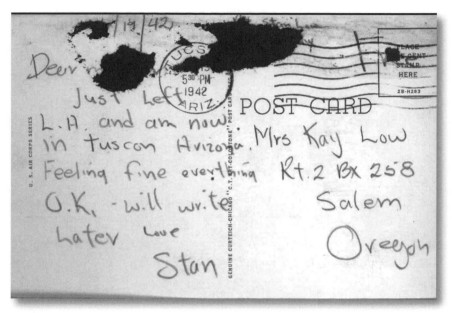

Clifford Stanley Low's first postcard, June 19, 1942. Courtesy of the Low family.

* * *

In a lifetime of three weeks, Stan and nineteen thousand other recruits entered, toiled through, and graduated from basic training at Sheppard Airfield on the barren prairie north of Wichita Falls, Texas, four hours east of Amarillo. Stan was one of half a million young men who would pass through the gates of Sheppard Field during World War II.

Today, July 12, 1942, was the day that determined his fate and future in the United States Army Air Corps. Stan looked at the sealed orders, turning them over, inspecting the packet, hoping to glean a hint of its contents. Stan wanted to fly, but he could just as easily end up as a cook's assistant. Finally, unable to wait any longer, he tore open the envelope, unfolded the document, and read its contents.

"Pfc. Clifford Stanley Low is ordered to report to Harlingen Aerial Gunnery School."

Stan let out a gleeful "Hurrah!" and then immediately became aware of the dozens of other recent graduates surrounding him with their assignments in hand.

"What did you get, Stan?"

"I'm going to Harlingen for gunnery training," Stan replied, unable to suppress a huge smile. "What assignment did you get, Earl?"

"Hey! You're looking at another red-hot gunner, Stan! I'm going to Harlingen with you!"

"No way! We're both going to be getting our wings? That's incredible."

Earl Byrd was a year older than Stan and was from Bryson City, North Carolina, in Swain County. Earl was the very first person Stan had ever met who spoke with a Southern accent. The boys loved to argue about which one of them had the accent. They both dreamed of flying. Since neither had gone to college, becoming a pilot, copilot, or navigator was out. Being a gunner got them into the sky just the same.

"I can't wait to shoot down some Zekes!"[1] Earl exclaimed, pumping his fist in the air. "And just in case I run out of ammo, I'll have my Colt .45 strapped to my leg!"

Stan laughed at his friend's bravado. Stan didn't show it, but he felt an all-consuming sense of pride just the same.

"With your Colt .45, we'll have this thing over by Christmas, Earl." Stan laughed as he recalled Wally's words and the taste of the dim sum at the Golden Pagoda. The three weeks since he'd left behind civilian life and Los Angeles might as well have been an eternity.

Harlingen, Texas, was six hundred miles due south of Sheppard Field via Fort Worth, Austin, and San Antonio. Col. John R. Morgan was the first commanding officer of the Harlingen Aerial Gunnery School, having arrived in August 1941. The first class of six hundred students—120 every week—had completed the five-week course and gone on to fight in the European and the Pacific theaters. By the time Stan and Earl arrived in July 1942, the demand for more gunners had increased the number of students to 188 per week. That number would rise to 475 gunners per week by November 1943. The five thousand

---

1   "Zeke" was the American code name for the Mitsubishi A6M Zero.

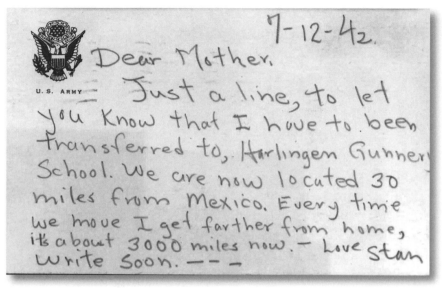

7-12-42.

Dear Mother,

Just a line, to let you know that I have to been transferred to, Harlingen Gunnery School. We are now located 30 miles from Mexico. Every time we move I get farther from home, its about 3000 miles now. — Love Stan

Write soon. — - —

Postcard from Clifford Stanley Low dated July 7, 1942. Courtesy of the Low family.

gunnery school graduates in 1942 were dwarfed by the fifteen thousand graduates just a year later in 1943.

Tech Sgt. Eldred Scott, a veteran gunner of the Doolittle Raid over Tokyo, greeted the new group of excited aerial gunnery students with a scowl that hid his amusement.

"So, you think you can shoot straight? I'll bet some of you country bumpkins think firing a .50-caliber machine gun is just like shooting squirrels back home in Arkansas, or wherever you pieces of shit come from!"

Not wanting or expecting an answer, he continued, growling, "Well, it's not! And if you don't pay attention and learn the difference, you are going to end up dead and coming home to your mother in a box! You got it?"

The silence was deafening as the men shuffled uneasily. "I said, you got it?!"

"Yes, sir!" they shouted in unison.

"That's better. Now, just remember this one thing, and you'll do all right."

The men stood motion-less, silently waiting to learn the key to aerial gunnery and their survival.

"Never ever shoot at the enemy!" Scott paused for effect and then continued. "Shoot at where the enemy is going to be.

"Lead, gravity, and quick reflexes, boys. These suckers are going to be coming at you out of the sun at four hundred miles per hour. If you hesitate or if you mis-calculate the angle, the dis-tance, the speed, or the effect of gravity, you and your crew will end up dead!

"And one more thing, in your panic—and you will be panicked—do not shoot down your friends!"

Earl Byrd, 1942. Courtesy of the Byrd family.

* * *

"Earl, what flight did you get assigned to?" Stan asked as they headed for the mess hall.

"Same as you, Stan. We both got TSgt. Scott for an instructor. Heaven help us!"

"Amen, to that, Earl. He's going to eat us alive and spit out the bones."

Later that morning, the twelve men in TSgt. Scott's flight stood at attention on the flight line as Scott introduced them to their weapon of choice.

"This here is your best friend. Treat her well, and she will keep you and your crew alive," Scott growled as he held up the .50-caliber Browning automatic machine gun.

"But you don't get my gun. You get this!" Scott smiled, pointing to a pile of parts on the ground. "That's your gun over there. When you learn how to put it together, then you can practice shooting it."

"You will have to become intimate friends with this gun. You will learn each part and know it like the back of your hand: bolt, barrel, cover plate, lever, slide, spring, pin, and stud. You will learn how to take the gun apart and put it together again, blindfolded. Now get to it!"

The men were perplexed, picking up each piece and turning it over, trying to fit the pieces together. It was hopeless.

Finally, Earl came forward, smiling. "It's easy, boys. She's just like a really big semiautomatic hunting rifle. Where I come from, we like our guns," Earl purred in his best Carolina drawl.

In no time flat, Earl had the Browning machine gun assembled. In turn, he taught each man in his flight how to quickly assemble the machine gun.

"Not bad, Pvt. Byrd. I see you know your way around an automatic machine gun. By tomorrow, I want you to have these men ready to do that blindfolded.

"Now, let's go to the indoor range and practice shooting."

As they entered the range, Scott handed each man a small BB gun.

"What's this for? I thought we were in gunnery school."

"You will learn the principles of shooting at moving targets on this range," Scott said, pointing at the small dark planes moving right to left at the end of the range. "You will learn to aim ahead of your target."

"Now gather around, and let me tell you what's going to happen in the next five weeks. Once you master this BB gun range, we'll go outdoors to the skeet range, where you'll shoot twelve-gauge shotguns. By then, tracking and leading the target will be instinctive.

"Next, we'll let you fire a .50-caliber machine gun, but I guarantee it won't work. Your first experience firing a machine gun will be on the malfunction range. Each time your gun jams and stops firing, you will have to figure out what's wrong and quickly fix it.

"You'll spend some evenings cleaning and repairing machine guns from other flights. You are going to come to know each machine gun better than your own mother.

"Studying enemy silhouettes may be the most crucial skill for you to learn. In a split second, you will have to accurately identify the airplane in your sight. If you shoot down a friendly, your career as a gunner is finished.

"Now, who knows the four key elements of accurate shooting?" Not waiting for an answer, Scott continued, "Estimation of the range of an enemy aircraft, determining its relative speed, giving it the right lead, and harmonizing the gun with the sight. This must all happen in a few seconds. If you pause or if you are wrong, you may end up dead.

"Remember, men: You fire your gun along a straight line, but gravity will cause your bullet to drop below the target. So, to compensate, the gun must be pointed up. Then the bullet will drop into the target.

"Next, you will learn how to operate and fire your machine gun from a moving, power-driven turret. Resist the temptation to be a Hollywood gunner and fire at everything in sight. These guns fire 850 bullets per minute at 2,950 feet per second. Not only will you run out of ammo, but the bullets also generate so much heat they'll melt the barrel! Fire your .50-caliber gun in short, accurate bursts. Got it?

"Finally, after all of that, if you haven't washed out, we'll take you up in a plane and have you practice shooting at a target being towed by another plane. If we like you, we'll give you a parachute.

"Remember, these bombers fly in cold, thin air at high altitude. You must be constantly alert, ready to spot and shoot down the enemy before he does the same to you and your crew. The lives of your crew depend on you and your big guns."

Stan and Earl looked at each other, shaking their heads at this whirlwind preview of their next five weeks of gunnery training.

* * *

The daily progress sheets recorded each student's score hour by hour. By the end of the third week, Stan and Earl were at the top of their flight. Years of experience hunting in the backwoods with his brother Clyde made shooting a moving target second nature for Earl.

"Don't tell Scott, but this gunnery stuff is a lot like shooting rabbits back home in the Carolina Smokies. We just use bigger guns and ammo," Earl whispered to Stan as they put on their flight suit and parachute, preparing for the in-flight gunnery practice.

Stan only had a little practice firing a hunting rifle with his big brother Gwunde on the farm in Salem, Oregon. But sighting a moving target and making the mental calculations about distance, speed, and lead all seemed natural to Stan. He was in his element, firing these machine guns.

"But you, Stan, how do you do it? I don't think you've done much

North American AT-6 Texan, used for gunnery practice. US Air Force photograph. Public domain.

hunting, but you never seem to miss," Earl marveled.

"I can't explain it, Earl. It just feels right. I see it all happening. Sometimes it all slows down, and I can picture the moving target and the bullets' path through the air as they rip through the target. I am sure it won't be this easy with real Zekes shooting back at us."

"You got that right, Stan."

Stan and Earl climbed into the North American AT-6 Texan plane's back seat, each wearing a flight suit, leather helmet, goggles, and parachute. Stan mounted his .50-caliber machine gun and took a few practice swings peering at a distant target through the reflective optical sight.

Once airborne, the four planes flew in formation, with two bogey planes towing targets. Stan's plane was piloted by Lt. Cole, who had been assigned to the young student to see how well he did with live action and a target moving in three dimensions. The bogey planes took off, climbing toward the sun and cloud cover.

"Keep a sharp lookout, Pvt. Low. It's your job to spot the enemy first. Don't let him get the jump on us."

"Yes, sir," Stan replied with his eyes peeled, looking for any speck in the distance that might be one of the bogey planes.

"Call out the enemy when you spot them, and I'll take evasive maneuvers. Remember, shoot at the target and not the tow plane, Pvt. Low."

The wind was violent, and the noise of the plane was deafening. Stan strained to pick up the enemy planes with the wind crushing his face and pressing the goggles into his eyes.

Suddenly, he spotted a dark speck overhead.

"Bogey overhead at ten o'clock."

Lt. Cole had seen the bogey and was ready to evade and attack. He banked the plane to the right and dove for the ground. As the bogey dove down on them, it picked up speed and was closing the distance rapidly. Cole pulled back on the stick and banked to the right as the bogey flew past them. Continuing to bank hard to the right, he maneuvered his plane behind the bogey, which was now the target.

"Low, sight him and take him out!" Cole yelled, forgetting protocol.

Stan already had the target in his sight. He knew the distance and speed. He aimed in front of the target, calculated the drop, and fired a burst from the machine gun.

The destruction of the target was instantaneous and complete. It was shredded.[2]

"Nicely done, Pvt. Low. We'll go in search of the other bogey now."

Stan smiled and kept his eyes peeled for the second bogey, but it was nowhere in sight. Earl had similar success hunting his bogey that morning, destroying the target with a single burst from his machine gun.

On the ground, TSgt. Scott had been briefed and approached Stan and Earl as they stowed their parachutes and machine guns.

"Good shooting, men. Keep it up, but we may have to separate you two, so the other men can get some practice shooting aerial targets," Scott laughed. "But don't get too cocky. You still have a lot to learn about gunnery tactics."

Stan and Earl smiled and accepted the praise in silence. "Did you hear what he said, Stan?"

"Yep, and that man is a true gunner's legend."

* * *

On Monday, August 10, 1942, the thirty-second and largest class ever graduated from Harlingen Aerial Gunnery School lined up on the flight line. Maj. Gen. Barton K. Yount, commanding general of the Flying Training Command, addressed them with pride.

"You are the men who will write the history of World War II in blazing gun smoke, in tracer bullets across the sky. You now wear the proud insignia of prime fighting men."

Stanley and Earl had been selected to lead their class onto the

---

2 Gunnery students fired rounds painted in different colors of ink, leaving colored rings as they hit the target. A 5 percent hit rate was required to pass.

TSgt. Eldred Scott pins Gunners Wings on SSgt Clifford S. Low of Salem, Oregon. 1942. Courtesy of the Low family.

stage where TSgt. Eldred Scott stood at attention in front of a huge American flag. Each gunner's name was announced.

"Sgt. Clifford S. Low."

Stan looked up and felt Earl give him a nudge. "Go on, Stan. We earned this. Get up there."

Stan walked across the stage and stood at attention, looking straight ahead.

"You did good, Stanley. You've become a first-class gunner. Shoot straight and make your country proud, son," Scott said as he pinned the gunner wings onto Stan's Army uniform.

"Thank you, TSgt. Scott," Stan replied as reporters for the *Valley Morning Star* took photos of the young Chinese American boy and the Doolittle Raid war hero.

As he left the stage, a reporter approached Stan. "What's your name, son, and where are you from?"

"Sgt. Clifford S. Low, Salem, Oregon, sir."

"No. I mean, where are you from originally?"

"I was born in Salem, Oregon, sir."

"You know what I mean. What country are you from anyway?"

Stan smiled as he realized what the reporter was asking. "I'm an American, sir. My father was born in China. But I am as American as you or any of these men, who are prepared to fight and die for their country."

The reporter scribbled furiously and then hurried off, searching for a few more quotes to write his story. He already had a title in mind: "Graduates of Gunnery School Receive First Wings; Heroes Aid in Ceremony."

Stan, Earl, and the rest of the thirty-second class of the Harlingen Aerial Gunnery School were the first gunners to receive aviators' wings in the history of the Army Air Corps. That morning, the pride of these flying fighters was enough to lift up an entire nation.

* * *

The evening's mail brought Stan news of a celebration of another kind.

Robert and Janet Chinn on their wedding day outside the Old First Presbyterian Church in San Francisco, August 1942. Courtesy of Bob Chinn.

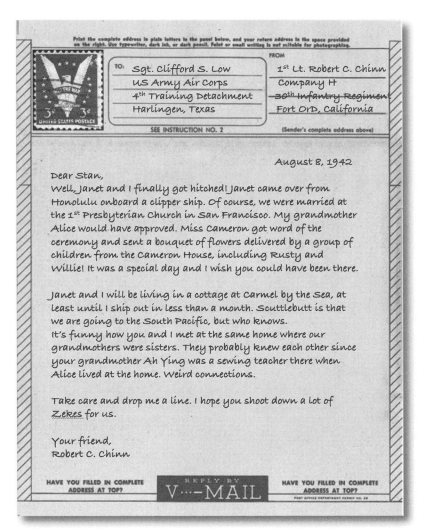

Print the complete address in plain letters in the panel below, and your return address in the space provided on the right. Use typewriter, dark ink, or dark pencil. Faint or small writing is not suitable for photographing.

TO: Sgt. Clifford S. Low
US Army Air Corps
4th Training Detachment
Harlingen, Texas

FROM
1st Lt. Robert C. Chinn
Company H
~~30th Infantry Regiment~~
Fort Ord, California

SEE INSTRUCTION NO. 2   (Sender's complete address above)

August 8, 1942

Dear Stan,

Well, Janet and I finally got hitched! Janet came over from Honolulu onboard a clipper ship. Of course, we were married at the 1st Presbyterian Church in San Francisco. My grandmother Alice would have approved. Miss Cameron got word of the ceremony and sent a bouquet of flowers delivered by a group of children from the Cameron House, including Rusty and Willie! It was a special day and I wish you could have been there.

Janet and I will be living in a cottage at Carmel by the Sea, at least until I ship out in less than a month. Scuttlebutt is that we are going to the South Pacific, but who knows. It's funny how you and I met at the same home where our grandmothers were sisters. They probably knew each other since your grandmother Ah Ying was a sewing teacher there when Alice lived at the home. Weird connections.

Take care and drop me a line. I hope you shoot down a lot of Zekes for us.

Your friend,
Robert C. Chinn

HAVE YOU FILLED IN COMPLETE ADDRESS AT TOP?   REPLY BY V---MAIL   HAVE YOU FILLED IN COMPLETE ADDRESS AT TOP?

Letter from Robert C. Chinn, dated August 8, 1942. Courtesy of the Low family.

CHAPTER 3

AIR CORPS CADET TRAINING

JANUARY–APRIL 1942

Simultaneously, another group of young men converged on Maxwell Field, located a thousand miles to the east in Montgomery, Alabama. They were selected as aviation cadets to undergo five weeks of preflight training at the Southeast Air Corps Training Center.[1] Those who successfully passed through this program would proceed to advanced training as pilots, navigators, and bombardiers. Most had completed at least two years of college and had passed rigorous physical and academic tests.[2] The air at Maxwell Field was so thick with their desire to fly that you could cut it with a knife. Flying was their dream. Washing out was simply not an option they wanted to consider. In truth, up to 50 percent of the would-be pilots washed out between preflight school and advanced pilot training.

---

1 In 1941, 9,272 men applied for pilot training as aviation cadets. The very next year, the number of applicants exploded to 550,000, of which 52 percent were accepted.

2 Three days after the attack on Pearl Harbor, the college requirement for aviation cadets was replaced with an Army Air Force Qualification Examination designed to test intelligence and the ability to absorb training center instructions. One million men took this test; one-third of them failed it. The ban on married applicants was also removed.

The training was tough and rigorous. The indoctrination began before the cadets even set foot on Maxwell Field.

* * *

The lieutenant greeting the new cadets at the train station in Montgomery did nothing to reassure the anxious recruits.

"You worthless zombies! Line up and stand at attention!"

The men looked around, not sure what to do, waiting for the next guy to make a move.

"Are you deaf?" the lieutenant roared. "Move it!"

Scott Regan, a blond-haired boy from California, smiled, stepped forward, and snapped to attention, eyes forward. The other men quickly followed his example. Regan, educated in the Lasallian tradition at St. Mary's College High School in Northern California, was used to the Brothers' discipline, order, and focus.

"There are three rules of the Air Corps! Only three. Learn these, and you will survive. Forget or ignore them, and I guarantee you will wash out! Now, which of you zombies knows the three rules?"

Regan stepped forward again. "Yes, sir. No, sir. No excuse, sir!"

The lieutenant approached Regan. "All right, wiseass. Where are you from, zombie?"

"Oakland, California, sir."

"Well, pay attention, keep your nose clean, and maybe we won't have to send you back home to your mother!"

"Yes, sir!"

The lieutenant, looking directly at the new cadets, continued, "You will be punished for any and all infractions. Gigs will be given, and tours walked for inattention in the ranks, for sounding off, for inattention in the mess hall, for failure to obey orders, for failure to shine your shoes or tuck your shirts, or for dozens of other infractions that you can't even imagine!"

The men looked around nervously.

"Eyes forward, zombies!

Postcard of the train station in Montgomery, Alabama. Courtesy of the Low family.

"You will learn to march everywhere in formation at 140 paces a minute without breaking stride. You will learn to sit and eat in the mess hall like cadets, without talking.

"You will look, act, and think like aviation cadets. And so help me God, you will honor the uniform and code of the United States Army Air Force! Do I make myself clear?"

"Yes, sir!" they shouted in unison.

* * *

Maxwell Field had a long history in aviation, having been selected by Wilbur Wright as a flying school site in 1910. In the five-week preflight program, cadets were given intensive physical and academic training in the mechanics and physics of flight, chemical warfare, and the use of gas masks. Required courses in mathematics and science followed practical applications in aeronautics, deflection shooting, and thinking in three dimensions. The program served as a boot camp and an initial screening to eliminate those with no aptitude for flying. Over the course of the war, Maxwell Field transformed a hundred thousand aviation cadets into Army Air Force aviators.

Preflight cadets Regan, Lesser, Kerby, and Crane were unlikely friends. In any other world, they would probably never have crossed paths, let alone depended on one another for their future. In a sea of a thousand aviation cadets at Maxwell Field, they had somehow found each other. Each man's strengths perfectly complemented those of the others. Whether they would serve in the Army Air Corps as pilots, bombardiers, or navigators was about to be determined by the three-pronged Aircrew Classification Battery. The composite stanine score, based on a physical examination, a psychomotor test, and the dreaded psychological assessment, would determine their assignments.

Scott L. Regan was the natural leader, cool as a cucumber and unemotional; he was never flustered and was always in control. John Crane's love of math, science, and philosophy made him the intellectual of the group, having graduated magna cum laude from Notre Dame in 1940. Jerome Lesser was a natural athlete with boundless energy and uncanny hand-eye coordination. He possessed incredible attention to detail and a love of mechanical devices, math, and photography. His ability to communicate, lead when necessary, and make decisions would be essential. The fourth man in the group of friends, George D. Kerby, was a natural flier and a gifted writer but was less of a born leader than Regan. In the end, Kerby may have been the best student in the group.

Regan awoke on cue at 0455. The barracks were pitch-black, and the soft sound of snoring from the rows of beds was somehow comforting. He lay in his bed, hands behind his head, waiting for the raucous, staccato noise that would mark the start of another day at Maxwell Field.

"John, wake up!"

When Cadet Crane did not move, Regan reached over and shook his bed. Crane hated reveille and the shock it brought to his system every blessed morning at 0500.

Crane groaned, "Another day? It's still dark out there. I just got to sleep."

Just as he pulled the covers over his head, the blasted and incessant reveille bugle filled the air. The men all groaned in unison.

"It's too early!"

At the other end of the barracks, Jerome Lesser bounded out of bed.

"Another day! Up and at 'em! This makes us one day closer to getting our wings!"

"Shut up, Jerome!"

Not bothering with a reply, Jerome took a broom handle, assumed a fencing pose, and lunged his makeshift saber at the offending cadet.

"On guard, Bender!" He gently poked his friend, lifting the covers off the sleepy cadet.

"Lesser, cut it out!"

Each day of preflight training was ordered with the now-familiar

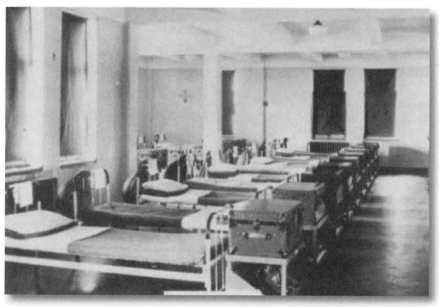

Maxwell Field dormitory, 1942. Wikimedia Commons. Public domain.

routine: 0500 reveille; 0545 morning assembly with calisthenics; return to barracks to shower, shave, and make up beds; march to breakfast; back to the barracks to prepare for 0700 inspection, followed by classes in math, physics, map reading, aircraft recognition, and Morse code.

After classes, the cadets marched back to their barracks, then did an hour of military drills and athletics. After dinner, they engaged in evening classes, worship for the religious, or sports and recreation, including card games. The final inspection occurred just before taps at 2130. Throughout the day, uniforms were kept spotless, and shoes were polished at least ten times. Order and discipline demanded that the men march everywhere in formation. The cadets addressed underclassmen as "Mister."

The stress of the upcoming Aircrew Qualification Exams was mounting, as each man knew his future hung in the balance.

Maxwell Field cadet inspections, 1942. Wikimedia Commons. Public domain.

Calisthenics at Maxwell Field, 1942. Southeast Army Air Force Training Center. Public domain.

"I don't get this geometry and physics stuff. It gives me a big headache!" Regan complained.

"Me too," Kerby lamented. "I don't need that stuff to fly a plane. I can't believe they gave us twenty-one books to read cover to cover!"

"Here, let me help you guys," Crane offered. "It's pretty easy if you start with the basics and build up from there."

"OK, genius. Show us how to pass the math part of the test, and we'll help you with the psychomotor evaluation," Regan offered.[3]

"That's my specialty," Jerome objected. "Hand-eye coordination is what fencing is all about."

"Yeah, we've seen you playing around, but how good are you really, Jerome?"

---

3   The psychomotor evaluation assessed steadiness, balance, equilibrium, reaction time, and ability to think clearly and read directions under conditions of confusion.

"Well, when I was in high school, I didn't like my parents getting into my business. One Saturday evening, I came home really late, and my parents started grilling me. They wanted to bust my chops. I ignored them and went right to my room and shut the door. Well, the next morning, they were reading the *Times* and were plenty shocked to see my photo in the sports section as the New York City high school fencing champion![4] They paid a little more attention to my sports after that. A couple of years later, I won the New York City college fencing title. So, yeah, I'm pretty good."

"OK, Zorro. You can show us your stuff. All this psychomotor stuff is pretty worthless in my mind," George Kerby lamented.

"It's that damned psychiatric exam that's got me spooked," Crane confided. "What's the shrink going to ask me, anyway?"

"Just answer the questions calmly. Tell the truth. Don't exaggerate, and do not make stuff up," Regan explained. "We can practice. I'll be the shrink and show you how to ace the psych eval."

"Well, George, how can you help us? What's your gig?" Jerome asked.

"The Kerbys have been in the newspaper business for generations. Before the war, I worked at the proof desk of the *Charlotte News*. So, all that vocabulary testing on the exam is pretty easy for me. I'll teach you guys how to memorize tons of new words. In fact, it works for any kind of memorization."

The four friends tutored one another for the next few weeks until they were all confident and prepared for the classification battery. Their teamwork paid off, as their stanine scores were at the top of the class.

In the end, each man's assignment fit him perfectly.

"Hey, Errol Flynn! What assignment did you get?" Regan asked Jerome Lesser.

"I'm going to bombardier school. It looks like I was too smart to be a pilot." Jerome laughed.

"How about you, Professor Crane?"

---

4   In April 1935, Jerome Lesser was the New York City Saber Fencing Champion as a member of the Textile High School fencing team.

Jerome Lesser in a fencing competition at Maxwell Field, Montgomery, Alabama, 1942. Wikimedia Commons. Public domain.

"I'm headed for navigator training," John Crane replied.

"How high was your stanine score, John?"

Crane, who had aced the testing, replied modestly, "Pretty high."[5]

"Well, I guess we know who the pilots are," Lesser added.

Regan and Kerby smiled and nodded in agreement.

"Looks like now we have a full crew," Regan added. "Let's promise to hook up again after our training and then go out and save the world."

The four men stood in a circle and put their right hands together, promising to join up after specialty training.

"Here's to the Four Musketeers." Jerome smiled.

"How about, 'To the Four Aviators!'" Regan suggested.

* * *

The graduation ball was the most talked about and highly anticipated event of the five-week program and was the social high point for

---

5   Navigators required the highest stanine score because of the math skills required for navigation.

Montgomery. The week before the ball, a vanguard of young women from across the country began arriving with their evening gowns and high heels. Many were attached to young men about to graduate from preflight training. Others flocked to Montgomery with the hope of snaring a young American aviator. Available hotel rooms were nonexistent. They held smaller dances at the officers' club. For a shindig of this magnitude, they had to convert Hangar 6 into a monstrous dance hall. Announcements were printed at the base print shop and sent out to young women across the nation. The Glenn Miller Orchestra and the Skinnay Ennis Band, famous as the orchestra for Bob Hope's radio program, provided live music for the evening.

"Are you inviting Louise to the graduation ball, John?"

"Yep, she's taking the train tomorrow from her parents' place in Morris, Illinois," replied Crane.

"When are you two getting hitched?" Jerome asked.

"We set a date for the middle of August. By then, we should have completed all of our training."

"Are we invited?" Kerby asked.

"Sure thing. It's going to be at the chapel on the Notre Dame campus. I'll expect you guys to be there."

"How about you two? Who are you bringing?" Kerby asked, looking at Regan and Lesser.

"I met a young woman named Joyce in Montgomery," Regan revealed without offering more details.

"And you, Errol Flynn? Who are you bringing, Jerome?"

"I may bring two or three young women!" Jerome laughed.

"I'll try not to steal your dates with my charm."

"Get out of here, Romeo!" The other three laughed as they pelted Kerby with their dirty underwear.

The evening of the ball, the young couples arrived and passed under the "Saber Arch" formed by the training wing's cadet officers. The dancers foxtrotted, waltzed, and jitterbugged to the live music strains until late into the evening. Each young woman wore a corsage known as a "Victorage," which was composed of wire stems,

Maxwell Airfield graduation ball. Public domain.

with ten-cent war stamps knitted into red, white, and blue ribbons. The evening was perfect in every way. In the end, Jerome Lesser only brought one date to the Maxwell Field ball, a young woman named Ruth Hirshfield.

At the preflight graduation ceremony, the next day's final review was a moment of intense pride for all the cadets. It was now second nature to march in stride as one unit. As they passed the reviewing stand with their saber salute, all eyes snapped to the right. The drama and feeling of solidarity unified the men. The zombies from a mere five weeks ago had become hardened fighting men and proud aviators in the United States Army Air Force.

Maxwell Field aviation cadets, preflight, April 1943. Public domain.

CHAPTER 4

SUNNY SANTA ANA: GROUND SCHOOL AND MOVIE STARS

APRIL 1942

The passing Southern California landscape was nothing like Montgomery, Alabama, and certainly was a world apart from the Bronx. In a rare moment of reflection, Jerome Lesser gazed absently out the window and thought about how far he'd come in the four months since leaving behind his life in New York City. *If Grace could see me now! What a life it is in this man's Army Air Force.*

The red Pacific Electric Railway car was packed with aviation cadets from the Santa Ana Army Air Base, each clamoring to pay the $1.15 round-trip fare. On their first weekend pass, they were in full dress uniform and were dying for some action.

"Jerome! Check out the orange groves! They're everywhere," Scott Regan exclaimed.

Admiring the endless rows of lush orange trees, Jerome replied wistfully, "I could really go for a cold glass of fresh-squeezed Sunkist OJ."

"Can you believe all the California sunshine?" George Kerby added. "I sure don't miss all that Alabama rain and humidity."

"Yeah, check out my California tan," Jerome bragged, showing off his bare, sun-darkened forearms. "I was working on an Alabama tan, but with all that rain, it was pretty hopeless."

"Where's Crane?"

"The professor is reading a book on navigation," George replied.

"John, put the book down and join the party. We've been doing nothing but studying for the past two weeks," Scott admonished his friend.

John looked up, smiled, and returned to his book.

"Hopeless." Jerome laughed.

"No problem. When we get lost in our B-24, we'll need John to bring us home."

"Can't wait to see Hollywood, boys," Jerome said, rubbing his hands together. "Let's have some fun!"

"I want a big, thick, juicy steak, with mashed potatoes, gravy, and all the fixings," John added, looking up from his book.

"Finally, we got your attention by appealing to your stomach," Jerome laughed.

"You boys have fun this weekend, but behave yourselves like cadets," Scott warned.

"Yes, Father Regan," the boys replied, rolling their eyes.

The Army Air Force West Coast Training Center at the Santa Ana Army Air Base was brand-new. The first fifty cadets arrived on February 25, 1942. By March, the place was crawling with five thousand aviation cadets. Housing was still being built, so three thousand cadets were living in a temporary tent city. Cadets Lesser, Regan, Crane, and Kerby arrived as upperclassmen, having already completed preflight training at Maxwell Field in Alabama. The immediate benefit was their assignment to quarters in the newly constructed barracks—home sweet home.

Oddly, Santa Ana Field was an airfield without planes or a runway. It was strictly for classroom academic lessons and a ground school. The studies were rigorous, with required physics, math, navigation, aerial photography, and Morse code courses. And that was just the

Pacific Electric "Red Car" 1216 to Santa Ana, 1940s. Orange County archives. Creative Commons 2.0.

first week. However, this weekend, the cadets forgot about all the end-less studying. Hollywood was calling!

The trip from Santa Ana, just over thirty miles, took almost two hours with frequent stops. Needing a place to stay, the boys decided to check out the exclusive Rosslyn Hotel on West Fifth Street in down-town Los Angeles.

"I hope this place doesn't cost too much," Scott worried, looking around the very luxurious Rosslyn Hotel lobby. "We haven't been paid yet, and I'm a bit short on cash."

Jerome smiled. "We've got the rooms covered, Scott. Don't worry about the cost."

They approached a pretty receptionist at the desk. Taking the lead, Regan explained, "We would like to check in, ma'am. We'll need two rooms."

The young woman smiled at the soldiers and handed Regan a pen, directing him to the ledger. "Sign in here, please. And don't put down Santa Ana as your residence. That's your air base, not your home."

After each cadet entered his name and hometown, she continued,

"The two rooms are on the tenth floor, and each includes two full beds, a private bathroom, and a sitting area. I also gave you upgraded rooms with a swell city view and a complimentary breakfast."

Regan looked around nervously. "How much will that be? We don't have a lot of cash on us."

Jerome was laughing in the back. "Maybe we should have you sleep in the closet, Scott."

The receptionist smiled. "That will be four dollars for one night."

"Do you mean four dollars for each of us?" Regan asked. "I think we can cover that."

"No, it's four dollars total for both rooms! One dollar a night for each of you. That's our special rate for soldiers. And you men certainly qualify," she gushed, admiring their uniforms.

Jerome and John burst out laughing. "Pay the lady, Scott, before she changes her mind!"

"Where are you from, soldier?" she asked, looking directly at Regan.

"Oakland, California, ma'am."

"If you promise to stop calling me ma'am, I would love to show you around."

Jerome cut in, "Sure thing, miss. We would love your company. I'm Jerome, this is George, John, and the California boy with all the dough is Scott."

"It's a pleasure to meet you, boys. My name is Beth. Why don't you go and check into your rooms? I get off work in thirty minutes. Can you meet me back here at 6:00 p.m.?"

"We'll be ready and waiting, Beth," Scott replied as they headed for the elevator.

* * *

Not wanting to be late, the boys were waiting in the lobby at 1750. Promptly at 1800, Beth appeared dressed to kill with her hair done up and her makeup freshly applied. Heels and a white satin evening dress had transformed her from a receptionist into a vision.

"Wow, Beth! You're a knockout! How did . . . ?"

"Nowadays, a girl always has to be ready for an evening out. You never know when a lonely soldier's going to need some company."

"Well, it looks like you'll have four flyboy escorts this evening." Jerome laughed.

"Actually, I invited my friend Cathy. She'll be meeting us at the restaurant. I hope you don't mind some more female company."

"Not at all." Scott beamed. "Where are we going for dinner?"

"Mike Lyman's Grill, of course. It's in Hollywood and is the hangout for all the movie stars and starlets. And I'm glad you wore your uniforms. You're in for some very special treatment tonight. Los Angeles loves our boys in uniform!"

* * *

Mike Lyman's Grill at 1627 North Vine was in the heart of Hollywood, next door to the Huntington Hartford Theater. The building's funky, Tudor-style roof harkened back to its days as a tavern. However, the large red neon sign proclaiming "Mike Lyman's" left no doubt that this was Hollywood. Inside, the green ceiling and patterned green carpeting offset the red upholstered booths and barstools. But no one came to look at the carpeting. Lyman's was about good food and people. The rich and famous, and the not so rich or famous, all came to see and be seen at Mike Lyman's Grill. Tonight was no different.

The menu boasted an astonishing array of 322 eclectic dishes, including "Kosher Stuffed Kishke" and "Gefilte Fish"; dozens of seafood options, including "Fried Louisiana Shrimps" for 75 cents and "Lobster Newburg" for $1.50. Steak and meat choices were plentiful, including "Filet Mignon" for $1.50, or perhaps "Two Lamb Chops," extra thick, for $1.35. And to finish off the meal, Mike Lyman's offered thirty-five tempting desserts.

But to start things off right, the front of the menu advertised Lyman's custom cocktails with bourbon or rye, plus Martinis, Old-Fashioneds, Manhattans, Bacardis, and a crowd favorite, the Lyman's Daiquiri. No one was going home thirsty.

The host showed Beth and her four uniformed escorts to their table at the front of the dining room, where Cathy was waiting. Her sparkly red dress and hair to match contrasted Beth's quieter demeanor.

"Hi, Cathy! These young men are our responsibility tonight. We have Scott, John, George, and Jerome. Fellas, this is my friend Cathy."

"Well, Beth. I'm glad you decided to share your young soldiers with me tonight."

Cathy smiled as she gave each soldier a warm Hollywood welcome and a kiss on the cheek.

Jerome and Scott held the girls' chairs as they were seated. "Thank you, gentlemen."

Jerome looked around the room in awe. "Boy, if you aren't in uniform, and you're not working here, then you must be a movie star!"

"You pretty much nailed it, Jerome." Cathy smiled.

"Look at all those stars! There are Abbott and Costello, and there's Clark Gable!"

"Yes, it's a shame about Carole Lombard."[1]

Jerome was watching a woman across the room with her head partially turned away. "Is that—"

"Yes, of course. That's Jeanette MacDonald!" Cathy interrupted before Jerome could get it out.

"Wow! I'm a huge fan and have seen all of her movies."

"Do you want to meet her?" Cathy asked, grinning.

"Would I ever. But I wouldn't want to bother her. She probably gets pestered by fans all the time."

"Nonsense. I'm sure she would love to meet one of our young men in uniform. Tonight, you're the star, Jerome," Cathy explained, getting up from the table and motioning for Jerome to follow.

"Beth, order us Mike's Special Steak Dinner with everything included."

"Is that OK with you, Jerome?"

"Perfect. Make mine charbroiled, medium."

---

1   Carole Lombard died in a plane crash on January 16, 1942, after a war bonds fund-raising event in Nevada in which she raised $2 million for the war effort.

Cathy led Jerome across the restaurant, stopping beside Jeanette MacDonald's table.

"Excuse me, Miss Mac-Donald. This young soldier, Jerome, is dying to meet you."

Jeanette turned and looked up at Jerome with a smile that lit up the room and won Jerome's heart.

Jerome extended his hand tentatively. "It is such an honor to meet you, Miss MacDonald. I never imagined . . ."

Still smiling, Jeanette grasped Jerome's hand. "Please sit down and tell me about yourself, Jerome."

Jeanette MacDonald, 1930s. Public domain.

Sitting, Jerome began, "Well, for starters, I have seen all your movies, and I love your singing. You are the most beautiful actress on the screen. All the guys say so."

"Thank you, Jerome. Which is your favorite movie?"

"I loved *San Francisco* with Mr. Gable."

"Yes, did you see Clark tonight? Perhaps you can meet him later."

"And I really like your musicals with Nelson Eddy. *The Girl of the Golden West* and *Sweethearts* are my favorites."

"Nelson and I are working on another movie coming out this summer. It's going to be called *I Married an Angel*. If you're in town, you must be my guest for the grand opening at Grauman's Chinese. We'll have dinner with Sid. But first, tell me more about yourself, Jerome."

"I'm from the Bronx. My younger sister, Grace, and my brother, David, are also big fans of yours. I like sports, especially fencing, and I was studying to go into the textile industry when Uncle Sammy came calling. So, I enlisted and am now an aviation cadet."

Jeanette, listening intently, had not taken her eyes off the young cadet.

"I knew there was something about you that was familiar! You are the spitting image of my friend Errol Flynn. He's also a fencer, at least in the movies! He's something of a swashbuckling romantic in real life, too."

Jerome blushed. "The guys do call me Errol Flynn when they're kidding around. Not that I look like him. Just that we both like fencing."

"No, Jerome. You definitely have Errol's good looks and confidence. You must be popular with the young ladies."

Now Jerome blushed but confessed, "I did meet a young woman named Ruth. She is—well, she's special."

"I hope that we finish off this war quickly and that you and Ruth will be happy together, Jerome."

Continuing, she added, "You know, I grew up in Philly, not far from your family in the Bronx. I love Hollywood, but sometimes I miss my old life in Philly. It's hard to find a decent Philly cheesesteak around here." She laughed.[2]

In a brief fifteen minutes that felt like a lifetime, Jerome fell in love with Jeanette's smile and caring personality.

"When you write home, be sure to send my regards to your parents, your sister, Grace, and your brother, David. Tell them how proud we are in Hollywood of you boys in uniform. You are the real heroes, Jerome."

The steak dinner was sumptuous, but Jerome's highlight was meeting his new girlfriend and admirer, Jeanette MacDonald.

When the waiter brought the check, Scott picked it up and frowned. "There must be some mistake. I think they forgot to charge us for the dinners. Look, our bill is only $8.40! Call the waiter back so he can fix the bill."

Beth and Cathy were trying hard not to laugh. "This is the best part of the evening! Your steak dinners were $1.40. I told you Los Angeles loves our boys in uniform!"

---

2   Pat Olivieri invented the Philly cheesesteak in the 1930s.

"Thank you, Mr. Lyman!" the boys murmured, shaking their heads in disbelief.

"Now where to, girls?" Scott asked.

"Earl Carroll's famous Hollywood nightclub is our next stop."

"Lead the way, ladies. We're ready for a night out on the town."

"Should we get a cab?" Scott asked, looking down Vine Street.

"Oh, no. It's only two blocks. Come on, boys," Cathy called out. "It's a perfect evening for a stroll, and we want to be seen with our soldiers!"

Walking south on Vine, they took in the sights, passing by the Brown Derby and the Santa Fe Railway Building.

At the corner of Vine and Sunset, Beth instructed, "All right, now turn around."

The view was magical, with the giant neon signs advertising the Broadway Hollywood Plaza Hotel and Wallichs Music City.

"Wow! What a view. And look where we're standing," George exclaimed. "This is NBC Studios!"

"Come on. We're almost there. Earl Carroll's is just down Sunset," Beth called out as she led the way.

Postcard view of Vine Street at night, 1950s. Courtesy of the Low family.

The lavish Earl Carroll Theatre was built in 1938 for five hundred thousand dollars. It was a showcase for the Earl Carroll musical comedy revues, and as the sign proclaimed, "Thru these portals pass the most beautiful girls in the world." A twenty-four-foot neon silhouette of Earl's companion, Beryl Wallace, dominated the entrance. Extravagant Earl Carroll's theater was an example of Hollywood's golden age at its very finest.

At the ticket window, a smiling brunette greeted them. "That will be $1.65 each, fellas. There's no cover charge and no drink minimum."

"That must be another special price for soldiers," Scott guessed.

"Yes, of course. Plus, each of you and your dates can go to the bar for a complimentary sandwich and a coffee."

"Thank you. I'm getting to like this city," Scott noted as Beth and Cathy led them up the massive red-carpeted staircase to the main hall of the theater.

Inside, soldiers, Hollywood celebrities, and Angelenos seated at rows of white-tableclothed tables filled the 7,200-square-foot theater. A black patent leather ceiling, graceful fabric-covered walls, and surrounding neon light sculptures completed the art deco interior.

"Look at that huge rotating stage!"[3] Jerome called out as their hostess escorted them to their table. "We have the original Earl Carroll Theatre on Broadway back home, but I've never been there."

"Who cares about the stage? I want to see the showgirls," Crane said.

"Well, now we know how to get your nose out of that navigation book!" Scott laughed.

"Remember, you're getting married this summer," Jerome quipped.

The hostess passed up dozens of empty tables, finally stopping right in front of the stage.

"Mr. Carroll reserves this table for Beth and her favorite young soldiers. Enjoy the show."

Scott turned to Beth.

"How did you arrange this special treatment?"

---

3   The Earl Carroll Theatre featured a specially designed massive stage with a 60-foot-wide double revolving turntable and staircase.

Earl Carroll Theatre. Courtesy of the Low family.

Beth smiled. "I have friends. Uncle Earl takes good care of me."

The two-and-a-half-hour floor show was a musical extravaganza. The Earl Carroll Vanities and Burlesque Show was full of music and dancing by sixty of the world's most beautiful women. Statuesque and scantily clad, they had the boys' full attention.

For the evening, Jerome, Scott, John, and George forgot about being aviation cadets. Tonight, they were four young men out on the town with their dates, having the time of their lives.

After taking Beth and Cathy home, they stumbled into their rooms at the Rosslyn Hotel at 0430 in the morning. Jerome was so excited that he couldn't wait to tell his sister Grace about their evening.

After the weekend out on the town, it was back to the grind studying in Santa Ana.

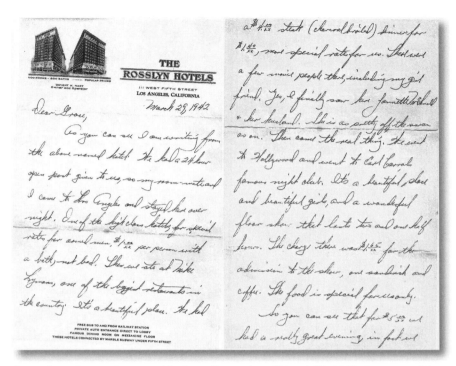

Letter from Jerome Lesser to his sister, Grace, dated March 29, 1942. Courtesy of the Lesser family.

"All we do around here is go to class and study, and we're still so far behind it's not even funny," Jerome complained.

"Chin up, boys. We'll get through this," Scott said.

"Yeah, but they do pile on the classes around here," George agreed.

"Physics is killing me," Scott admitted.

"One formula at a time, guys. I'll give you a hand with physics after mess this evening at 1730. That will leave us four hours to cram until lights out at 2130," John offered.

"All of this studying will be worth it when we receive our wings and finally get to fly. Let's keep our eyes on the prize," Scott encouraged.

By mid-April, grades were posted. The cramming had paid off. All four cadets had passed every class and were given assignments for the next phase of their aviation training. John Crane was headed back to the East Coast for navigator training at Turner Field in Georgia. Scott Regan and George Kerby were going to San Antonio, Texas, for pilot flight training at Brooks and Lubbock Fields. Finally, Jerome Lesser, headed for bombardier school, had his bag packed for the short trip to Victorville, California, in the western Mojave Desert, just north of Los Angeles. It was finally time to fly!

Aircraft identification training, WWII. US government photo. Public domain.

Aviation cadets at Santa Ana Field, West Coast Army Air Force Training Center. Wikipedia. Public domain.

CHAPTER 5

INTO THE WILD BLUE YONDER

MAY–SEPTEMBER 1942

Having survived the weeding-out process of preflight, two thousand young men descended upon Brooks Field in San Antonio, Texas, for primary flight training. They were still fresh off the farm or from countless Podunk small towns across America. Flying was their dream. In truth, many had never even driven an automobile.

* * *

The silver PT-17 Stearman biplane slowly taxied to a stop with its Continental 220-horsepower radial engine purring. Instructor Smith climbed out of the front seat, stepping onto the wing.[1]

Giving his student in the rear seat a thumbs-up, Smith yelled, "Take her up. Make two touch-and-go landings, and then bring her back here in one piece. You're ready."

Smith hopped down onto the ground, stepping back to give Regan plenty of room to taxi the Stearman for his first solo flight.

---

1   Primary flight training instructors were usually civilian instructor pilots.

Stearman PT-17 primary flight trainer. Wikimedia Commons. Public domain.

Regan took a deep breath and slowly exhaled as he adjusted his goggles. He'd flown ten hours in the Stearman, with the last couple from the rear seat. Gripping the throttle with his left hand and the stick with his right, Regan's feet were positioned high on the rudder pedals, firmly pressing the brakes. Releasing the brakes and gently advancing the throttle, he slowly taxied toward the runway, making S-turns for better visibility. Feeling a slight crosswind, Regan put the stick into the wind to keep the wing from being lifted and locked the tail wheel to keep her taxiing straight.

As Regan approached the runway, he checked for incoming planes before turning. Applying the left rudder and a burst of the throttle, he turned left onto the runway and set the aircraft on its takeoff course. Locking the tail wheel, he checked again for landing planes.

Regan lowered his seat to the flying position, dropped his heels to the deck, checked the tower for course signals, and made a last check for incoming planes.

Advancing the throttle smoothly and positively all the way forward, Scott felt the torque as the plane surged forward. His heart was racing.

You can do this, Scott!

With the tail wheel firmly on the ground, the Stearman rapidly picked up speed on its takeoff roll. He eased the nose down into the takeoff attitude, and the tail wheel rose off the ground.

OK, hold that attitude!

As the biplane picked up more speed, it became airborne.

Pulling back on the stick, Regan talked himself through: "OK, ease the nose up a little into the normal climbing position. Keep the plane straight and wings level."

Regan smoothly retarded the throttle to the climbing position. At two hundred feet, he began a climbing turn to the left. Leveling off at two thousand feet, Scott finally exhaled and looked out of the cockpit. The view was the same as before, but the sensation of flying solo was exhilarating.

"All right! I'm flying solo!"

Making corrections Regan observed: *Left wing's too low . . . Pull her nose up . . . Watch the tachometer—she's revving too high . . . Ease back on the throttle . . . Hold a little right rudder.*

All right, that's better. Banking the plane slightly to the left, he looked down at the airstrip below with its crisscrossing runways. What a beautiful sight! Flying the Stearman was a visceral experience. With the wind in his face, the smell of the engine in his nostrils, and the roar and vibration of the engine coursing through his body, Regan was one with this flying machine. All those countless hours of studying, drills, and more studying had finally come to this moment. He had escaped the bonds of Earth's gravity and was free to fly like a bird.

"Stop daydreaming, you idiot! You still have to land this thing!"

Regan set up for the turn onto the base leg, checking the wind sock for a crosswind. The turn onto the final approach was smooth and controlled.

Regan took in a deep breath as he lined the Stearman up with the runway and began his descent. He pulled the power back to idle, with mixture set to rich,[2] and held the attitude as he felt the plane sink like a refrigerator.

Unable to see over the front of the plane, Regan sighted the landing spot and used his peripheral vision to keep the airplane centered on the runway.

OK. Don't bring the nose up at all; take yourself over the runway, lower the nose a bit. Hold it. Hold it. Now start rounding out; round it out gradually. Keep it centered.

The Stearman gently touched down for a perfect three-point landing. As he advanced the throttle for a touch-and-go landing, the plane picked up speed and was again airborne in a few hundred feet.

Few experiences can compare to a pilot's first solo. For Scott Regan, the soaring biplane was only matched by his soaring spirit as he circled the airfield in San Antonio, Texas. He was a pilot at last.

* * *

After their solo and the traditional dunking,[3] the cadets became familiar with various aerobatic maneuvers. Slow rolls, snap rolls, loops, spins, chandelles, Immelmanns, and lazy eights were part of the concentrated training program.

"All right, cadets. The Stearman is gentle as a kitten in level flight. Now we're going to teach you to 'yank and bank' so you feel some real g-forces as she becomes firm and aerobatic. Who wants to puke first?"

In the air, Regan was back in the front seat, flying straight and level.

"Let's start with a simple inside loop. Just like we showed you in class. Ready?"

"Yes, sir," Regan responded, gripping the stick and throttle.

"Line up with the road—that's your reference. When you finish

---

2   The mixture control sets the amount of fuel added to the intake airflow.

3   Following their solo flight, the cadet was initiated with a large barrel of water poured over his head by his fellow cadets.

the loop, you are still going to be lined up with the road."

"Got it."

"OK. Move the stick forward and open the throttle to start your dive."

The Stearman dove and picked up speed.

"OK. Push the throttle all the way forward and ease back on the stick to start climbing."

The Stearman responded, starting an upward arc.

"At the top of the loop, hold it until you have your wings perfectly level in an inverted position."

"OK, now retard the throttle and line yourself up with the road!"

Scott finished the loop, advanced the throttle, and pushed the stick to level off.

"OK, Cadet. Do you still have your breakfast? How was that?"

"Great! Let's do it again."

"Let's try a split S. It's like half an inside loop with a 180-degree roll at the top into the upright position. So, from the inverted position at the top of the loop, you give it full left rudder and full left aileron to flip her over."

The rest of the afternoon was a nonstop series of rolls, loops, spins, figure eights, and combination aerobatics. It was just like being a kid on the Big Dipper roller coaster at Venice Beach for Regan.

Now we're flying! Scott thought as he brought the Stearman back to earth.

As they assembled for a post-session debriefing, it was evident that not all the cadets had made it through the day with their lunch and pride intact.

Regan spotted Robert Bender across the room. "Robert, how did it go today?"

"Do you mean how much puke did I get in my hair?" he replied, still looking green. "The cockpit was a mess. I doubt they'll let me fly fighters after that fiasco."

"Don't give up so easily, Robert. You might get to love aerobatics with more practice and less breakfast."

Aviation cadets pose in front of their PT-17 trainer. Courtesy of Douglas 63rd Preservation Society, Inc. https://WWIIFlightTraining.org.

"Don't talk to me about food," Robert groaned.

Maxwell Sullivan and George Kerby smiled as they overheard Bender's laments.

"How did you boys do today?"

"Not too bad," George replied. "The flying was a kick in the pants! No barfing, although I came close more than a few times."

"Yeah, can you imagine doing the same aerobatics in basic training with a BT-14? That plane will pull some Gs and will totally kick butt. And it's forty miles per hour faster than our Stearman!"

The challenges of flight training were unyielding and relentless. By the end of primary flight training, 30 percent of the class of two thousand had already washed out.

In a few short weeks, those who remained were transformed into flying cadets, aviators in the United States Army Air Force. The next phase, basic flight training, would challenge them with larger and more powerful flying machines. The potential for washing out or for deadly accidents loomed ever larger in their headlong quest for aviator wings.

* * *

Randolph Field east of San Antonio, the "West Point of the Air," was the world's most beautiful training center. The base administration building was known as the Taj Mahal. Aviation cadets, or "dodos," entered a new world that was strictly military, beginning the process that would shape them into military fliers. Achieving this goal meant mastering more complex maneuvers in ever more powerful aircraft.

The men, who had arrived in civilian duds, were quickly transformed into Air Force aviators. They stood rigidly at attention on the flight line, dressed in flight suits, leather helmets, and goggles. Each man had his seat-pack parachute strapped to his behind.

"So, you dodos think you can fly because they let you circle the weed patch in that pathetic Stearman baby trainer! Well, I got news for you. My mother can fly that plane. It's slow. It's forgiving, and it's made just for dodos like you!"

Having thoroughly deflated the cadets' egos, Lt. Hale paused for effect, staring down the nearest dodo.

"Here at Randolph, you will fly the fixed-undercarriage North American BT-14.[4] She's fast, powerful, and complex beyond anything you've experienced. Those of you who are lucky will survive and wash out. Those who are less fortunate will learn why we call this plane the 'cadet killer'! She does not forgive your errors or stupidity. Do I make myself clear?"

"Yes, sir!" the cadets shouted in unison.

"Now split up into your squadrons and meet up with your assigned instructor at your plane. Move it!"

---

4   The North American BT-14 had a 450-horsepower Wright R-985-25 engine, a maximum speed of 177 miles per hour, a range of 765 miles, and a ceiling of 21,650 feet.

Cadets Regan, Bender, Kerby, and Sayre[5] gathered around their assigned plane, looking for the instructor.

"Looks like we're on our own," Sayre quipped.

Just then, Lt. Hale came around the front of the BT-14. "So, you think you can fly this plane, Cadet Sayre?"

"No, sir."

"Then shut up and pay attention."

"God help us," Kerby murmured to Regan.

"I will be your instructor for the next nine weeks. My job is to teach you to operate this machine. You will learn to control her in VFR conditions, and then we will teach you to fly in formation, to use your instrument to fly in bad weather, and everyone's favorite, you will learn to fly and land this beast at night in pitch-black conditions! Oh, and I almost forgot. I will make you barf, and you will clean it up. Now who wants the first crack at this plane?"

The next few weeks flew by in the blink of an eye. Military discipline was ever-present, with reveille at 0600 and taps at 2130. In between were endless drills, marching in formation, calisthenics, ground school courses, and time in the cockpit of the BT-14. The cadets marched everywhere in formation. They ate together in the mess hall, standing at attention at their table until given the order to sit, which they did as one.

The underclassmen acted as waiters, keeping the senior cadets' plates and glasses full.

"Dodo, pour me some juice," Bender demanded. "Hurry up! And don't spill it."

"Give him a break, Bob. Have you forgotten what it's like?" Scott admonished his friend.

"We put in our time. Now it's their turn to suffer."

"How'd you do with the aerobatic flying today, George?" Scott asked, changing the subject.

---

5   Lt. Paul F. Sayre, from Athens County, Ohio, was a B-24 pilot in the 320th Squadron of the 90th Bomb Group. Like Regan, he was an early replacement pilot in the 90th Bomb Group. His plane and crew were lost on April 16, 1943, in the Eastern Highlands of New Guinea.

BT-14 trainers preparing for a night flight, 1942. US government photo. Public domain.

"I can do the maneuvers just fine, but my stomach does not like that upside-down flying with high Gs. I even made Lieutenant Hale queasy with my flying."

"Maybe you should take something before you go up," Paul Sayre suggested.

"Yeah, we hate the smell of your puke." Bender laughed.

"Well, my instrument flying is spot on. Hale says I have the brain-power to fly by instruments."

"Tomorrow, we have our night flying session," Scott reminded them.

"I don't mind taking off and flying at night. It's landing in the dark that spooks me," Paul confessed.

"You got that right," Bender agreed.

* * *

Link flight trainer. Courtesy of Michael Barera.

For weeks the cadets had practiced instrument flying and night approaches on the Link Trainer.[6] It was hardly the real thing but still resulted in repeated crash-and-burn landings. The real-life night landing of the BT-14 would be even more challenging, and the scuttlebutt in the barracks was full of stories of missed approaches, accidents, and deaths.

On the flight line that evening, Lt. Hale was even more tense than usual.

6   Edwin Link invented the Link flight trainer in 1929. Known as the "Blue Box," it was the first commercially available flight simulator. Using his experience from his family's piano and organ business, Link used the mechanisms from two player pianos to turn the plane with realistic movements of pitch, roll, and yaw. The first customers were amusement parks, then the Army Air Corps purchased 10,000 Link Trainers for their aviation cadet program in 1940. Cadets were taught instrument flying in poor weather conditions with limited visibility.

"Gather round. Let's go over this one more time. Each of you will practice night landings with me in the back seat. We'll do a check ride, and those of you who pass will do a solo night landing. Any questions?"

The four nervous cadets were silent.

"OK. Let's review it one more time. At night your eyes will play tricks on you. In the dark, you will not have the usual visual cues. You will probably think you're higher than you really are, resulting in a low approach. If you don't fix it, you will crash, and you will die. Dark runways are hard to spot and judging distance and slope gets tricky. Brightly lit runways make the runway appear closer, resulting in a high approach."

"How about the parachute flares?" Kerby asked.

"Yes. We will practice dropping the parachute flares to light the ground. But those can also be deceiving. Ultimately, it is up to you to keep your wits about yourself and to land this plane safely at night."

"Now, who's first?"

Regan stepped forward. "I'm ready, Lieutenant."

"OK, Regan. There's nothing like a volunteer in this man's Army."

* * *

It was pitch-black outside as the BT-14 turned onto the strip's final approach at Randolph Field.

Geez! It's tough to see the runway!

"All right, Regan. Talk me through this landing."

"Elevation three thousand feet. Powering back on the throttle. Three percent glide slope," Regan called out. "Keeping the nose down. Airspeed ninety miles per hour."

"Can you see the landing strip, Cadet?"

"Negative."

"Check your elevation and speed. You're coming in too steep."

"Elevation one thousand feet. Airspeed eighty miles per hour. We look higher."

"Trust your instruments, Regan. Now fix it!"

Parachute flares. US Army Air Force training film. Public domain.

Unsure of what to do, Regan continued the same glide path. It looked perfect.

"Fix it, Cadet, before we crash!"

Suddenly, the vague outline of the landing strip appeared. He was coming in too steep.

"Advancing the throttle. Pulling up the nose. Airspeed seventy-five miles per hour."

"OK, Regan. That's better. Just take it slow and land her normally."

Easing back on the throttle, he reported, "Airspeed sixty-five miles per hour. Rounding out."

Regan waited for the wheels to touch down. Nothing.

"Give it some power, Regan."

Regan advanced the throttle gently. The plane touched down with a bounce and rolled forward on the runway.

"A bit tricky at night, isn't it?"

"Yes, sir. It's hard to judge distances."

"You did OK. We got down in one piece. Just trust your instruments, and don't be afraid to go around if you're not sure."

"Let's try a landing with the parachute flares. They're OK to use in an emergency landing, but you shouldn't need them for routine night landings."

After taking off for another attempted night landing, Lt. Hale instructed Regan on the use of the parachute flares.

"The trick is to drop these at an elevation over the end of the runway. You want to time it so the parachutes will be over the runway as you're making your final approach."

"Sounds like a plan."

"It's a lot harder than it sounds. But let's give it a go."

Regan circled over the runway and dropped the self-igniting parachute flares at four thousand feet. He continued to circle, watching as the flares ignited, glowing bright yellow as they slowly floated down toward the airstrip. He was mesmerized by the slowly descending flares glowing in the Texas night sky like beacons to the wayward traveler. He wondered how long it would be before they touched down.

After his second circle, Lt. Hansen broke into his trance. "Isn't there someplace you need to be about now, Cadet Regan?"

Regan spotted the altimeter rapidly counting down the feet. *Holy crap, Scott! Wake up!*

"Yes, sir!" Scott called out as he headed for the base leg of his approach.

As Regan turned into the final approach leg at three thousand feet, the two flares were positioned perfectly over the end of the runway about a thousand feet up.

"Looks like you lucked out on this one, Cadet."

Regan pulled the throttle back, powering off as the BT-14 sank toward the runway. The flares lit up the strip beautifully, giving him a target to land the plane.

"Wow! Those flares really light up the runway!"

"OK. Bring her in, and don't bounce the landing this time!"

The BT-14 glided in perfectly, passing the flares as they descended onto the field.

Regan rounded out the landing for a perfect touchdown.

"All right, Regan. Get off the runway and drop me off by the tower. You're ready to do your solo night landing."

"Yes, sir!"

Regan perfectly executed his solo night landing without flares. He trusted his instruments and picked up the airstrip in time to make a perfect landing in the dead of night. Just after his plane touched down, as it was rolling down the runway, there was an explosion on the adjacent runway. A flaming BT-14 smashed into the ground and spun end over end in a massive fireball.

"My God! Who is that?"

Regan taxied back to the tower, unable to take his eyes off the blazing inferno. The sirens completed the story as the crash team sprang into action, but there was nothing they could do. The only thing worse than washing out of the program was ending it like this, as a massive fireball flameout. The truth was that accidents in the air cadet flight training program were a known risk and were very common.[7]

* * *

The next morning the death of Cadet Wendell Wilson hung over the base, bleak and impenetrable, yet no one spoke of the accident. The cadets were quickly learning to compartmentalize death and to move on.

The end of the nine-week course had snuck up on the cadets. Regan stared at the envelope that would determine his next assignment in advanced flight training.

Please, God. Let it be single-engine training.

---

7   Throughout the war, the Army Air Forces suffered more than 6,500 fatal accidents in the continental United States, resulting in the loss of 7,114 airplanes and the deaths of 15,530 personnel. This was an average of ten deaths and nearly forty accidents, fatal and nonfatal, each day.

He slowly opened the letter, pulled out and unfolded the orders, took a deep breath, and read: "Cadet Scott L. Regan is to report for multiengine flight training at the Lubbock Army Air Corps Advanced Flying School, Lubbock, Texas."

"Aaagh! How can this be?"

"Did you get single or multiengine, Scott?" George Kerby asked from across the room.

Scott groaned, "Multiengine! Bombers with ten-hour missions!"

"How can that be? You were first in the class. No one was even close."

"No idea, George. Guess I'll hunt down Lieutenant Hale and get the scoop. What did you get?"

"Multiengine. For me, that's fine. I don't want to be a hotshot fighter pilot. Not my style."

* * *

Lt. Hale was expecting Regan. "At ease, Regan. What can I do for you?"

"You know why I'm here, sir."

"I have a pretty good idea."

"I worked my butt off to be number one in the class. You knew I wanted to fly fighters. Why did you put me in for bombers?" Scott fumed.

"You were the best flier in the class, Regan. But it's about more than the flying."

"Well, what else, sir?"

"The needs of the Army Air Force, for one! But beyond that, the personality of the cadet is critical."

"You don't like my personality?"

"No, I mean your personality as a pilot. Scott, you are precise and controlled. You never miss a vector. Your formation flying is perfection."

"So, what's the problem?"

"Fighter pilots need to be aggressive and reckless. You are neither. You could fly circles around those guys in a check ride. But in a dogfight, you need more than precision."

Scott was quiet, contemplating his fate. He was too perfect. Too controlled.

"But the real reason I recommended you for multiengine training is your stanine psych evaluation. You are a natural leader, Regan. More than any cadet I have come across. Frankly, you've been pegged as a leader from your early days at Maxwell. It's in your file."

Scott was stunned. His vision of being a fighter pilot was melting away. All he could muster was, "Yes, sir."

"Be the best damned bomber pilot and take care of your men. They will need you, and the Army Air Force needs you. I know it's not glamorous, Regan. But this war will be won by men like you, doing the heavy lifting."

"Yes, sir!" Regan replied with a bit more enthusiasm.

"And a word of advice: do not ever again question a superior officer about an order. This is the Army, not a fraternity. Now, report to Lubbock Field and learn how to fly that Curtis twin-engine AT-9.[8] She's hard to fly, but you can handle her, and she goes two hundred miles per hour!"

---

8   The Lubbock Army Air Corps Advanced Flying School was ten miles west of Lubbock, Texas. Class 42-G graduated in August 1942. Lt. George D. Kerby graduated with the highest academic standing from the advanced twin-engine bomber training school.

Curtis AT-9 twin engine trainer, equipped with two Lycoming R-680-9 engines, 295 horsepower each. Maximum speed 197 miles per hour. Range 750 miles. Ceiling 19,000 feet. National Museum of the United States Air Force. Public domain.

CHAPTER 6

BOMBARDIER SCHOOL

MAY–JULY 1942

Victorville, California, fourteen hundred miles due west, was home of the Victorville Army Air Force Bombardier School. Positioned on the Mojave Desert's southwestern edge, the location benefited from 360 days of sunshine every year and abundant wide-open spaces, making it an ideal location to train future bombardiers. Groundbreaking ceremonies for the 2,200-acre base took place on July 12, 1941. Cadet Jerome Lesser was among the first bombardier students to report to Victorville, arriving at the end of April 1942.[1] The twelve-week bombardier school training program[2] began with course work, in which they learned the theory and physics of dropping a bomb from a moving plane. A ground-based simulator looked like a mobile self-propelled painter's scaffolding. The bombardier student steered the simulator over the target, learning the basic principles and use of the Norden bombsight.

Jerome Lesser was the oldest student in the bombardier class, but after their first two-hour exam with 130 questions, he had the second-highest score.

Flight training utilized the twin-engine Beech AT-11 Kansan

---

1 During World War II, the seventeen Army Air Force bombardier schools graduated 47,236 bombardiers.
2 Bombardier training was later increased to an eighteen-week course.

Victorville Army Flying School postcard. Courtesy of the Low family.

Bombardier training apparatus at Victorville Bombardier School. Wikimedia Commons. Public domain.

fitted with a plexiglass nose and bomb bay.

The weapon of choice was the hundred-pound sand bomb spiked with a small amount of black powder. By the end of May 1942, the students flew two and a half hours every day, working in pairs. One student would be bombardier and the other would be the photographer.

"OK, Lesser. You have control of the plane," Lt. Zimmerman informed Jerome from the cockpit.

Peering through the Norden bombsight, Jerome adjusted the knobs to bring the target into the center of the crosshairs.

"Target's in my crosshairs. Opening bomb bay doors."

"Make this a good run, Jerome," Mandell Cypress encouraged his friend, with the camera ready to record the bomb drop.[3]

"No sweat, Mandell. Killing the drift here," Jerome reported as he adjusted the turn and drift knobs to correct for a crosswind.

Jerome held the mark steady on the Norden bombsight and watched the sight angle narrow as they approached the target. Making minute adjustments, he held the target in the crosshairs.

"Bombs away!" Jerome called out as he watched the hundred-pound bomb fall away toward the target.

"There she goes! It's looking good," Mandell reported with the camera running.

"Don't miss the explosion. This one's going to be right in the pickle barrel."

"You have to maintain your average. We're leading the class," Mandell boasted.

The sand bomb struck the target, with the detonator setting off small charges marking the bomb strike's location.

"Perfect! That was about ten feet from the shack!" Jerome exclaimed.

"Man, that's going to bring your average down even further. What's your average? Like 120 feet?"

"Over the last twenty bombs, my average is 103 feet from

---

3   Mandell L. Cypress (1918–2006) was a distinguished bombardier aboard a B-24 Liberator in the Pacific War. He flew over four hundred hours of combat missions with the 307th Bombardment Group of the 5th Air Force and was awarded an Air Medal with multiple Oak Leaf clusters by Admiral Chester Nimitz.

A Beech AT-11 Kansan bombardier trainer, with two Pratt and Whitney R-985 450-horsepower engines, a maximum speed of 215 miles per hour, a cruising speed of 150 miles per hour, a range of 745 miles, and a service ceiling of 20,000 feet. US Army Air Force. Public domain.

the target."

"Well, we Jewish bombardiers drop the meanest bombs! And you have that wicked hand-eye coordination, Jerome."

"We do have an all-Jewish crew today. But frankly, outside this plane, I'd rather be known as a hotshot all-American bombardier," Jerome replied.

"I know what you mean, Jerome. I don't want to encourage that matzah-ball comedy routine I've been hearing. I heard a lot of that bullshit growing up in Tennessee."

"Yep, I am going to fight and maybe die as an all-American aviator. Here, let's switch places. You have to keep our average at the top of the class!"

Jerome Lesser at Bombardier School, Victorville, California, 1942. Courtesy of Donna Eschen.

"No worries. With this new bombsight, you can't miss!"[4]

* * *

Later that afternoon, Jerome and Mandell were in the kitchen peeling potatoes.

"I do love KP duty!" Jerome groaned, peering at the mountain of potatoes they still had to attack with their Army regulation potato-peeling knives.

"You just have to have fun with it. Look at Ernie over there. He's

---

4   The new Norden bombsight was a top-secret development.

the singing potato peeler! Not a care in the world for that Tennessee boy!"

Jerome glanced over at Ernie Ford, another bombardier student, and laughed, "That guy can sure sing a deep bass! But he's messing up my potato peeling concentration."

"Ernie says he's going to be famous someday!"

"Yeah, sure. A famous potato peeler, maybe!"

"No, really. Ford told me he met Roy Rogers on his ranch near here, and Mr. Rogers likes Ernie's singing."

Ernie Ford. US Army Air Force photograph. Public domain.

"Well, I guess there's no accounting for taste, as they say. Besides, what do I know about good singing?" Jerome laughed as he attacked another spud with his knife.

"Hey, Ernie! Get to work! That pile of potatoes isn't getting any smaller!"[5]

* * *

By early June, the bombardier students were undergoing cross-training as pilots and navigators. As Jerome wrote to his kid sister Grace, "So, now you can see who the most important man in the plane is."

---

5   Ernest Jennings Ford, aka Tennessee Ernie Ford (1919–1991), after his training at Victorville Army Airfield, served as a bombardier on a B-29 Superfortress. Later Ernie Ford and Mandell Cypress returned to George Air Force Base in Victorville as bombardier instructors. According to Cypress, Roy Rogers did help Ernie Ford with his singing career.

AIR CORPS ADVANCED FLYING SCHOOL
VICTORVILLE, CALIFORNIA

June 9, 1942.

Dear Grace,

Well, now that we are almost bombardiers, we have to be navigators and pilots, to say nothing of being gunners. So now you can readily see who the most important man in the plane is. Yes, its no other than the the bombardier. Yep, we can also navigate with the bombsight.

Maybe you heard the new bombardier song? It's pretty good. Don't believe all you read about "washout" pilots being turned into bombardiers. Right now the bombardiers are the pick of the cream. You really have to have it to be a good bombardier. And don't think for a minute the pilots & navigators aren't getting mad because we

Letter from Jerome Lesser to his sister, Grace Lesser, dated June 9, 1942. Courtesy of the Lesser family.

"Hey, Lesser! Are you writing to your kid sister again? When do I get to meet her?" Ernie Ford asked.

"Never! She's too smart for you anyway, Ernie. She wants to major in stuff I never even heard of. Something called econometrics."

"I like smart girls," Ernie protested.[6]

"No way, Ernie. Besides, she goes to all-girls' schools, and she can defend herself with my fencing foils!"

"All right, but be sure to mention me in your letter," Ernie persisted.

* * *

"Another good day for dropping bombs. It's sunny, clear, and hot as the dickens!" Mandell reported.

"Yeah. Yesterday was miserable out here. The updrafts from the desert heat had our plane bouncing around all afternoon. It was bumpy as hell."

"You still did pretty good, but everyone except you was puking their guts out!"

"Today is smoother. Let's maintain our average for distance to the target. I'm still hovering around a hundred feet," Jerome said.

"You know, Jerome, you only need an average of 230 feet to qualify. You are way overqualified to be a bombardier in this man's Army Air Force."[7]

The day started out well, with Lesser's first bomb landing forty feet short of the shack.

"All right! Way to go, Jerome!" Mandell shouted. "Keep it up! They'll be assigning us to come back as instructors."

From there, the day went downhill rapidly. The next bomb landed 250 feet beyond the target.

"Crap! What happened on that one? I made the same calculations as the first bomb!"

"No worries, Jerome. Just shake it off, and let's go around and try again."

---

6   Ford married Betty Heminger on September 18, 1942.
7   For qualification, a bombardier student flew seven bomb runs—four during the daytime and three at night—and had to place his bombs within 230 feet of the aim point.

Lesser watched the third bomb fall away toward the target. "Come on, baby! Hit the target!"

As the bomb began to drift off target, Jerome's heart sank. "Oh, no! Not another boner bomb!"

The sand bomb exploded 280 feet from the shack. "Man, what am I doing wrong?"

"Shake it off, Jerome. Just think positive thoughts and go around again."

Lesser's performance that afternoon was nothing to write home about. Looking despondent, he shook his head as he reviewed the day's damage.

"Five bombs. Two hundred and thirty feet average from the target! I give up! I could have done better with my eyes closed."

"Don't worry, Jerome. It's only one day and five bombs. It won't mess up your average too much."

"I guess we all have bad days."

Victorville Bombardier School students returning to base after a day of training. Public domain.

Lesser returned to form the next day and was spot on for the rest of the bombardier training. He, Mandell, and Ford were at the top of the class as they prepared to graduate and receive their wings.

"Hey, Jerome! Ernie says we have Hollywood company coming to entertain us tonight."

"Who's that?"

"Well, a friend of mine from high school named Dinah Shore!"

Dinah Shore, 1940s. Wikimedia Commons. Public domain.

"You've got to be kidding. You know Dinah Shore?"

"Yep. She graduated one year ahead of me in Nashville. Back in high school, she was Fannye Rose Shore. Nice girl. She'll be here with some guys named Bob Hope and Jerry Colonna." Mandell laughed.

"Wow! Real headliners. Maybe Dinah Shore will let Ernie sing with her."

"Who cares about Ernie? I just want to ask her for a dance."

"OK, that I want to see."

* * *

The show that evening for the aviation cadets was the highlight of the twelve-week course. Hope was in rare form, and the gorgeous and talented Dinah Shore had the boys begging for more. She sang all of their requests.

As she finished her set, a cadet in the front row shouted, "Dinah, we have a friend of yours who wants to say hello!"

Dinah looked out into the crowd as the cadets pushed Mandell up onto the stage.

"Dinah, I don't know if you remember me from high school . . ."

"Of course, I remember you, Mandell! It hasn't been that many years since Hume-Fogg High in Nashville!"

Beaming, Mandell made his request. "May I have this dance, Dinah?"

"Of course, but first come over here and give me a big Tennessee hug!"

The men cheered wildly as Mandell and Dinah Shore waltzed to the music of the school's orchestra. It was a night to remember.[8]

As the evening wound down, Dinah took Mandell's hand. "Be sure to write me a letter when you get overseas. We are all so proud of you boys."

* * *

The legend of that summer evening was not quite complete. As the entourage was leaving the base, they stopped at the guard gate. The sentry on duty spotted Dinah.

"Good evening, Miss Shore. I sure wish I could have heard you sing tonight. I'm a huge fan."

Dinah smiled. "What's your favorite song, soldier?"

"I love all your music, but my favorite is 'Silver Wings.'"

Without missing a beat, Dinah opened the door and stepped out of the car. "Well, I'll sing it right now. This one is just for you. Although some people say he's just a crazy guy, to me he means a million other things . . . he wears a pair of silver wings."

Dinah Shore sang "He Wears a Pair of Silver Wings" and many other favorites that evening under a starlit sky in a private concert that one soldier will never forget.

---

8   Interview with Lt. Mandell Cypress in *Flying Flak Alley* by Alan L. Griggs (McFarland & Company, Inc., 2008).

HEADLINERS OF SCREEN, RADIO THRILL CADETS

Bob Hope, Dinah Shore, Host of Others Entertain Soldiers At Victorville Base

Stars of the stage, radio and screen including the irrepressible Bob Hope and Jerry Colona and the lovely Dinah Shore, paraded across the stage at the Victorville Flying school Saturday night as Lieut.-Col. Roy D. Butler, the commanding officer of the post, was host to the officer and enlisted personnel.

Virtually the entire force on duty at the field, where are trained bomber pilots and bombardiers, attended the show, presented on the athletic field. The school's band opened the entertainment with a 30-minute concert.

Among the guests were newspaper and press association writers who were invited by Colonel Butler to a tour of the field in the afternoon, dinner with the cadets and bombardiers and to the officers' club for the evening.

THORESON IN CHARGE

Lieut. Harold P. Thoreson, public relations officer of the post and former San Bernardino postmaster, arranged the program and greeted the guests for Colonel Butler.

From 8 o'clock until midnight, the stars entertained the thousands of men, the officers, their ladies and guests. Hope acted as the master of ceremonies, aside from appearing with Jerry Colona in a series of skits taken from their radio programs. Miss Shore, the singing star of the Eddie Cantor radio show, literally stopped the program, sing for the soldiers all the numbers they requested.

There's one young soldier who's never going to forget Dinah Shore and her graciousness. The lovely young WSGN-BLUE Network songstress topped off a four-day trip to Uncle Sam's desert training camps last week by giving a private performance for a lonely sentry. Dinah had finished singing for the boys at the last camp visited—had sung every song they had requested, and more. The party was over and she was traveling back to Hollywood when her car was stopped in the middle of the desert outside Victorville, Calif. When the sentry recognized the BLUE Network singing star he told her to drive on. Then he added: "Gosh, Miss Shore, I surely wish I could have heard you sing tonight. but I guess somebody has to do sentry duty. I hope you will sing "Silver Wings" on your program again some time

DINAH SHORE

soon." "I'll do it right now," the gracious lady replied. Not only that, but Dinah sang others of the sentry's favorites. "I never really got to see his face," she said afterwards. "But I know he liked the songs because he stood so still while I was singing them." Miss Shore is heard

The San Bernardino Daily Sun, *July 20, 1942.*

Daily Mountain Eagle, *October 15, 1942.*

CHAPTER 7

SEEING AMERICA FROM A TROOP TRAIN

AUGUST 1942

In early August, the aerial gunners continued the five-thousand-mile train trip across America, courtesy of the US Army, heading north from Harlingen, Texas, with stops in Sedalia, Missouri; Omaha, Nebraska; Cheyenne, Wyoming; and Denver, Colorado. Along the way, their ranks swelled as they picked up new gunners from East Coast gunnery schools, including Sgts. Paul Vinson, Albert Cowles, and Francis Fox. Every town they passed through gave the boys a friendly reception.

Each of the cities was home to at least five hundred thousand people, and every one of them was conveniently the site of an Air Force base. In Wyoming, they almost died from the heat, and the next day, in Colorado, they were freezing. The train was scheduled to pull into Salt Lake City, Utah, on Saturday, August 15, after a ten-hour train trip from Colorado. Stan's and Earl's sealed orders confirmed their final destination, Geiger Field, in Spokane, Washington, where they would meet the rest of their crew and finally begin training in the Consolidated B-24 Liberator.

In Denver, the boys headed for the popular USO Hall at the

Stan's 5,000-mile train trip across America courtesy of the US Army Air Corps, 1942. Google Maps.

University of Colorado near Colorado Boulevard.

"Come on, Stan. Let's find some girls to dance with." Earl grinned.

"I'm not much of a dancer, Earl," Stan begged off. "You go ahead. I need to find some postcards."

"You sure, Stan? The girls will be all over that uniform. Besides, we've spent way too many weeks around smelly guys. A little perfume and female company are just what we need."

"You go ahead, Romeo."

With the latest Glenn Miller tunes playing in the background, Stan wandered around until he found the USO canteen.

"You have any postcards, ma'am?"

"I'm not a ma'am!" the pretty young clerk replied with a

hurt expression.

"Sorry, ma'am. I mean miss," Stan stammered.

"Don't worry, soldier. I didn't mean to embarrass you. What's your name?"

"Clifford, but everyone calls me Stanley or Stan for short."

"My name is Deidre. And where are you from, Stan?"

Stan looked at the girl for the first time. Her long, wavy brunette hair offset her pretty face. Deidre's perfect complexion didn't need much makeup. Stan thought she might be eighteen or nineteen years old.

"Salem, Deidre."

"Like in Massachusetts?"

"No. Salem, Oregon. My mom lives on the family hop farm north of Salem in a town called Keizer."

"You know how to dance, Stan? I'm almost finished here and could use some fun tonight."

"Ah, sure, I guess," Stan replied, blushing.

"Don't worry. I'll show you how and we'll have fun. Come on, soldier."

"What about the postcards?"

"Here, take these USO postcards. They're free."

"Why didn't you say so?"

"Because then you'd have left, and I wouldn't have anyone to dance with." Deidre laughed, pulling Stan along onto the dance floor. The lights, movement, and music were intoxicating. Deidre was indeed a good dance teacher, and she had Stan moving around the dance floor like a pro.

After several nonstop dances, Deidre exclaimed, "You're a natural, Stan. Where did you learn to dance like that?"

"On the hop farm. After the harvest every September, we threw a huge party for the three hundred hop pickers and their families. It was a tradition that the whole town looked forward to. Anyway, there was always plenty of food, drinks, music, and of course, dancing."

"Well, you learned really well. Now, that was fun. Let's give it another whirl. What do you say?"

"Sure thing!"

It was the most fun Stan had had in months. The drudgery of basic training and the intensity of aerial gunnery tactics melted away, leaving a young boy and girl slow dancing in each other's arms on a summer evening. Stan felt the warmth of Deidre's body, the touch of her hair against his face, and the scent of lilac in springtime. They both closed their eyes, and for a brief moment, the chaos of war faded away. Later that evening, as Stan walked Deidre back to her apartment, she slipped her arm into his and rested her head on Stan's shoulder.

When they arrived at her place, Stan turned to say good night.

"Good night, Stan. I had a lovely time," Deidre whispered as she rose on her toes to give Stan a long, soft kiss on his lips.

Blushing, Stan stammered, "Thanks for the postcards, Deidre, and the dances."

Smiling, Deidre slipped a piece of paper into Stan's hand and whispered into his ear. "Here's my address and phone number, Stan. Don't lose it. I will expect one of those postcards from you very soon."

"When this is over, I'll come back to find you, Deidre."

"Shush, Stan. Don't make any promises. Just don't forget me."

With that, Deidre entered her apartment, softly closing the door while Stan stood on the dimly lit sidewalk basking in the warm glow of a young romance that might have been.

The next morning Stan pulled out the postcard and fulfilled his promise to his mother while omitting the details of the prior evening's female companionship. By the end of the letter, he was daydreaming about Deidre. The memory of her soft kiss made him momentarily forget where he was headed.

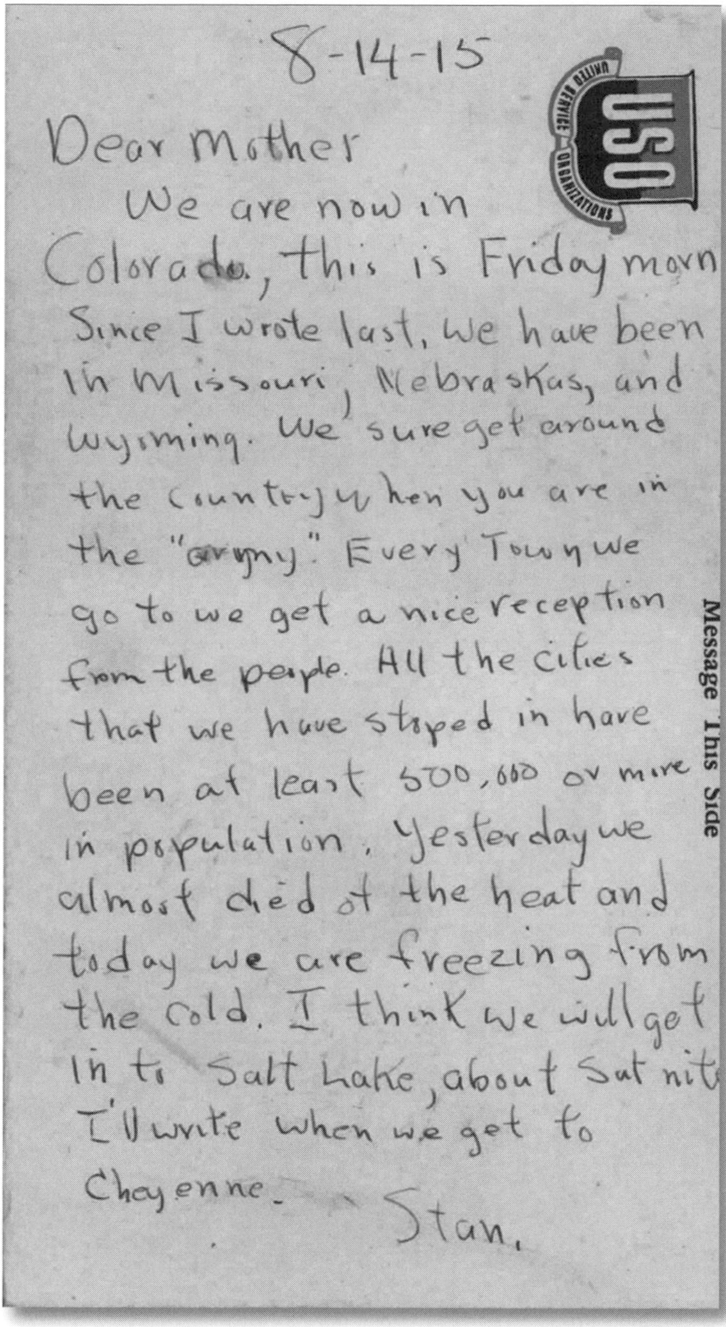

8-14-15

Dear Mother
    We are now in
Colorado, this is Friday morn
Since I wrote last, we have been
in Missouri, Nebraskas, and
Wyming. We sure get around
the country when you are in
the "army." Every Town we
go to we get a nice reception
from the people. All the cities
that we have stoped in have
been at least 500,000 or more
in population. Yesterday we
almost died of the heat and
today we are freezing from
the cold. I think we will get
in to Salt Lake, about Sat nit
I'll write when we get to
Chayenne.   Stan.

Message This Side

Letter from Clifford Stanley Low to his mother, dated August 14, 1942.
Courtesy of the Low family.

CHAPTER 8

B-24 TRAINING
IN SPOKANE

AUGUST–SEPTEMBER 1942

Geiger Field, seven miles west of downtown Spokane, was a primary World War II training base for the Army Air Corps.[1] The 8th Air Force, 34th Bomber Group, composed of the 4th, 7th, 18th, and 391st Bomb Squadrons, used the field as a group training site for the B-17 Flying Fortress and B-24 Liberator heavy bombers. In 1942 and 1943, Geiger Field was training the replacement crews of the Consolidated B-24 Liberator bombers built 1,300 miles to the south in San Diego, California, as well as in Michigan and Texas. With a top speed of over 300 miles per hour, a range of 3,000 miles, and a ceiling of 35,000 feet, the B-24 Liberator became the most produced American wartime aircraft in history. At peak production, the Consolidated factory turned out a new B-24 every 100 minutes, seven days a week, delivering more than 18,500 aircraft for the wartime effort.[2]

By mid-August, Air Force B-24 Liberator crews began to assemble at Geiger Field. Following specialized training across the country,

---

1 Today, Geiger Field is Spokane International Airport.
2 There were 8,685 B-24s produced at Ford Willow Run in Detroit, 6,506 at Consolidated San Diego, 2,745 at Consolidated Fort Worth, and 966 at North American Dallas.

Consolidated B-24 Liberator factory. Wikimedia Commons. Public domain.

pilots, navigators, bombardiers, and gunners all converged on Spokane to begin the process of quickly melding into one fighting unit. Initial crew assignments were based upon arrival at Geiger Field, to get the men in the air as soon as possible.

The men who arrived with Stanley Low and Earl Byrd were assigned to twelve bomber crews, each with eight or nine men. The assignments were posted on a bulletin board outside the ready room. The men all gathered around, straining to see their crew numbers.

"What plane did you get, Stan?" Earl asked.

"Crew 2 piloted by Robert Bender.[3] How about you, Earl?"

"Crew 1 with Scott Regan. It looks like I'll see you from a distance in the skies, Stan."

---

3   Robert P. Bender (1918–1956, from North Carolina) became a B-17 pilot in Europe with the 95th Bomb Group. Bender had the distinction of losing four B-17 planes although his crew was uninjured.

"Yeah, I wish we could have gotten the same plane. Would have been good to have a friend on board. At least we're both in the 391st Bomb Squadron."

"Well, I reckon they had to split up the two best gunners in this group." Earl grinned. "Sgt. Scott probably phoned ahead and told them two hotshot gunners were coming their way!"

Stan laughed. "Yeah, you're probably right, Earl. I'll be sure to wave when we're beating you to the targets!"

"No way, Stan. We'll beat you guys and shoot down more bogeys along the way!"

* * *

Mail call was the high point of the day at any base. A word from home or a sweetheart could make the entire week for these young men in flight suits. They crowded around as the lieutenant called out the names.

"Regan, Scott; Bender, Robert; Byrd, Earl . . ." The names droned on for fifteen minutes. As each waiting airman failed to hear his name, hopes sank, but there was always tomorrow.

"Hey, Earl. Who's your letter from? Your girlfriends back home? Can I read it?" Stan asked, hoping for something to lift his spirits vicariously. He hadn't seen a letter in over a week.

"Sure thing, Stan," Earl replied. "Anything for a bud, but let me have first crack at it."

Taking Earl's letter, Stan gushed, "You're a real Romeo! Who are those two girls you've got your arms around?"

Earl smiled. "Just friends from back home in the Smokies. We're canoeing on the Tuckasegee River."

The excited men tore open letters and packages as the rest of the squadron started scattering.

"Low, Clifford," the mail officer called out.

"Come on! Has anyone seen Sgt. Low?"

"Hey, Stan! Wake up! You got a package!" Bender called out. Stan looked up and found the whole room of airmen was staring at him.

Earl Byrd and girlfriends in Bryson City, North Carolina, along the Tuckasegee River. Courtesy of Bob Byrd.

Stan stumbled up to the front of the room.

"Here you go, soldier! Make sure you save some of whatever is in that box for me!"

"Ah, sure, and thanks," Stan mumbled.

Stan turned the package over, inspecting the writing and address. The lack of any return address just added to the mystery. Finally, unable to contain himself, he tore off the wrapping paper and opened the box.

"Cookies!" Stan called out.

The men crowded around while Stan passed out the cookies to his crew and friends.

"Thanks, Stan. You're swell. Peanut butter cookies with pecans."

At the bottom of the box, Stan found what he was hoping for, an envelope with "Stan" written in cursive. He inspected it slowly to make the excitement last. Stan put the pink envelope up to his face and inhaled.

Lilacs in spring! Stan's heart leapt. His hands were trembling as he carefully opened the envelope, pulled out the letter, and silently read the words.

August 21, 1942

Dear Stan,

I received your USO postcard soon after you left
Denver. The day you left I waited on the train
station platform and saw lots of soldiers and
lots of troop trains, but I couldn't find you. I
stayed around just in case you might see me
from your train.

Stan, thank you for a fun evening of dancing
at the USO hall. I will always remember my
young solider from Salem, Oregon, the one who
learned to dance at the hop farm. I wish we
had more time to get to know one another, but
these days you take what you get. Every moment
and every experience is so precious.

I am so glad I met you, Stan. Please remember
me and look for me after this dreadful war is
over.

PS. Hope you like the cookies!

Love,
Deidre
Denver, Colorado

THE YOUNG MEN'S CHRISTIAN ASSOCIATIONS • THE NATIONAL CATHOLIC COMMUNITY SERVICE
THE SALVATION ARMY • THE YOUNG WOMEN'S CHRISTIAN ASSOCIATIONS
THE JEWISH WELFARE BOARD • THE NATIONAL TRAVELERS AID ASSOCIATION
U S O IS FINANCED BY THE AMERICAN PEOPLE THROUGH THE NATIONAL WAR FUND

*Letter from Deidre to Clifford Stanley Low, dated August 21, 1942. Courtesy of the
Low family.*

***

The crews barely had time to get acquainted with each other and their new B-24 Liberators. Within two weeks, on August 31, the men were transferred to Topeka, Kansas, where they joined up with the 8th Air Force, 333rd Bombardment Group, 467th Squadron. Topeka Army Airfield was used for operational training of heavy-bombardment B-17 Flying Fortress and B-24 Liberator crews before they were deployed overseas. The Army activated the newly constructed airfield on July 15, 1942. The airmen traveling by train with Stan from Spokane in August were among the first to arrive at the new Topeka air base.

The men had been reorganized into four B-17 crews and twenty-six B-24 crews. They were to become the first replacement crews for the 8th Air Force. Stan's crew at Geiger Field was broken up. He joined the B-24 crew 68-Z-2, piloted by 1st Lt. Scott Regan and copiloted by 2d Lt. George D. Kerby. The navigator was 2d Lt. John L. Crane, and the bombardier was 2d Lt. Jerome A. Lesser. The enlisted men included Sergeants radio operator Albert S. Cowles, engineer/gunner Earl L. Byrd, and the three designated gunners, Francis R. Fox, Paul C. Vinson, and Clifford S. Low. Each man had a story.

Lt. Scott L. Regan, 1942. Scott was an accomplished athlete. He played halfback for the St. Mary's College High School Panthers and was a star on the St. Mary's Gael intercollegiate golf team.Courtesy of Cary Borba Perrin.

***

In the mess hall the next morning, Stan spotted his friend from gunnery school, Earl Byrd.

"Hey, Earl! I can't believe I got assigned to your B-24 crew,"

Stan exclaimed.

"Yeah, my lucky day! Now we can go to town shooting down Zekes!"

"You will have to move fast to keep up. You have to do all that flight engineer stuff before you can pick up your .50-caliber guns in the top turret."

"Don't worry about me. I'll get my share of Zekes. You just keep the front of the plane clear of incoming enemy fighters from the nose."

Stan laughed. "We both have dual .50-caliber guns. So, it'll be a pretty even competition."

"Here, let me introduce you to the other guys in the crew. This here is the golden boy, blue-eyed, blond-haired 1st Lieutenant Scott Regan, our pilot. He wanted to be an actor in Hollywood but settled for some time in the cockpit leading this motley group."

"Good to meet you, sir," Stan said as he saluted 1st Lt. Regan.

"Relax, Stan. We're all friends here. No saluting and no sir stuff while we're alone. Good to have you on board. Earl says you fire a mean .50-caliber gun."

Stan grinned and stuck out his hand, shaking Scott's vigorously.

"This is Lieutenant George

Lt. John L. Crane, Jr. in his junior year at Notre Dame. Notre Dame Yearbook 1939. Courtesy of Sheila Jaffray.

Lt. George D. Kerby. Kerby was born in Greenwood, Mississippi, on February 22, 1917. Family photograph.

Lt. Jerome A. Lesser. Lesser's father was German, and his mother was Russian Jewish and Hungarian. He chose to keep his German and Russian heritage hidden. Lesser family photograph. Courtesy of Barbara Rotenberg.

Albert Cowles was the radio operator and one of the waist gunners on the B-24 Liberator. Photograph taken in the fall of 1942 in Oahu, Hawaii. Courtesy of John Lowell.

Kerby. At six two, he's too tall to be a gunner, so he had to settle for being the copilot. He'll keep an eye on Scott to make sure he's flying the plane straight and level. George is from Baltimore, but he's a Southern boy from Charlotte, North Carolina.

"John Crane is our crew philosopher and navigator. John was his class president and captain of the varsity basketball team before he went to Notre Dame. He's got a degree in philosophy and some fancy cum laude title. Have him show you a photo of his wife, Louise. She's a doll.

"Next up is 2nd Lieutenant Jerome Lesser, from the Bronx. Jerome's Jewish and says his grandparents came from Hungary, but he's an all-American bombardier and drops a mean bomb on enemy targets.

"This young man was a champion fencer back in New York City.

B-24 Liberator ball turret gunner. Air Ministry Second World War Official Collection, CI1028.jpg. Public Domain.

Jerome is also our resident chemist. I think that means he can make us a still."

"Glad to have you onboard, Stan. Just don't call me Jerry."

"Enough of the officers. We enlisted grunts keep the guns blazing. My name's Albert Cowles. I operate the radio, but as the waist gunner, I plan on shooting down lots of Zekes. I'm also from the Bronx."

"Albert is the other thespian on our crew," Crane added. "That's a fancy word for an actor for you country boys. Cowles claims to have a contract with MGM in New York City. I imagine we'll be seeing him and Scott on the big screen real soon."

"I've never met an actor before. Are you famous?" Stan gushed.

"Don't listen to those guys, Stan," Albert replied, embarrassed by the sudden attention. "I was in a bunch of community theater plays, and the MGM deal is real, but I'm no Clark Gable."

"We'll be needing you to shoot down Zekes, not quote Shakespeare over the radio!" Jerome laughed.

"Yeah, yeah. Next, you'll want my autograph! I'll bet you know my job." The next man grinned.

"You're the ball turret gunner!" Stan replied.

"You got it, Stan. If they ever install those cramped ball turrets, I'm the guy they'll squeeze into it! At five one and 106 pounds, there's only one place they're going to stick me! For now, I'm the belly gunner. My name's Francis Fox."[4]

"Francis is the other California boy on board," Regan added.

"Actually, I'm a Southern jockey," Francis added, laughing. "I live in Burbank, California, but was born in Missouri."

"You're a real jockey?" Stan asked in amazement.

"Yep! I rode thoroughbreds with the best in the world. I was an apprentice to a jockey named Euclid Leblanc."

Sgt. Paul C. Vinson, 1940. Paul Vinson was from western Kentucky, an area called the "land between the rivers." During Prohibition, the region was so famous for its high-quality moonshine that it became the favorite source of illegal alcohol for the legendary Chicago gangster Al Capone. Courtesy of Robert Prescott.

"This here is our tail gunner, Paul Vinson. We call him Vinni. He's our resident moonshiner and the old man in the group. Paul is from New Hampshire, but he never really lost his rural Kentucky roots. Paul says he was a lab technician, whatever that means. I think he likes cows and stuff."

---

4 Early B-24s did not have the ball turret. They started with a terrible contraption that involved the gunner facing forward in the fuselage, looking through a periscope. It was very disorienting and made people sick; it was also pretty useless. These were taken out and there was nothing there at all until the ball turret came along. In the meantime, for a belly gunner, a frame with a single center mount could be swung into place at the entry/camera hatch further aft. The first ball turret was not installed until June 1943.—Bob Livingstone

Sgt. Earl L. Byrd. Courtesy of Bob
Byrd.

Clifford S. Low, 1942. Courtesy of the
Low family.

"Yeah, I went to the Mass State Agricultural College and worked for the Tolland County Dairy Association," Paul interjected. "We left Kentucky when I was born, so I can milk a Holstein cow but don't know much about moonshine."

"He's also the other married guy," John Crane interrupted.

Paul grinned. "Got hitched six months ago to my gal, Emily. But for these fellas, I'm the guy who protects their ass as the tail gunner. At six feet, I barely fit into that cramped tail turret."

"Why do they call you the old man?" Stan asked.

"Paul will turn thirty next year!" Albert explained.

"Wow! That is old!"

"All right, old man. You better figure out how to make us some Kentucky moonshine, because we don't have much use for cow's milk!" Earl laughed.

"You know me. I'm your North Carolina top turret gunner/flight engineer. I was supposed to be an airplane mechanic but made my way into gunnery school with you. I have a brother, Clyde, in the merchant marines, and a half brother, Carrol Gouge, in the Army Air Corps. I plan on shooting down more Zekes than any of you!" a grinning Earl boasted.

"And what's your story, Stan?" Scott asked.

"I'm from Salem, Oregon, but live in Northern California now. I have a brother, Loren, in the 7th Air Force. He's an aviation engineer in the South Pacific, building the runways guys like us will be landing on."

"We count on those engineers. Glad to have him on our side," Scott replied.

"Where you really from, Stan?" Jerome inquired.

"You mean, am I Hungarian?" Stan laughed.

"Yeah, that's right."

"I am a Chinese American. My dad came over from southern China a really long time ago, like in the 1870s. He grew hops in the Willamette Valley in Oregon and made lots of money and friends along the way. I can't say I'm much of a farmer, although I did pick some hops. Like you boys, I always wanted to fly."

Earl raised his glass. "Well, here's a toast to our all-American crew! We have a California golden boy aspiring actor, an Ivy League philosopher, two Bronx Bombers, three Southern boys, a Kentucky moonshiner, and the son of a Chinese hop farmer!"

"Here! Here! To the all-American crew!"

"I think we just named our B-24, boys," Scott said with a smile as he downed his glass of apple juice.

CHAPTER 9

B-24 LIBERATOR TRAINING IN TOPEKA

SEPTEMBER 1942

In five short weeks, the B-24 crew of nine men needed to become proficient in takeoffs and landings, simulated bombing runs, formation flying, flying with multiple engine failures, night flying, and aerial gunnery. They needed to learn to think and act as one. Their lives depended on it. Once the crew perfected one skill, they practiced it repeatedly for hours on end. They flew their simulated missions for fourteen hours a day. When each day finally came to a close, the men were ready to drop. The last thing they wanted to do was to talk or think about flying or dropping bombs. Back home in the new green wooden barracks at the Topeka Fairgrounds, the conversation often turned to their families.

"Stan, where did you say you were from? You're Irish, right?" Jerome joked. "And how long have you been here, anyway?"

"Family is from China. I've never been there and don't plan on going anytime soon. We've been here for a long time, like for three generations. My grandfather came to work on the railroad in the 1860s."

"Three generations! That's nothing!" Earl replied. "Byrds have been in America for ten generations. It started with a guy named Colonel Thomas Bird, who left London and came to Virginia in the 1690s. At least that's our family story."[1]

"Wait a second. My English family was in Virginia at the same time," Francis added. "That was about ten generations ago for the Foxes."[2]

"You're not going to believe this, but I have a connection to Virginia, too!" Paul exclaimed. "Vinsons were there more than ten generations ago![3] I don't know the guy's name, but we started out in Virginia. Maybe our families knew each other!"

"Better make room in Virginia for another family. Kerbys were also there in the 1600s!"[4] George chimed in. "I think the guy's name was Henry Kerby from England."

"Well, I got you all beat." Albert smiled. "There were five members of the Cowles family on the *Mayflower*. They came from England, and some went to Connecticut and settled in Hartford."[5]

"We may have to change the name of our plane to *Old Dominion*," John Crane added. The eight puzzled stares prompted John to add hurriedly, "That was King Charles II's nickname for the Virginia colony."

"Thanks, Professor," Francis smirked.

"How about you, Cap? How long have Regans been around here?"

"We're newcomers compared to you guys. I'm third-generation Irish. Grandparents settled in Ohio, where my dad, Frank, was born in 1898," Scott replied.

"I thought you were from California," Stan said, puzzled.

"We moved around a lot. My dad worked for Standard Oil, and we lived in El Paso, Texas, before going to Oakland, where I was born."

"Well, boys, our cockpit is filled with the luck of the Irish," John Crane interjected. "My great-grandfather, Michael Crane, came over from Ireland in about 1850. So, we have a pilot and navigator with Shamrock green in their veins! I hope we two can keep your Lib flying

---

1   Col. Thomas Bird (1653–1710) of London, England, immigrated to Virginia in 1691.

2   Henry Isaac Fox (1650–1714), born in London, immigrated to the Virginia Colony.

3   Thomas Vinson Sr. (1650–1713) of Virginia.

4   Henry Kerby (1670–1751) was born in England and immigrated to Virginia. George Kerby was a tenth-generation American.

5   Albert Cowles was the tenth generation of the Cowles family in Connecticut.

straight and level so Jerome can drop those bombs smack dab in the middle of the target."

"Well, boys, you know my story," Jerome finished up. "I'm your all-American bombardier."[6]

* * *

The next day, after he and Kerby completed the preflight checklist, Regan taxied the B-24 Liberator toward the runway, calling out to the crew to check in over the interphone.

"Copilot ready," Kerby mumbled as he adjusted the engine speed.

"Navigator here," Crane called in as he rechecked his route one last time.

"Bombardier ready," Lesser called in, adjusting his Norden bombsight.

"Nose gunner here," Low followed as he swept his twin .50-caliber guns side to side.

"Engineer ready, Cap," Byrd called in.

"Radio operator, here," Cowles answered.

"Belly gunner ready. Let's get this show on the road!" Fox shouted.

Static flooded the intercom as they waited and then waited some more.

"Tail gunner, are you there?" Regan called out.

"Yeah! Yeah! I'm here, Scott. Damned tail turret is too cramped. I can't fit a parachute and flak jacket in here!" Vinson replied.

"Lose some weight, Vinni," Francis chided. "Wait until they put in those ball turrets. It'll be like being a sardine in a can!"

"All right, men, cut the chatter. Let's look sharp today. No screwups. Do your jobs."

* * *

Scott adjusted his headset. "OK, George. She's all yours," he called

---

6   There were 550,000 American Jews who served in the US military in WWII, about 11.5 percent of the total American Jewish population of 4,770,000.

out to his copilot. "Just talk me through the takeoff, so I know what you're doing."

"Sure thing, Scott," Kerby replied as he took control of the wheel and lined the plane up with the runway.

As George released the brake and advanced the throttle, the plane roared down the runway, gathering speed.

At ninety miles per hour, Kerby called out, "Applying back pressure."

At 115 miles per hour, the ship left the ground and became airborne.

"Holding the nose down to pick up speed. Raise the gear, Scott."

"OK, George. Gear up," Scott called out.

"Speed is up to 135 miles per hour."

"Raise the flaps and reduce the power to 45 inches manifold pressure at 2,550 revolutions per minute," Kerby instructed. "I'm synchronizing the propellers to distribute the load equally to the four engines."

Climbing out at 1,000 feet per minute at 150 miles per hour, Kerby checked the gauges for any sign of problems. Everything looked perfect.

"Manifold pressure 45.5 inches at 2,550 revs per min. Oil pressure

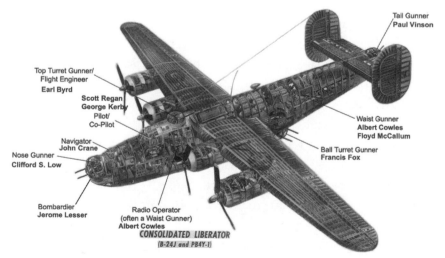

Modified flying cutaway by Reynold Brown depicting B-24 Liberator crew assignments. Flying, October 1945. Public domain. Creative Commons.

B-24 Liberator cockpit. National Museum of the United States Air Force. Public domain.

84 pounds. Fuel pressure 15 pounds per square inch. Oil temperature 80 degrees. Cylinder head temperature 210 degrees."

"You're in the groove, George. That was a textbook takeoff."

"Let's resynch the propellers."

"Setting mixture controls to auto lean; turning off booster control; closing the cowl flaps," Kerby called out as he set the plane up for level cruising.

"OK, George. Take her up to 9,500 feet so you can drop her down into a cruising altitude of 9,000 feet."

"Taking her over the hump," Kerby called out as they climbed and then put the B-24 into a shallow dive, picked up speed to 185 miles per hour, and leveled off at 9,000 feet.

Scott set the turbochargers to maintain thirty-one inches of manifold pressure.

"Nice flying, George. Let me take her out to the bombing range so Jerome can get in some practice with those hundred-pound sand bombs."

The Liberator headed east toward the bombing range. As they approached the range, the outline of a city painted on the ground came into view, with targets indicated by a large white X.

"Lt. Lesser, do you have your bombsight turned on? It's going to be your show in here in a few minutes," Regan called out to his bombardier.

"Yeah, Scott. The Norden bombsight is on, and the gyros have been warming up. I'm ready. I hope the ground crew loaded my sand bombs," Jerome replied.

"You should have checked the ordnance yourself."

B-24 Liberator. Wikimedia Commons. Public domain.

"Aye, aye, Captain."

"A bombardier with no bombs is not much use to us."

Lesser felt the vibration of the gyros as he peered through the bombsight's telescopic eyepiece. He entered the plane's precise elevation and the required ballistic information, which enabled the Norden bombsight to calculate wind direction and velocity, drift angle of the aircraft, ground speed, and the exact angle to deliver the bombs to their target.

"I have the target in my crosshairs, Scott."

"OK, Jerome. You have control of the plane," Scott replied. "She's all yours."

"Opening the bomb bay doors."

The target began to drift off the crosshairs as a crosswind affected the plane's course.

"Killing the drift here," Jerome called out as he adjusted the turn and drift knobs, crabbing the plane into the wind. The target came back into alignment within the crosshairs.

The Norden bombsight calculated the drift angle and cross trail distance to compensate for the crosswind's effect on the falling bombs by flying upwind of the target.[7]

Peering through the eyepiece, Jerome held the target steady and watched the sight angle narrow as they drew closer to the target.

"It's looking good, Cap," Jerome called out.

At the precise moment when the sight angle of the bombsight matched the calculated drop angle, a switch activated, releasing the hundred-pound sand-filled bombs.

"Bombs away!" Jerome called out.

He watched through the eyepiece as the bombs fell away from the plane. After forty seconds, they struck the ground, and detonators set off small charges to mark the location of each bomb's strike.

---

7   The Norden Bombsight was a top-secret development of the 1930s used in World War II and the Korean War. It was a mechanical computer with a complex system of gears, levers, motors, pulleys, cables, and gyroscopes that made the calculations to deliver the bomb to the target.

"Bull's-eye," Jerome reported.

"That's another bombing run right into the pickle barrel![8] Nice work, Jerome," Regan said.

"Way to go, Jerome," Stan called out from his nose gunner position next to the bombardier. "You have to show me how you do that bombardier stuff."

"Sure, Stan. I'll give you a crash course. You never know when you might have to drop the bombs for us someday."

"That's right! Cross-training boys. Every man needs to be able to step into another seat in an emergency," Regan advised his men. "Let's go around and do it again from a higher altitude."

"OK, Lieutenant Crane. Plot us a course to pass south of the airfield and bring us back to the bombing range at twenty thousand feet," Scott called out to his navigator.

In a few moments, Crane called the heading over the interphone, "Heading one-eight-zero degrees for fourteen minutes."

"It's going to be cold up there, men. Have your electric flight suit heaters plugged in, and turn up the rheostat.[9] Check your oxygen masks," Regan advised his crew over the interphone.

The B-24 Liberator was neither pressurized nor heated. The temperature and air pressure in the plane were the same as the outside air. At twenty thousand feet, the temperature was -12°F. The temperature dropped to -47°F on missions at thirty thousand feet. Above ten thousand feet, the men used supplemental oxygen.

"Darn heaters don't work half the time, Scott," Cowles called out from the waist gunner's position.

"Stop complaining, you wimp! The tail's colder," Vinson replied. "We'll be doing our oxygen check every fifteen minutes. Call out your number loud and clear. Don't make me ask who's unconscious! Cowles,

---

8   Actual accuracy for the Army Air Corps bombardiers in 1940 was a circular error of about 400 feet from an altitude of 15,000 feet.

9   A rheostat is an adjustable resistor that is able to provide varying resistance in an electrical circuit. In this application, the rheostat controls the temperature of the heated flight suit.

you're responsible for the O2 checks on this mission."[10]

"Got it, Lieutenant," Albert responded.

Dark thunderhead clouds in the distance were the first warning. As the Liberator climbed through the clouds, the swirling gusts buffeted the plane.

"Hold on, men. We got some turbulence coming," Regan called out.

With the plane bouncing up and down, Vinson grabbed onto his .50-caliber gun as the drops of rain pelted the tail's plexiglass turret. "Pretty rough ride back here, Cap!" Vinson replied. The flash of lightning lit up the sky, followed by the thunderous clap that shook the plane and the men's nerves.

"That was close. Let's get out of here," Jerome called out from the nose. "Forget the darn sand bombs!"

Sheets of rain ripped in through the open waist gun windows. Cowles was getting drenched.

Suddenly the floor dropped out and the Liberator plummeted two hundred feet, then shot back up like a roller coaster.

"Forget the aerobatics, Lieutenant. Let's find some smooth air," Byrd yelled, holding on to his .50-caliber gun.

"Roger that, Cap! Enough of the roller coaster ride. I felt that one in my stomach," Vinson called out from the tail.

"Cut the chatter, boys! We'll be out of this thunderstorm in a jiffy," Regan said. "John, plot us a course out of this weather. Let's find some smooth air and drop those bombs."

Crane had been plotting their course and watching the developing weather. "Turn to heading nine-zero degrees and climb to twenty thousand feet. That should take us out of the storm and above the clouds."

As predicted, the ride smoothed out, and the rain died down as the Liberator lumbered on toward the bombing range.

In the tail, Vinson looked back toward the receding thunderstorm, admiring the lightning show. "It's kind of pretty from a distance. Glad

---

10 The oxygen checks were a deadly serious business. Faulty oxygen equipment or a disconnected hose could cause death in minutes.

we escaped that one!"

"OK, Jerome, she's all yours," Regan called out as they approached the bombing range. "Albert, do your oxygen check. We're at twenty thousand feet."

"Aye, aye, Captain. Men, call out your numbers."

"One!"

"Two."

"Three."

"Four!"

"Five."

"Six . . ."

"Tail gunner, check in!"

"Sorry about that, Albert. Seven."

"Eight and nine from the cockpit. Keep checking your oxygen masks, men. And turn those heaters up."

"Roger that! It's freezing back here," Cowles reported from the waist gunner position.

From the front of the plane, Lesser had the target in the crosshairs of the Norden bombsight. Adjusting the path for the crosswind, he flew the Liberator upwind.

"Opening bomb bay doors."

At the precise moment, the electronic trigger released all seven sand bombs.

"Bombs away! There they go!" Jerome called out.

The men were hypnotized by the falling bombs as they watched from the bomb bay doors and the waist gunner windows.

"There's no way you're going to hit the target from up here. You'll miss by ten miles!" Vinson reported from the open bomb bay door.

"You have no faith, Vinni. Just watch and learn!" Jerome laughed. Sure enough. It was another perfect clustered bull's-eye.

"What did I tell you, boys? They taught us well at Victorville. We bombardiers can fly the plane, drop the bombs, and navigate our way back home. All without breaking a sweat!"

"How many bombs did you drop? You're supposed to drop two, right?"

"Oops! Looks like all seven sand bombs hit the target. It must have been a malfunction or my twitchy trigger finger." Jerome smiled.

Regan congratulated his friend. "Great job today, Jerome. Thanks to you, we'll be getting home a bit early today."

"Now, if Stan will just show me how to shoot his .50-caliber machine gun, I'll be a one-man show!"

"Any time, Jerome," Stan replied. "Come on up into the nose gunner's station,[11] and I'll show you how to shoot down some Zekes." He swung the guns right to left, sighting imaginary enemy fighters.

"Can't wait, Stan. I'll take you up on your offer."

"OK, John. Plot a course to take us home."

* * *

Back in his room that evening after chow, Paul Vinson had orders to change barracks but couldn't wait to tell his wife, Emily, about their adventures. It was all in a day's work in the Army Air Corps.

September 8, 1942
Dearest Emmy,

Just got back from a bombing practice flight. After an hour or so of flying around in circles, it sort of got monotonous. But you're too high to get out and walk home. It was pretty rough up there today. First you'd drop and then shoot up. Enough so that you could feel it in your stomach. So, guess the distance was more than a few feet.

The bombardier got a couple of bull's-eyes, so I guess he feels pretty good about it. He had seven bombs left to drop. He must have gotten nervous, because all of the sudden as we

---

11 The first nose-turreted B-24 was built on June 30, 1943, so this crew would have trained and flown a "glasshouse-nosed" B-24.—Bob Livingstone

were over the target he let all seven go at once. As a result, we came home that much quicker. The bombs are only a hundred pounds: five pounds of black powder and enough sand to bring the weight up to a hundred pounds. When they drop, we watch them out of the open bomb bay doors and the gun windows. They look as though they would land ten miles from the target. Still, they don't. They come pretty close, I'll say.

Love,
Paul

U.S. ARMY AIR FORCES
GEIGER FIELD, WASHINGTON

468ᵗʰ Bomb. Squad.
Army Air Base
Topeka, Kansas
Sept. 8, 1942

Dearest Emmy,

I've got to move to-night – a new barracks. Don't know what the idea is yet but guess I'll have to do it any way.

Just got in from a bombing practice flight. After an hr. or so of flying around in circles it sort of gets monotonous but your too high to get out & walk home. It was pretty rough up there to-day, first you'd drop & then shoot up, enough so that you could feel it in your stomach so guess the distance was more than a few ft.

The bombardier got a couple of bulls eyes so guess he feels pretty good about it. He had seven bombs left to drop & he must have gotten nervous because all of a sudden as we came over the target he let all seven go at once. As a result we came home that much quicker.

The bombs are only 100 pounders, 5 lbs of black powder & enough sand to bring the weight up to 100 pounds. When they drop we watch them out of the open bomb bay doors and the gun windows. They look as though they would land 10 miles from the target. Still they don't, they come pretty close I'll say.

Oh honey, I won't be a radio man from what I get here. They give us just a smattering so we could run a set in a pinch. Just in case the radio man should get knocked off.

Letter from Paul Vinson to his wife, Emily, dated September 8, 1942. Courtesy of Joanne Davidson.

CHAPTER 10

THE TENTH MAN: A SHORT TRIP HOME

SEPTEMBER 1942

The eighty-acre McCallum homestead in central Michigan, nine miles south of Evart, was poor, rural America, but for Eldon McCallum, this was his home. He loved it here. For four generations, the McCallums had been struggling to eke out a living as farmers, growing hay and corn, using horse-powered hay loaders and human sweat to get the job done. The days were long, and the harvests were often meager.

Eldon, or Eldie as the townsfolk knew him, had little interest in farming. He was an outdoorsman to his very core and a bit of a legend in these parts. As a teen, Eldon had bagged the first deer ever taken in the county. Known for his quick smile and outgoing personality, fun-loving Eldon was always ready to take anyone hunting, fishing, or swimming. He was the ultimate sportsman, and these backwoods were his playground.

With his shotgun in hand and Zeke, his retriever, at his side, Eldie headed for the "big swamp" along the western edge of the farm. The ground was soft from the early fall rain as he quietly stepped through the thickets in his regulation Army Air Force flying boots. He hadn't intended to wear the fleece-lined boots, but his departure from the base had been a spur-of-the-moment decision. The rubberized boot soles were perfect for the muddy field, but his green flight suit was already a mess.

Zeke had come out to greet him as he exited the last ride. Zeke's frantic excitement and wagging tail made the previous four months melt away. Hitching rides was pretty easy in these parts, filled with more trust than good sense. Even leaving the base without a pass had been easy. He just strolled right through the gate and he was free, at least for now. It took three rides and four hours to cover the almost two-hundred-mile trip northwest from Willow Run to Evart. Frankly, if he'd had to, he would have walked home. Gazing at his muddy boots brought into focus how he'd come to be here.

There's going to be hell to pay later.

"Come on, boy. Let's go hunting," Eldie whispered.

He slipped into the barn with Zeke and found his best hunting shotgun and a few shells. He hadn't even been up to the old house on the hill. He knew his parents would be up there, but there would be too much explaining to do. It was easier this way.

"You don't need any explaining, do you, boy?" he told Zeke.

The thick brush surrounding the swamp was a perfect hiding place for partridges, his favorite game. Zeke went ahead a few yards, stopping to sniff every bush and rock. Suddenly, the dog froze. A second later, Zeke ran into the brush, flushing out a flock of partridges. The startled, flapping birds made a whooshing sound as they took flight.

Eldon instinctively raised his gun, sighted the birds in flight, led them perfectly, and pulled the trigger, all in one practiced motion.

Bam! The recoil pushed the shotgun's stock into his right shoulder. The sound was deafening, but it was the glorious echo of the shot ringing through the air that made Eldie feel at home, at last.

"Got one!"

Zeke tore off into the brush, rooted around for a second, then came bounding back with the bird held softly in his mouth.

"Good boy!" Eldie encouraged his boyhood companion with a pat on his head that made Zeke's tail wag even faster. Eldie placed the partridge into his flight suit. He knew it would be only a few minutes before his parents spotted him, so he unloaded his shotgun and headed up the hill to the two-story gray asphalt-covered family home.

On the trudge up to the house, his thoughts turned to his parents. Eldon was not a pacifist like his father, Floyd Senior, who had never fired a gun, gone hunting, or killed another living thing in his life. As a young man, to avoid the draft during World War I, he moved his whole family to Billings, Montana, where his daughter Helen was born. Floyd was as patriotic as the next man; he just didn't see sense in killing another human being. After he learned that his friend Joseph Guyton was killed on Germany's front lines in May 1918, he never again questioned his decision.[1]

Eldie hated the name Floyd. He never used it, ever, until he was drafted into the Army. The military insisted on calling him Floyd E. McCallum. It made him cringe being called Floyd. Lots of things about the military got under his skin. Basic training at Fort Custer had been a real pain.[2] He'd come down with a bad case of the flu, which didn't make things any easier. At twenty-six, he was the old man in boot camp. Being years older than the other recruits, Eldon had a real problem with military rules and regulations.[3] He frankly didn't see the sense in having some snot-nosed kid tell him what to do.

The steps of the old house brought him back to the present. He couldn't wait to see his mom, but grimaced in anticipation of the scolding he was going to encounter. Edna May had been a school-teacher who ordered her world with strict rules and discipline. She lovingly imposed order on Eldie's childhood, reining in his wild side.

For a brief, odd moment, Eldie considered knocking at the front door, not sure to which world he belonged. Shaking his head, he turned the handle, opened the wooden door, and passed back into

---

1   Joseph W. Guyton, from Evart, Michigan, was the first American killed on German soil, on May 24, 1918.

2   During World War II, Fort Custer had an area of 16,005 acres, and quarters for 1,279 officers and 27,553 enlisted personnel. More than 300,000 troops trained there. Fort Custer later served as a POW camp for 5,000 German soldiers, until 1945.

3   Floyd Eldon McCallum was born June 30, 1915. He was twenty-six years old when he was drafted on January 30, 1942.

his former life. The old three-bedroom home hadn't changed much in four months. Frankly, it hadn't changed much in decades. The parlor was dark and eerily quiet until the sneak attack. Struck from behind, Eldie was facedown on the carpeted floor.

"Gotcha, Eldie!" a delighted Bill cried out, pouncing on his older brother's back. Eldie tried to roll over, but Bill had him pinned down.

"Bill, you've been eating too much of Mom's cooking. You weigh a ton." Eldie laughed.

Letting his big brother up, Bill hugged Eldie like he never wanted to let go. Eldie was his hero. He was a hero to all of Bill's friends, but today Eldie was his and his alone. Bill had been devastated when Eldie had left home for Camp Custer, certain that he would never see him again.

"I think you squashed our dinner." Eldie laughed, pulling the partridge out of his flight suit. "Where's Mom?"

"Out back picking greens for supper."

"And Dad?"

"Who knows? Maybe in the privy. Probably out with his friends. He expects me to do all the farm work now that you're away, and Hardie's married!"

Eldie tousled Bill's hair and laughed. "Don't complain! It'll make a man out of you. But I remember what it's like. Hang in there. How old are you now, Bill? Maybe about twenty years old?"

"I'm fourteen, and you know it, Eldie!"

"OK. But you do weigh a lot for a kid. You been taking care of Zeke for me?"

"Yep. We go hunting every chance we get. I've been using your guns. I hope that's all right."

"Sure, Bill, but I'll have to tell you about the big .50-caliber guns I hunt with now. We'll be hunting Japanese Zeros real soon."

Bill was about to reply when the back-porch door opened and Edna May came in with a basket full of collard greens and tomatoes. She looked up with a shocked expression and dropped the basket, scattering the greens over the linoleum floor

"Eldon! My son! What are you doing here? Why didn't you call? You just gave me a dreadful fright. I thought I was seeing a ghost!" she exclaimed, rushing into the front room to embrace her son.

"Sorry, Mom. I left Willow Run in a bit of a rush," Eldie explained, hoping that would be the end of the explanation.

"What do you mean, Eldon?" Edna May asked suspiciously. "How long are you on leave?"

The room was silent as Eldie looked first at his mother and then at the floor.

"Eldon, what's going on here?" she asked quietly.

"Mom, I had to come home. I couldn't take being there anymore. I had to see you and Bill and Helen and Hardie and Dad."

"Let me see your pass, Eldon," Edna demanded, like a school-teacher asking to see a student's hall pass.

"Don't have one, Mom. I just walked off the base and started hitching rides. I hitched all morning to come and see you. I don't know what happened. When I saw the gate, I couldn't help myself. I just left."

Edna was quiet as she considered what her son had just told her. She knew what he had done was wrong, and it violated every fiber of her rule-oriented being, but she was overjoyed to see her son, and who knew when or if he would ever be home again.

"I'm glad you came home, Eldie," she whispered, embracing her son again as he let out an audible sigh of relief. "Are you staying for dinner?"

The rest of the afternoon and evening was a blur of laughter, back-slapping, good company, and Edna's delicious home-style cook-ing. All the family and many of the neighbors arrived as word of Eld-ie's surprise visit spread like wildfire. By early evening, well-wishers filled the home, spilling out onto the porch.

"What's training been like?" Eldon's older brother Hardie asked.

"Gunnery school was a breeze. Just like shooting partridges with a really big gun that spits out ammo faster than anything you can imagine, like eight hundred bullets a minute!"

"Man! That's a lot of firepower," Bill exclaimed with envy. "Can I see your gun someday?"

"They don't let us keep it. We have to turn it in every day after we clean and oil it."

"How about your crew? What are they like?" his sister, Helen, asked.

"They're OK, I guess. We all hooked up at Barksdale Field in Shreveport, where the 90th Bombardment Group formed. In June, we transferred to Greenville Army Air Base in Greenville, South Carolina. They assigned me to a B-24 crew as a gunner. Now we're at Willow Run picking up our new Liberator at the plant."

"What are the guys like?" Helen persisted.

"Well, we're all single guys. Not a married man in sight. Frankly, it seems unfair that only the single guys will be fighting and dying for their country."

Eldon paused, wishing he could take back the last part as he stared at his married older brother, Hardie, who had stepped into the parlor. "I'm sure there must be some married guys, but I haven't seen any," he added hurriedly.

"How long are you staying, Eldie?" asked Collin Campbell, his old boss at the Barryton Press.

"Not long, Mr. Campbell. Are you keeping my old job open for me? I still remember how to stack, fold, and deliver newspapers." Eldie laughed.

"You'll always have a job at the Barryton Press, Eldie. Or maybe you still want that position with the state police."

Eldon smiled, remembering his dream of entering law enforcement. Not much chance of that now.

Later that evening, after the guests had finally departed, heading back to Evart and the surrounding farms, Eldon found himself alone with his mother in the kitchen, scrubbing pots and pans.

"Mom, I need to talk to you."

"What is it, Eldon?"

"I don't think I'm coming back. I'm not scared, but I have a bad feeling. If anything happens to me, I want you to know that I'm going to be OK."

Edna May quietly embraced him, trying to resist a mother's instinct to reassure her son. "I know you'll be fine, Eldon. I'll be waiting for you here or on the other side, son," she whispered as a single tear trickled down her face.

*　*　*

The next morning Eldie had his limited gear packed as his family gathered around. The air was thick with unspoken worry and longing, covered up with well wishes and bravado.

"Give 'em hell, Eldie!" Hardie encouraged.

Helen smiled as she embraced her brother without uttering a word.

Bill simply hung on to his big brother and refused to let go.

"We know you're tough, Eldon," his father said as he shook his son's hand for the last time. "Remember what we taught you, and use whatever it takes to get through all of this."

Eldon caught a ride from Evart with Mr. Smith, who was heading up to Detroit on business. The trip back to Willow Run was quicker than the trip home.

*　*　*

As Eldon expected, there was indeed hell to pay back at the base. As soon as he passed through the gates at Willow Run, MPs arrested him and threw him in the brig. He was quickly found guilty of going AWOL and demoted two ranks. Staff Sgt. Floyd E. McCallum would be Cpl. Floyd E. McCallum for the rest of this war. Worst of all, they removed him from his assigned crew, who flew off in their new plane. But this was wartime, and Uncle Sam desperately needed every able-bodied soldier, even those with momentary lapses of judgment.

On October 4, 1942, Cpl. Floyd Eldon McCallum found himself on his way to Topeka, Kansas, with orders to join B-24 crew 68-Z-2 piloted by 1st Lt. Scott Regan. He would have to hightail it to Topeka, as Regan's Liberator was scheduled to depart for Long Beach, California, the next day.

* * *

At Topeka Army Airfield, McCallum presented his orders to the commanding officer of the 333rd Bombardment Group, Col. Leo De Rosier, who was frowning as he quickly scanned the papers.

"If you want to join Lieutenant Regan's crew, you better get a move on, Corporal. They may be on the taxiway as we speak! You are going to have to run." He pointed toward the airstrip. Col. De Rosier wasn't kidding. Regan's crew was loading up their gear and boarding their Liberator.

Cpl. Floyd E. McCallum, Fort Custer, Michigan. Courtesy of George Corwin.

"Well, who do we have here? A Johnny-come-lately, I see," Earl Byrd commented, sizing up the new man on the tarmac. "What's your name and specialty, soldier?"

"Cpl. Floyd Eldon McCallum, and I'm a crack gunner," Eldon replied, waiting to see the response. *The last thing I need is another group of regulation-spouting officers and blindly obedient enlisted men.*

The other men gathered around, looking at McCallum with suspicion.

It's not going to be easy to break in with this group.

To his surprise, Earl grinned. "Well, welcome aboard, Crackpot! Get on up here."

"I said I was a crack gunner, not a crackpot," Eldon objected.

"I heard you, Crackpot. We all go by nicknames, and now you have one, too. The guys call me Early Bird. How good a shot are you, anyway?"

"Back home in Michigan, I can hit a running squirrel at two hundred yards with a .22-caliber rifle."

"Well, we're not shooting at squirrels, and we're not firing pop guns out here," Vinson growled.

"Well, us country boys don't need a .50-caliber automatic gun to go hunting in the woods," Eldon replied.

"I thought I heard some country in you, boy! You're going to fit right in to this group," Earl Byrd said, grinning and extending a hand.

"Come on up to the flight deck and meet the lieutenants," Cowles said, leading the way along the nine-inch catwalk running down the center of the plane.

"Lieutenant Regan, this here's our new gunner, Corporal Floyd McCallum. And Floyd, this is our copilot, Lieutenant George Kerby, and navigator, Lieutenant John Crane. You'll have to meet our bombardier, Lieutenant Lesser, later. He's busy up front along with our nose gunner, Sergeant Low."

"Welcome aboard, Floyd," Regan said. "Do your job, and we'll all get along."

"Sir, do you mind calling me by my middle name, Eldon or Eldie? I hate Floyd."

"No problem. Eldie it is. When we're in a private company, we can drop the formalities."

The enlisted men were finishing up stowing their gear and going over checklists to prepare for the cross-country flight to the West Coast.

"So, what else do you bring to our all-American crew, Eldie?" Francis asked.

"What do you mean?"

"Well, this crew has a bit of everything that's American. We have a California golden boy, an Ivy League philosopher, two Bronx Bombers, three Southern boys, a Kentucky moonshiner, and the son of a Chinese hop farmer!"

"So, where is your family from, Eldon?" Cowles asked.

"I grew up on a farm in Evart, Michigan, but I don't think that's what you're asking."

"That's right. Where did the McCallums come from, Eldon?"

"I'll let you guess. But here's a hint. I'll be wearing a kilt when I shoot down all those Zekes!" Eldon laughed as he attempted his best Scottish McCallum brogue.[4]

The men laughed at Eldie's Scottish accent, clapped him on the back, and got back to loading their ammunition. Eldie felt at home for the first time since he'd left Evart to see the world.

Shooting big guns and being a warrior with this group of guys is going to be all right.

* * *

Before they left Topeka, Stan had rushed over to the base commissary, picked out his mother's favorite See's Candy, and scribbled a message home. On the rack, he spotted a postcard of a bomber and proudly placed it in the package, hoping his mom would understand how he'd be arriving in Long Beach. It wasn't a B-24, but it would have to do, and she wouldn't know the difference.

---

4   Floyd McCallum was a fourth-generation Scottish American. Floyd's great-grandfather Malcolm (1799–1872) was from Skipness, and his great-grandmother Margaret McNaughton (b. 1812) was from Argyllshire. Malcom immigrated to Ontario, Canada, where his son William was born in 1844, and then to Mecosta County, Michigan, where he died.

Postcard sent by Stan to his mother, August 1942. Courtesy of the Low family.

CHAPTER 11

LONG BEACH, CALIFORNIA

OCTOBER 1942

The ring of the doorbell brought Kay out of her daydreaming. As usual, she was thinking about—actually, she was worrying about—Stan. Gwunde had been away from home in the South Pacific for almost two years, but he was older and could take care of himself.

Aiyaah! Stanley is too young. He's still the baby in the family. I should never have signed those papers to let him enlist. What was I thinking?[1]

Running to the front door, MeiMei called out, "I have it!" At seventeen years old, she was pretty much her mom's constant companion.[2]

Opening the door, she took the package and smiled as she immediately recognized the scrawled printing.

"Mom, it's a package for you!"

Kay took the package, carefully removed the paper wrapping, and smiled broadly at its contents.

"Stanley always remembers my favorite See's Candy."

She opened the box and offered a piece to MeiMei and her

---

1 In mid-January 1942, the minimum age to sign up for the Army Air Corps cadet program was reduced from twenty to eighteen. Stanley initially tried to enlist in 1941 when he was nineteen.

2 MeiMei is Cantonese for "little sister."

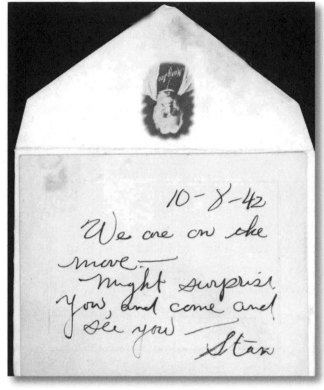

10-8-42
We are on the
move.—
Might surprise
you, and come and
see you —
Stan

See's Candy card sent by Stan Low to his mother in October 1942. Courtesy of the Low family.

older sister, Isabel, who had just entered the parlor of her home in Los Angeles.

"Here's the card, Mom."

"You read it to me," Kay ordered as she bit into a caramel-covered candy with almonds.

"I think Stan's coming for a visit," MeiMei revealed. "It says, 'We are on the move. Might surprise you and see you. Stan.'"

Kay squinted at the card, searching for Stan's name. She had glasses but was much too vain to wear them.

Ding dong! Ding dong!

"Who could that be?" MeiMei asked as she bounded out of her chair.

"Maybe more candy." Isabel laughed.

As MeiMei opened the door, she let out a squeal of delight at the sea of olive green filling the front porch. "Mom, you better come see this!"

"What is it, MeiMei? I can't eat any more candy," she replied, getting up from the couch, her curiosity piqued.

"Just come to the door."

What Kay encountered was a mother's joy. "Stan!" she gasped as she grabbed her youngest son and embraced him.

Embarrassed, Stan gently pulled away. "Mom! Let me introduce you . . ."

"Hug your mom, Stan!" Jerome said.

"Yeah, BFW. Do it for us!" the men chided him in unison. Stan embraced his mother fully.

"That's enough! My turn now," MeiMei interrupted as she embraced her best friend and older brother.

Isabel waited patiently, hugged her little brother, and asked, "What's BFW?"

"Never mind. Maybe I'll tell you later."

Ignoring Stan's objections, Earl blurted out, "It's our nickname for your brother. We call him Baby-Faced Warrior."

"But that's too long, so we shortened it to BFW," Albert explained.

"Who are your friends, Stan?" MeiMei asked, smiling at the sea of airmen.

"First, please come in," Isabel instructed.

Inside, Stan began the introductions: "Mom, this is Lieutenant Jerome Lesser—"

Jerome interrupted. "It's a pleasure to meet you and Stanley's family. Please call me Jerome."

"And this is my friend from gunnery school, Earl Byrd. These guys are Albert Cowles, Paul Vinson, and the newest member of our crew, Eldon McCallum."

"Hey! What about me?"

"Sorry, I missed you back there. This guy is our belly gunner, Francis Fox. He lives in Burbank, not far from here. Francis is a famous jockey."

"Not famous, ma'am, but I do ride thoroughbreds, and I am from Burbank." Francis grinned as he shook hands with Kay and Stan's sisters.

Sitting with their caps in hand, the men, dressed in their olive-green uniforms, filled the apartment's front room. The conversation was animated as each, in turn, told of his family back home. The others sat politely as they quietly thought of their own mothers and siblings.

Finally, Isabel interjected, "You must be famished. Let's go out for lunch!"

"Great idea, and I know just the place." Stan grinned. "It's called the Golden Pagoda in Chinatown."

"Maybe your friends want some American food, Stanley," Kay suggested.

"No, ma'am. We like Chinese. We get American grub every day! It's like eating K rations."

"Stan's older brother, Gwunde, taught me that word, 'grub.' " Kay smiled.

"Well, boys. Let's get you some good Chinese grub," Mei-Mei laughed.

* * *

On the way into Chinatown, the taxis turned onto Alameda and passed by Union Station. Stan gazed out the smudged window and remembered his friends dropping him off here. It seemed like an eternity had passed since then.

The meal of dim sum at the Golden Pagoda hit the spot for the boys, who had had more than their fill of Army mess hall meals.

At Isabel's insistence, they called the air base in Long Beach and told the Lieutenants Regan, Kerby, and Crane to join them at the restaurant. Now the entire crew was united with Stan's family.

The waiter recognized Stan immediately. "Who are your new friends?" he asked.

"This is my B-24 crew. We have been training and just flew in from Topeka, Kansas," Stan replied proudly.

"You know this guy?" Lesser asked the waiter.

"He's a famous gunner," Earl added.

"He too skinny," the waiter said. "Here. You eat more Chinese food." He piled more food on Stan's plate.

Regan stood with a teacup in hand, "Here's a toast to Stan's family and our all-American crew!"

"Here! Here!" the men repeated the toast. "To Stan's family! Our families are the reason we're going to war."

The waiter returned. "You have to pay today—no free food. Your Army friends eat too much dim sum," he explained with a worried expression.

"No problem. The Chinese food was delicious," Kerby exclaimed as they pulled out their wallets to pay.

"No! No!" Kay objected. "We pay. You boys are Stanley's friends and our guests."

"But we overate. It will be expensive," John Crane objected. "Let us take care of the bill."

"I said no!" Kay replied.

"You better let my mom pay. It's a matter of pride," Mei-Mei explained.

"Thank you, Mrs. Low," each of the men said, showing their gratitude for the excellent food and the company.

"Our families thank you for showing us a nice afternoon," Scott Regan said. "We won't forget you."

Outside, Stanley posed briefly for photos with his mom and sisters, then prepared to rush back to the base.

"Don't rush, Stan. You never know when you'll see them again," Kerby advised.

"Besides, your kid sister is cute!" Jerome smiled.

"Cut it out, Romeo! You still think you're Errol Flynn." Francis laughed.

The ride back to Long Beach Army Airfield was quiet as the men thought of their homes and families, now so very far away. They were one step closer to the war in the South Pacific.

MeiMei, Stanley, Kay, and Isabel Low, Los Angeles, October 1942. Stan and his B-24 crew were on their way to Hamilton Air Force Base in Novato, California, and then on to Australia and the war in the South Pacific. Courtesy of the Low family.

CHAPTER 12

HAMILTON ARMY AIRFIELD

OCTOBER 1942

Hamilton Airfield in Novato is positioned along the western shore of San Pablo Bay. The base, twenty-five miles north of San Francisco, was designed in the Spanish eclectic style, with white stucco buildings of hollow tile or reinforced concrete construction and red mission tile roofs. The land sloped gently up to a verdant plateau from the airfield, where the base resembled a Spanish hacienda. At the end of a palm-lined avenue, headquarters was housed in a mission-style building.

During World War II, Hamilton Airfield was a staging area for B-24 crews before they flew their new B-24s overseas to the European and Pacific theaters.

The 450-mile flight from Long Beach to Novato took Regan's Liberator up the Central Valley, passing just west of Bakersfield and then heading for the Bay Area. Stan was excited to show the guys his home state from the air. From the glasshouse in the nose, the view was spectacular.

"Hey, Jerome. I grew up in Stockton, just over these hills to the east of here."

"This place doesn't look like the Bronx," Jerome laughed. "You

Hamilton Airfield. US Army Corps of Engineers. Wikimedia Commons. Public domain.

guys have so much open space out here. It's unnatural!"

The B-24 took a westerly heading toward the Bay Area.

"Keep watching. We'll pass over this Diablo Range, and then we should see San Francisco Bay."

"I can't wait to check out the Golden Gate Bridge. Maybe Scotty will buzz it for us!"

"Hey, Crane, can you take us right over the Golden Gate?"

"You guys think this is a tour bus?" John laughed. "Sure, Jerome. Anything for a boy from the Bronx."

Twenty minutes later, Jerome got his wish.

"Woah! What a sight! That is not the Brooklyn Bridge!"

"Hey, Scottie. Can you take us down a little closer?"

"Sure thing, men. This may be our only chance to get an up-close and personal view."

Regan kept it legal but got down close enough to see the soldiers with their dates on the bridge pointing and waving at the Liberator as

Golden Gate Bridge, San Francisco, California. Wikimedia Commons. Public domain.

she roared overhead.

"Man, that's the most fun a guy can have in a B-24," Vinni called out from the waist gunner window.

"Hey, Early Bird and Eldie. Did you guys see the Golden Gate?"

"Sure did. Let's go around again," Eldon said.

"Sorry, boys. One buzz of the Golden Gate is our limit today. Now, get ready for our landing at Hamilton," Regan instructed his crew.

As they headed north over Marin County, the scenery did not disappoint.

"Look! There are Tiburon and Sausalito," Stan pointed out. "I think that water is called Richardson Bay."

The show was over quickly as Regan called into the control tower at Hamilton Field and began to descend for the final approach.

After reporting to the base commanding officer, the lieutenants were taken to the officers' quarters while the rest of the crew was escorted to their enlisted men's quarters next door.

Before they split up, Regan told them, "Let's meet up for chow in an hour and then plan our stay here."

* * *

After dinner, the men gathered outside the mess and took in the Bay Area's delightfully chilly evening air.

"Think of all the places we've been since leaving home. We should just stay here for a while," Francis mused.

"Yeah. This place is so peaceful and quiet," Early Bird agreed. "Kind of reminds me of home."

"Hey, Cap. Will we have time to go into San Francisco?"

"We have orientations, physicals, and immunizations tomorrow. After that, we should have a lot of time off. Just be sure you are on the flight line every morning at 0900 for roll call. You guys behave yourselves. We've come too far to screw the pooch now."

"Aye, aye, Captain!" Eldie saluted.

"I mean it, Eldie. Don't be late."

* * *

The next morning the ringing phone startled Francis, who was still half asleep. "What? Who do you want? Oh. OK."

"Stan, it's for you. There's someone downstairs to see you."

"It's probably my mom and sister. They went back up to Stockton."

"Nah! It's probably some dame you knocked up!" Early Bird joked.

"Shut up! Let me get dressed."

Stan quickly dressed in his uniform, grabbed his garrison cap, and ran down the single flight of stairs to the reception area. He approached the private on duty.

"Sgt. Low here. I have a visitor?"

"Well, you can take your pick, Sergeant," the private replied, pointing at five women seated in the visitors' area. "I have never in my life seen so many women show up at the same time."

Stan was turning to greet his mom and MeiMei when the private interrupted his thoughts. "You better get the rest of your crew down here. There are visitors for Regan, Lesser, Crane, and Vinson. Did I forget anyone? Man, you Romeos must have a lot of what women want."

Blushing, Stan replied, "You call up there. I'm going to visit with my mom."

"Good luck with that, Sergeant."

Stan entered the waiting area and was face-to-face with five anxious young women.

"Has anyone seen my mom and sister?"

Ruth Hirshfield (1922–2011).
Courtesy of Donna Eschen.

The room was silent. Stan was turning to go back and check with the private when a soft voice called out, "I'm not your sister, and I'm certainly not your mother, but maybe I can stand in for them."

Stan turned, and his heart soared, "Deidre!"

"Remember me, soldier?"

Stan couldn't stop smiling. "How did you know I'd be here?"

"I go to school in New York City, and my sorority sister knows a young man on your plane. Stan, this is Ruth."

"Nice to meet you, Ruth. How do you know me?" Stan asked, puzzled.

"Well, my Jerome has been writing to me about this young Chinese gunner who grew up on a hop farm in Salem. I told Deidre, and we figured you must be her Stan!"

"So, here we are! I hope you aren't disappointed."

"Disappointed? I can't imagine a better surprise than you, Deidre."

"Actually, we are all here to visit a young airman on your plane. This is Peggy, Scott Regan's sister, and these two are Emily Vinson and Louise Crane. I think you better get the rest of your crew down

90th Bombardment Group Special Collection. Used with permission from the San Diego Air and Space Museum.

here for this reunion, Stan, before these girls explode with anticipation!" Deidre laughed.

It was indeed a reunion for the ages. The lieutenants rushed over from the officers' quarters missing ties and proper pants. Once the hugging and other forbidden public displays of affection ended, the couples went outside for photos. It was a moment to never be forgotten.

George Kerby, Peggy and Scott Regan, and John Crane posed and were beaming arm in arm.

"Here, let me take the photo," Jerome offered as he leaped up onto a wall to get a better view. "John, your pants don't match!"

"At least I put on a tie. Just take the photo, Jerome, before I tell Ruth about all those women in Hollywood that night!"

"OK! OK! Look this way and smile. One, two, and three!"

***

By noon the crew had completed physicals and vaccinations at the base dispensary.

"That cute nurse gives a mean shot," Kerby complained, rubbing his arm.

"How many shots did you get?"

Regan rattled them off: "Hepatitis, measles-mumps-rubella, flu and typhoid, and yellow fever.[1] We should be good to go!"

"Just a little sore, Cap." Vinni laughed.

"At least we're free for the rest of the day. Let's get the girls and head into the city," John suggested.

* * *

"I thought I'd take you guys to the Forbidden City[2] Chinese nightclub on Sutter, but with the girls and wives, I think the Copacabana on Powell will be a better choice," Stan said.[3]

"Yeah. You're too young for exotic dancers anyway, BFW," Early Bird laughed.

"I'm twenty years old, just like Albert. Besides, this uniform gets me past any doorman."

"You still look like a baby-faced warrior to me," Vinni smiled.

"If you promise to behave yourself, maybe we can take you to both clubs, Stan," Jerome said, grinning.

That evening, the girls were dressed to kill in evening dresses and heels, with perfect makeup and perfect hair. No one said it, but each

---

1   The yellow fever vaccine developed in 1937 was responsible for a hepatitis B outbreak that struck 50,000 American soldiers in World War II. Made from contaminated blood serum, the vaccine infected up to 330,000 soldiers with hepatitis B from 1941 to 1942. One in seven became sick.

2   Forbidden City, at 363 Sutter Street, was an Asian-owned, managed, and staffed nightclub and cabaret that featured Asian singers, dancers, chorus lines, magicians, strippers, and musicians.

3   Joaquin Garay's Copacabana at 2215 Powell Street was a favorite of Hollywood stars, including Humphrey Bogart and Lauren Bacall, who frequented the Copa during their honeymoon. Garay was a popular radio and nightclub entertainer from the 1940s to the 1960s.

Cover for Copacabana night club souvenir, San Francisco, California. Courtesy of the Low family.

understood that this might be the last night out with the guys for some time to come.

After dinner and the floor show, the dancing started at the glamorous Copacabana. Jerome took Ruth's hand as they stepped onto the dance floor.

"The last time we danced, we were at the Maxwell Field graduation ball."

"You must be a good dancer, Jerome. I traveled three thousand miles for a second dance."

"The guys call me the jive bomber bombardier."[4] Jerome laughed.

"You're pretty sure of yourself!"

"No room for self-doubt. Life's too short, and the evening's

---

4   "Jive bomber" is 1940s slang for a good dancer.

young." Jerome and Ruth waltzed and foxtrotted to the sounds of the Copacabana orchestra.

During a slow dance, as Jerome held Ruth close, she whispered, "I'll wait for you, Jerome, but promise me you'll come home safe."

"If you'll marry me when this is over, I promise to walk through purgatory to get back to you."

Her whispered one-word reply—"Yes"—made Jerome's heart soar.

"And Deidre will be my maid of honor. She is so sweet. Look at Stan and Deidre dancing cheek to cheek. They make such a cute couple."

Jerome smiled. *Looks like BFW has a steady girlfriend.*

As the orchestra played the Irving Berlin favorite, "Cheek to Cheek," Deidre whispered the words, "Heaven, I'm in Heaven."

Gazing into her partner's eyes, Deidre whispered, "Stan, this is our song."

Stan smiled, pulled Deidre close, and nodded as they foxtrotted to the music. Tonight, they were Fred and Ginger, dancing and in love.

* * *

True to his word, Jerome and the guys finished off the evening with the late show at the Forbidden City, the first all-Chinese nightclub in America. They tried not to stare at the gorgeous, scantily clad women, but when exotic dance sensation Joy Ching took the stage enclosed in her gilded cage, it was hard not to take it all in.

"Stop ogling the dancers, Jerome." Ruth laughed, poking him in the side.

"Think of this as a cultural experience," Jerome deadpanned as they were seated.

"Sure!" Deidre scoffed. "There would be more Chinese culture in a fortune cookie!"

Looking at the menu, Jerome quipped, "Hey BFW, you've been holding out on us! Your family owns this joint."

"What are you talking about, Jerome?"

"It says so right here. 'Charlie *Low*'s Forbidden City.' You must be rolling in dough and dames." Jerome whistled.

"Cut it out, Jerome. The name's just a coincidence."

"Let me see that," Albert and Vinni chimed in. "Wow! You have been keeping secrets, BFW."

"You mean your cousin works here?" Scott asked.

"No. His family owns the place. Didn't you see the sign out front? Charlie Low's Forbidden City," Francis added.

"You've got to be kidding. So, where's cousin Charlie?" Vinni asked.

"Yeah, maybe he can introduce us single guys to the chorus line girls. They're gorgeous and exotic looking," Early Bird and Albert said.

The bantering was interrupted by the evening's host, flanked by two beautiful chorus girls.

"Good evening, ladies and gentlemen. Welcome to Char-

Joy Ching, an exotic dancer at Forbidden City, in 1942. In the early 1940s, "The Girl in the Gilded Cage" was a nightclub sensation. Public domain.

lie Low's Forbidden City, where we will show you how to have fun in Chinese!"

He was interrupted by applause and a voice calling out from the audience.

"Hey, Mr. Low. We have someone who wants to say hello. Our Liberator nose gunner, Stan Low!"

Jadin Wong, a performer at the Forbidden City. Photograph by Romaine. Courtesy of the Low family.

The house spotlights swung to the audience, highlighting the ten servicemen and their dates. The audience grew quiet and then exploded in laughter when the spotlight found poor Stan blushing and sliding down in his seat.

"He says he's your cousin!" Early Bird called out.

"Stop it, guys!" Stan hissed, trying to hide from the spotlight.

Stan was relieved when the spotlight returned to the master of ceremonies, tuxedoed Charlie Low with a microphone in hand.

"This next act cost me a pretty penny, folks. Li Tei Ming is the best torch singer in America; she's also my ex-wife! I had to triple her salary so she wouldn't leave the show. So, give Tei Ming a warm welcome."[5]

As Charlie was exiting the stage, he stopped and looked right at

---

5   Li Tei Ming's crowd-favorite song was the ditty "You're a Sap, Mr. Jap."

Stan, who was still blushing.

"Cousin Stan! Is it really you? Why didn't you send word you were coming to the club?" he blurted out as he grabbed Stan and slapped his back, whispering in his ear, "Play along with me, Stan."

"Uh, I guess I didn't want to bother you, Charlie."

"What are you talking about? My club is your home away from home. Now, who are your friends?"

Stan proceeded to introduce his nine crewmembers and Deidre, Ruth, Emily, and Louise, but stumbled when he got to Scott's sister Peg.

Peg laughed as she stuck out her hand. "Pleasure to meet you, Mr. Low."

"It is an honor to have all of these men in uniform in my club tonight. A couple of months ago, I bought three thousand in war bonds right here in the Forbidden City to support the war effort."

"Thank you, Mr. Low. That won't buy us a plane, but it will cover a couple of five-hundred-pound bombs earmarked for the enemy!" Kerby grinned.

Holding up his hand, he continued, "It was a small gesture. Please call me Charlie. Tonight, your drinks are on the house! And here's a small gift from the gorgeous Mary Mammon." Charlie grinned, passing out matchbooks.[6]

Stan turned his over and read the logo aloud: "Strike 'Em Dead. Remember Pearl Harbor!"[7]

"Ladies, you're going to love this next performer. They call Larry Ching the Chinese Frank Sinatra."

Charlie turned to go back on stage accompanied by the gorgeous Dottie Sun.

Earl poked Stan. "What about introducing us to the girls?"

"Cool it, Romeo." Scott laughed. "Enjoy the show, but hands off

---

6   Any serviceman on his way overseas was always seated first at the Forbidden City. The cover charge for these servicemen was the price of a glass of water, i.e., free.

7   The matchbooks were part of a patriotic campaign sponsored by the Citizens Win the War Committee at 85 Post Street in San Francisco.

Mai Tai Sing, Jade Ling, Larry Ching (the "Chinese Frank Sinatra"), Diane Shinn, and Li Tei Ming, in 1942. Photograph courtesy of Larry Ching's son, David Gee. David recalls going to the club as a young boy: "The first time I saw this picture was at the Forbidden City nightclub with a lot of other famous pictures of celebrities on the wall as you enter at the top of the stairs, and to your left the wall of pictures of a lot of famous people that went to that club back then. It was a long walk up those stairs to the top entrance."

the merchandise. I don't want to have to bail you out of some city jail."

The rest of the evening was a blur of dancing, singing, and freely flowing drinks. The girls' favorite were the glamorous dancing Mei Lings with Mary Mammon, Jackie Mei Ling, and Dottie Sun. It was a night out that they wouldn't soon forget.

"We have one more special guest performer tonight," Charlie announced. "She is a young but very special talent who will be making waves on our nightclub scene. This kid is talented beyond belief and even sews her own costumes. Please welcome Coby Yee!"

As they were leaving, Charlie came over to say goodbye.

"I trust you servicemen and your dates had a night to remember the Chinese way!"

"Thank you, Charlie. We had a swell time," Scott replied.

"You are welcome in the Forbidden City anytime you are in town. Stan, give my love to your mom and family. We are all so proud of you." Charlie smiled as he shook Stan's hand, delivering a small keepsake and message for his cousin.

The rest of the week was a whirlwind of more orientations and time spent with the women on trips touring Marin County and San Francisco. The windswept Marin Headlands and Tiburon offered

Coby Yee. Yee later owned and managed the Forbidden City. Courtesy of Patricia Nishimoto and Shari Yee Matsuura.

Souvernir photograph holder. Charlie Low's Forbidden City. Creative Commons.

spectacular views of the City by the Bay. Excursions into the city for seafood on Fisherman's Wharf and dim sum in Chinatown made everyone forget the looming war. Stan enjoyed sharing his part of America with the crew, and they were happy to have a tour guide to one of the most beautiful and exciting cities they had visited on their trip across the United States.

In Golden Gate Park, Stan took them to see the Japanese Tea Garden near the de Young Museum. The couples posed on the Japanese drum bridge.

"This bridge has been here since 1894. My grandparents came here during some big fair they had back then," Stan said. "You should see this place when the cherry trees are in blossom."

"You guys have any livestock in this park, Stan?" Vinni asked.

Stan laughed. "Funny you should ask. Follow me!"

The stroll through the park past Stow Lake and Spreckels Lake was relaxing and longer than Stan had remembered.

"Where are you taking us, Stan?" Scotty asked.

"You'll see. This surprise is for Vinni, our dairyman."

Vinni smelled the herd before they could see it. As they approached the bison paddock, Vinni exclaimed, "Now that's my kind of treat! Emmy, look at those beasts! They're magnificent!"

Emily laughed. "I guess we know who the dairy farmer is in this crew."

"You wouldn't have him any other way, would you?" Ruth asked.

"No, Vinni is just like my dad. Back in Massachusetts, we're all dairymen, but Vinni is the local Holstein expert. He loves large farm animals."

"Not as much as I love my wife!" Vinni laughed as he pulled Emmy close, still unable to take his eyes off the bison herd.

Paul and Emily walked hand in hand through the park. Emily smiled as she felt Paul checking out her diamond wedding ring.

"You like your ring, Emmy?"

"Almost as much as I like you, Paul Carter Vinson." Emily laughed.

Later that afternoon, on a tour that took them down crooked Lombard Street and up elegant Nob Hill, Stan pointed out the sights, including Cameron House, where his journey had begun.

"Ruth, see that brick building? That's Cameron House, where my grandmother stayed after she was rescued."

"Rescued?"

"She was a child slave in the 1800s, but she was one tough cookie."

Ruth looked at the square brick building and wondered what stories must be hidden within its walls.

On the way back down Sacramento Street, Ruth took Jerome's

Bison herd in Golden Gate Park, San Francisco, California. Photograph by Michael Durand. Wikimedia Commons.

hand as she gazed out at the gorgeous San Francisco Bay. A sunlit fog bank partially covered the Golden Gate Bridge.

"I love this city, Jerome. Maybe someday we can come back here to live."

"Two kids from da Bronx living in San Fran? Wouldn't that be something? I might miss the Yanks and a good pastrami on rye, but for you, Ruth, I'd live anywhere."

* * *

All good things must come to an end, and on the evening of October 12, 1942, the sky was dark with scattered stars, and Jupiter and Venus were low on the western horizon. Twenty-five Liberators were lined up on the tarmac at Hamilton Field. After the preflight visual inspection with the crew chief, Burkhardt, Regan and Kerby climbed up through the bomb bay onto the flight deck. The other crew members took their places, secured their gear, and prepared for departure. Regan and Crane knew their first stop but hadn't yet told the crew. Their final destination was still unknown. Sealed orders would determine their fate and heading after they left San Francisco.

On the flight deck, Regan and Kerby completed the checklist. Using internal power, the two began the process of starting up the four massive Pratt and Whitney R-1830 Twin Wasp radial engines.

"OK, George, let's crank this thing up. Starting sequence engines 3, 4, 2, and 1."

"Copy that, Scott."

"Propellers set to high rpm, throttles one half open, ignition on, and booster pump on."

"Priming and starter energized."

Engine 3 fired up with a cough and a puff of smoke. Regan set the mixture to auto lean. They repeated the process to start engines 4, 2, and 1 in sequence. Kerby set the engine speed to 1,400 rpm.

With all four engines running, Regan called the tower for taxi clearance. Releasing the brakes, the Liberator slowly rolled forward as they headed for the runway. While Regan held the throttle back to 800 rpm, the taxi speed was like a brisk walk. Using the outboard engines to steer the plane, Regan proceeded to the holding point.

"OK, George. Let's run up the engines to check the magnetos and propeller controls."

They performed the pre-takeoff checks and were number two for takeoff.

"Liberator 68-Zebra-2, you are cleared for takeoff."

"Men, assume the takeoff position. We are on our way at last!" Regan called out to his crew.

"OK, Scott. Let's get this show on the road," Early Bird replied.

Releasing the brakes, the Liberator surged forward on the darkened runway. Regan held the throttles wide open while Kerby kept an eye on the manifold pressure.[8] The plane picked up speed as the massive Liberator roared down the runway.

---

8   A 44-inch manifold pressure is ideal for takeoff.

With slight back pressure applied to the yoke, the nose wheel came off the ground and the Liberator assumed takeoff attitude. At 110 miles per hour, she became airborne as she flew herself off the runway.

"Speed 130 miles per hour. Gear up!"

As they ascended into the dark skies above Marin County, they flew over San Pablo Bay, heading south toward the Golden Gate Bridge.

"What a view!" Fox called out from the waist gunner position.

"Look at the lights of the city."

"Scott, let's buzz the Golden Gate again," Cowles called out from the radio operator's console.

"Not today, boys. But we can fly over her for one last look."

Out over the jet-black Pacific Ocean at five thousand feet, Scott pulled out the sealed orders.

"Take the controls, George. Let's see where we're going."

Regan opened the envelope, pulled out, and unfolded the orders: "'B-24 crew 68-Z-2 is ordered to report to Hickam Airfield, Honolulu, Hawaii, and then proceed to 5th Air Force HQ in Brisbane, Australia.' Men, we are headed for the South Pacific and Australia, but first, we have a luau stop in Honolulu."

The cheers from the crew filled the plane.

"Hula girls all around!" Francis shouted.

"You single guys can't have all the fun," Crane replied as he used the predetermined heading for the 2,400-mile flight to Hickam Field.

"OK, George, let's get her on the step at nine thousand feet for a smooth flight to Hawaii. John, plot us a course. You're going to need your sextant to shoot the stars for this trip."

"I'm already on it, Scott. I've got the A-10 out. Once we get to cruising altitude, I'll sight some stars to triangulate our latitude and longitude. We'll need some flame floats in a bit to determine wind direction so I can correct the track for our heading."

"Make it perfect, John, and keep checking our position. If we miss Hawaii by half a degree, there's nothing else out there but water. It'll be good night, Irene![9] You and George work on conserving fuel, and I'll get you a perfect heading to fly this Liberator straight to Hickam Field. We'll arrive in thirteen hours, early tomorrow morning."

Crane opened the dark-brown wooden box enclosing his Fairchild A-10 sextant. Suspending the sextant from the Liberator's astrodome, he proceeded to take his first timed star sighting.

No sweat. Honolulu, here we come!

---

9 Flights from Hamilton Field to Honolulu were usually made at night to allow for more accurate navigation by the stars. Crew would triangulate latitude and longitude with a sextant. When the war started, there had been only one transpacific flight, by Charles Kingsford Smith in 1928, so it was a big deal for quickly trained bomber crews to make this flight.—Bob Livingstone

The Fairchild A-10 sextant was used by the US Army Air Force in World War II. Courtesy of John Turanin at AeroAntique. com.

CHAPTER 13

LIBERATORS AND
HULA GIRLS

OCTOBER 1942

The wailing air raid sirens at Pearl Harbor and Hickam Field were deafening as soldiers and civilians sprinted to their stations. At Hickam Barracks Hospital, doctors and nurses, including Lt. Ann Fox,[1] stood by, ready to face the worst. The surgical and burn wards were prepped and fully staffed. Gunners stood ready at anti-aircraft emplacements as they scanned the skies for the approaching enemy. They were determined not to be caught off guard a second time.

"I see them! There must be a whole squadron of enemy bombers!" The same scene was occurring throughout Pearl Harbor. This time, there would be a fight.

***

The squadron of twenty-four bombers approached Pearl Harbor from the north at an elevation of ten thousand feet. They headed southwest

---

1   Lt. Ann Fox was the first woman to be awarded a Purple Heart for her actions on December 7, 1941, when she cared for the dying and wounded at the Hickam Barracks Hospital. That day the tiny thirty-bed hospital was flooded with 189 dead and over 300 casualties.

around Oahu, turning north to come up the channel's throat into Pearl Harbor. The bombers approached battleship row, but this time the Navy had moved the remaining ships to more secure locations.

Looking through the open bomb bay, the men could imagine the chaos they were causing. Pearl Harbor was gorgeous from the air, with the three fingers of West, Middle, and East Lochs and Ford Island. The bombers split up. Their target was Hickam Field.

A lone bomber descended as it approached Hickam Field with its target-rich runways lined by enemy aircraft.

The anti-aircraft guns filled the air with puffs of black smoke and explosions that rang out across the harbor.

"I hope those guys remember to shoot at the target we're pulling," Regan said.

'Enemy' Bombers To 'Attack' PH, Hickam Field

A simulated enemy bomber attack designed to test the air raid warning system of the Pearl Harbor-Hickam field areas will be held Wednesday morning.

United States army and navy planes will roar in a mock attack on the naval base and airfield between 8 and 10 a. m.

Some of the planes will tow targets which will be fired on by anti-aircraft guns.

Military authorities said the drill will apply only to Pearl Harbor-Hickam field areas and will be made as realistic as possible.

All civilian and military personnel in the areas will take part.

All other persons on the island are asked to continue their regular work.

Should an actual air raid occur during the drill, warning will be given over the regular air raid warning systems throughout the island and announcements will be made over Honolulu radio stations.

In so far as the drill is concerned, only the sirens in the Pearl Harbor-Hickam field areas should be sounded.

Article describing a simulated bomber attack on Hickam Field in Honolulu. Honolulu Star, *November 3, 1942.*

"No problem there, Cap. Those guys are shredding our target," Vinni called out from the tail gunner position.

"It's a good thing we got a long cable. I don't want some hotshot rookie gunners putting a hole in our tail section," Eldie replied.

"Men, we have to make two more passes," Regan said. "More practice for those trigger-happy gunners!"

"Next time, let someone else pull the darn target," Early Bird moaned.

The simulated attack was a success and a reminder of the constant threat that hung over Pearl Harbor. While the participating B-24 crews landed at Hickam, local reporters and photographers ran to submit their stories for the *Honolulu Star*'s November 4 edition. The previous day's *Star* had warned the citizens of Honolulu about the planned air-raid drill and mock attack.

Scott Luke Regan in Honolulu, Hawaii, in 1942. Courtesy of Cary Borba Perrin.

* * *

That afternoon on Hickam Beach, Lts. Regan, Lesser, Crane, and Kerby were lounging on the white sandy beach with tropical drinks in hand. The blue Pacific Ocean's lapping waves gently caressed the shore, while the warm onshore sea breeze cooled their sunburned faces.

"Man, will you look at that? I could reach out and touch those clouds," Jerome said.

"This place is paradise," Regan agreed, sipping his drink.

"Let's go for a swim," Crane suggested. "The water is so warm it feels like a bath."

"Where are the enlisted guys?" Kerby asked, looking back toward the base.

"I told them to come separately and to meet us here," Regan explained.

"Hawaiians are so relaxed. I doubt anyone is going to worry about fraternization around this paradise," Jerome said.

Just then, the guys showed up with Stan in front, leading a white dog by a seaweed rope.

"Hey, BFW! Where'd you find that dog?" Jerome shouted out.

"He found me, and he's been following us since we left the base."

"Nice leash, Stan. What kind of dog is he?" Kerby asked.

"Beats me. He's white, big, and friendly. I like him."

"Let's name him Roscoe. He can be our mascot," Francis suggested.

"OK. Let's see if Roscoe can swim." Jerome laughed as he ran into the surf, throwing a ball for Roscoe to fetch.

The guys cheered as Roscoe tore off into the surf, chasing Jerome and ignoring the ball.

Lying on the sunny beach, Vinni smiled. "This is the life: flying, lying around on the beach every afternoon, and swimming with the guys and Roscoe!"

"What's for dinner, Scott? Swimming and having people shoot at us all morning worked up an appetite," Crane said.

Reaching into his pack, Jerome pulled out two boxes. "Well, I have just the thing you need. Two pies made by my bud at the post bakery. Now, who wants cherry and who wants apple?"

The guys crowded around, each taking a piece of the pie in hand, devouring the treat. Even Roscoe got a piece.

"How'd you score the pies, Jerome?" Regan asked.

"I was snooping around the bakery when I spotted my old poker-playing friend from Brooklyn, Harry Joyce. PFC Joyce is now an Army baker. He was so happy to see a friendly face. He practically forced me to take two pies."

"What's the catch?" Regan asked.

"Harry wants to be a flying cadet. He may want us to give him a ride in our Liberator, if you want the hot pies to keep coming."

"Life in Bomberland is not so bad," Vinni mused as he finished the last of the cherry pie.

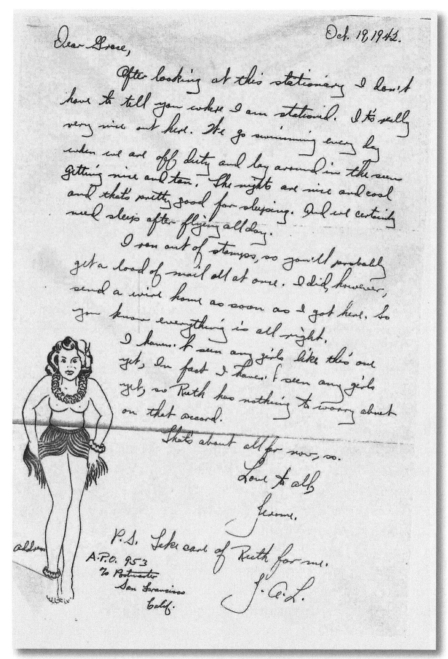

Letter from Jerome Lesser to his sister, Grace Lesser, October 19, 1942. Courtesy of the Lesser family.

The daily routine of flying on monotonous submarine patrols,[2] then working on their tans on the beach and swimming in the ocean, was the last fun the guys would have for some time.

Eventually, Roscoe's owners were found and came to retrieve the white German Spitz. It wasn't entirely clear who was sadder, the guys or Roscoe, *The All-American Crew*'s adopted mascot.

That evening, Jerome penned a letter to his sister, Grace.

* * *

Schofield Barracks, established in 1912, is located in Oahu's interior, twenty miles northwest of Hickam Field. Based at Schofield, the 804th Aviation Engineers had been on Oahu since April 1941. On December 7, 1941, the Aviation Engineers, under the command of native Hawaiian Col. Albert K. B. Lyman, had been in the thick of battle as the two waves of Japanese planes targeted Pearl Harbor and Hickam Field, Schofield Barracks, and the adjacent Wheeler Field and Bellows Field.

That morning, soldier-engineers became gunners during the attack, shooting at the attacking Japanese planes with whatever fire-power they could get their hands on. Later that afternoon, they began the monumental task of clearing the wreckage from Wheeler and Hickam Fields. Now, eleven months later, Schofield Barracks was crawling with the engineers who would go on to build vital air bases throughout the Pacific.

As Sgt. Loren Low approached the guard gate at Schofield Barracks, he sized up the situation and considered his options.

No pass. No problem. I'm not going to miss seeing Stan.

Loren approached a six-ton, six-by-six army-green truck as it waited to exit the base. Quietly slipping onto the running board along the passenger side, he squatted down and waited.

He spotted the corporal on the passenger side, looking down at him. Loren put his index finger to his lips. The corporal smiled and

---

2   The daily training submarine patrols were sometimes up to 850 miles out, requiring an eight-hour round trip with a cruising speed of 200 miles per hour.

World War II six-ton six-by-six truck. Photograph by Lars-Göran Lindgren. GNU Free Documentation License. Public domain.

looked away.

Outside the base, the truck turned onto Wilikina Drive, heading south. At the first stop sign, Loren hopped off the truck and waved to the corporal as they drove off.

Now I just gotta hitch a ride into Honolulu to visit Elsie, Loren thought as he stuck out his right thumb and smiled.

The first car, an old Studebaker, pulled over. No one was going to leave a tall, good-looking soldier in uniform on the side of the road. He was on his way.

"Aloha! Where to, soldier?"

Loren peered into the car at the smiling dark-haired woman dressed in a brightly patterned muumuu. "Goin' to Hillside Avenue above Waikiki. My sis lives there, and my kid brother is going to meet me."

"Well, hop in. For a family reunion like this, I'll take you all the way there. What's the address?"

Loren pulled a scrap of paper out of his shirt pocket and read: "It's 2747 Hillside Avenue. Mrs. Elsie Lam. That's my sis."

By the time they arrived forty-five minutes later, Loren, who

Elsie and her brother, Loren, aka Gwunde, in Honolulu, November 1942. Courtesy of the Low family.

could talk to anyone, had made another friend. Miss May Caldwell had learned about Loren, his family in Salem, Oregon, and even his Chinese name.

"Aloha, Gwunde! Enjoy your visit. Call me when you're ready to head back to Schofield Barracks."

May reached into the back seat and brought out a basket. "Can't arrive empty-handed. Here, take this for your sister, Elsie. It's delicious poi, made from taro root, and a few of my special papayas."

"Mahalo, May," Loren called out as he waved goodbye. Their chance encounter led to a family friendship that lasted for decades.

Set up against the Hawaiian hillside, the bluish-gray home with its slanting brown shingle roof was surrounded by lush tropical vegetation. Elsie, Loren's oldest sister, had come to Hawaii from Salem in 1925 as a recent Willamette College graduate. Even with her family's long-standing history in Salem, no one would hire an

American-trained teacher of Chinese descent. Fortunately, the territory of Hawaii had no such misgivings and welcomed her with open arms.

They likely had no idea of what they were getting into. Elsie taught English and drama to the students on the Big Island of Hawaii for several years before coming to Farrington High School in Honolulu. Elsie was proper in speech, manner, and dress, and demanded the same of each of her students, many of whom barely spoke Pidgin English. She taught her students how to speak, think, and behave with proper manners and etiquette.

Ms. Lee, as they called her, was like a being from another universe. Elsie had a well-deserved reputation as a taskmaster and soon became a beloved member of the Hawaiian community. Her students adored her.

Loren, on the other hand, was independent and adventurous and knew nothing of etiquette or proper speech. He taught their mother his bad habits and the colorful language he picked up on the playground. Thanks to Loren, words like "ain't," "grub," "Mulligan stew," and "lousy" became part of this proper Chinese mother's vocabulary. Perhaps because of his independence, Loren was Elsie's favorite.

The knock at the front door was loud and insistent.

"Sis, are you home? It's Gwunde!"

Elsie smiled and opened the door. She hadn't seen her younger brother for several years, but her tall, good-looking and irrepressible Gwunde hadn't changed a bit.

"My God! Have you grown even taller? People aren't going to believe you're Chinese."

"It must be the Army grub," Loren laughed. "There is certainly plenty of it."

They sat in the front room, catching up, with Loren looking around the house.

"Well, isn't he here?"

"Isn't who here?"

"Stan. He sent me a telegram saying he was flying to Honolulu

Stan and Loren in Honolulu while visiting their sister Elsie in November 1942. Courtesy of the Low family.

and would be visiting you today."

"That's odd. I haven't heard a word about it. I hope you're not too disappointed."

Loren was more than disappointed.

"He's the reason I went AWOL this morning. I was hoping to see Stan," Gwunde replied, looking glum.

At that moment, Stan came bounding out of the back bedroom. "Surprise! Ha! Got you, Gwunde!"

The brothers embraced, laughing and talking nonstop.

"Did you really go AWOL to come here today?"

"Well, a guy's gotta do what a guy's gotta do. And today, I had to see my kid brother."

They went outside to take photographs.

"You two put on your Army hats and shake hands," Elsie told them as she held up her camera.

"Perfect! Now, turn a little and smile more this time, Stan."

"OK, Lee.[3] That's enough photos."

"Well, you never know what's going to happen or when we'll have the opportunity to visit again."

"OK, but let's eat now. I'm starved," Loren said. Remembering his gift from May, he pulled out the basket. "This is from a lady named May Caldwell, who gave me a ride from Schofield Barracks. She said it's poi and papayas."

"Well, that will be a nice start for lunch."

During lunch, Elsie remarked, "You know, Gwunde, I have a lot of memories about your growing up in Salem."

"Probably naughty ones." Loren laughed.

"Well, all I know is when there was a puddle, you always ran through it, when there was a hole you'd jump in it, and when there was danger, by God, you'd go for it!"

"Yeah, I guess I was a handful."

"Yes, but a loveable one."

"And Stan, you were so little when I left home. I think you were only three years old. You were a sweet boy, very loving," Elsie reminisced.

"Next time, we'll have to get Bill to join us. He works the night shift. Bill has a new girlfriend named Amy, who is a nursing student at Queens Hospital."

The conversation went on for hours. Neither Stan nor Loren talked much about their life in the service. Somehow, it seemed out of place. Today was about home and family.

Later, Elsie revealed her plans for the evening.

"Have you boys been to a real Hawaiian luau?"

"Will there be dancing hula girls?" Stan asked.

"You're too young for that," Elsie replied. "But why don't you invite the men in your crew to join us? We'll be at Waikiki Beach at 6:00 p.m. sharp."

---

3   Lee was the family's nickname for Elsie.

Hawaiian hula dancers in 1942. Courtesy of the Low family.

The crew arrived in their dress uniforms and were adorned with leis by a beautiful Hawaiian hostess. Stan motioned for them to join the party as Albert was exiting the photo booth.

"Guys, this is my sister Elsie and my brother Loren. And, Sis, this is my crew. Scott is our pilot, George is copilot, Jerome is the bombardier, and John is our navigator. These guys are the important gunners: Albert, Eldie, Earl, Vinni, and Francis."

"Thank you for inviting us, ma'am," Scott said, offering his hand.

"We met your mother and sisters, MeiMei and Isabel, in Los Angeles," Jerome added.

"Aloha, boys! Welcome to our traditional Hawaiian luau." Elsie smiled. "Now, who wants a tropical drink?"

The mai tai was perfect, and the dinner was never-ending. They served a pu pu platter, rumaki, ono ribs, and shrimp ono nui, followed by the main courses of Hawaiian roasted pork, Hawaiian grilled fish, lomi lomi salmon, aloha sweet potatoes, and Loren's favorite, poi. For those who still had room, the dessert was macadamia coconut cake.

As good as the food was, it was the traditional dancing that captivated the guys.

The fire dancers were impressive, but it was beautiful hula dancers who had the boys spellbound.

"It's all in the hands, boys," Elsie advised. "They tell the story."

"Yes, ma'am," Albert replied, unable to take his eyes off the dancers' gyrating hips. "I don't ever want to leave this island."

"You got that right," Loren agreed as he polished off the rest of the luau feast.

* * *

When Loren finally returned to Schofield Barracks the next morning, he was greeted by MPs, who threw him in the brig. In his own words, he was busted down from sergeant to corporal and confined for two weeks, until the Army finally decided they needed him to get back to work.

* * *

On November 17, Stan's hastily sent telegram told his mom they were on the move.

"Hurry up, Stan! We gotta get back to the barracks, pack our gear, and get on the plane," Francis said.

"OK! I just gotta pay the guy. Almost done here."

Running back to the barracks, Stan shouted, "I wish we could take Roscoe with us."

"Forget about Roscoe. We're going to war!"

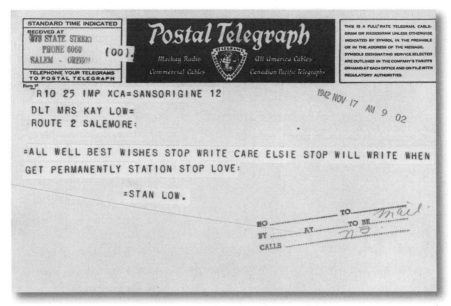

STANDARD TIME INDICATED
RECEIVED AT
878 STATE STREET
PHONE 6060   (00).
SALEM - OREGON
TELEPHONE YOUR TELEGRAMS
TO POSTAL TELEGRAPH

Postal Telegraph

Mackay Radio   All America Cables
Commercial Cables   Canadian Pacific Telegraphs

THIS IS A FULL RATE TELEGRAM, CABLE-
GRAM OR RADIOGRAM UNLESS OTHERWISE
INDICATED BY SYMBOL IN THE PREAMBLE
OR IN THE ADDRESS OF THE MESSAGE.
SYMBOLS DESIGNATING SERVICE SELECTED
ARE OUTLINED IN THE COMPANY'S TARIFFS
ON HAND AT EACH OFFICE AND ON FILE WITH
REGULATORY AUTHORITIES.

Form 1S

R10 25 IMP XCA=SANSORIGINE 12   1942 NOV 17 AM 9 02

DLT MRS KAY LOW=
ROUTE 2 SALEMORE:

=ALL WELL BEST WISHES STOP WRITE CARE ELSIE STOP WILL WRITE WHEN
GET PERMANENTLY STATION STOP LOVE:

=STAN LOW.

NO .... TO........ mail
BY .... AT........ TO BE........
CALLS .... no

Telegram from Stanley Low to his mother, dated November 17, 1942. Courtesy of the Low family.

CHAPTER 14

AMERICAN AVIATORS IN THE BUSH

IRON RANGE, AUSTRALIA

NOVEMBER 1942

Iron Range, along the northern coast of Australia, is on Cape York Peninsula. The narrow finger of land juts out into the Coral Sea as if pointing the way toward the enemy in Papua New Guinea, a mere ninety-three miles away across the Torres Strait.

For the 90th Bombardment Group, Iron Range was desolate, surrounded by impenetrable tropical rain forests. There wasn't a single farm, ranch, or even a dwelling nearby. A town with a pub was out of the question. The term "rain forest" was apt for the region, which, during the wet season, receives two hundred inches of rain in sixty days. Once, it rained for seventy-nine consecutive days, resulting in a foot of water on the runways. While southern Australia has four seasons, there are only two seasons on Cape York: wet and dry.

The air echelon of the 90th Bombardment Group arrived at Brisbane, Australia, on October 23, 1942. By November 13, the 319th, 320th, and 400th squadrons arrived at Iron Range with forty-eight B-24 Liberators. The 321st arrived six days later on November 19.

Map of Iron Range, Cape York Peninsula, Australia, and Papua New Guinea. Google Maps.

The dense jungle concealed the dirt runways, making them almost invisible from the air until the planes were right over the field.

The scuttlebutt about the primitive conditions at Iron Range didn't fully prepare the men for what they encountered. Hardy Australian engineers and the American 46th Engineers had arrived early to hew an air base out of the jungle. They'd chopped, blasted, and graded until the dense rain forest yielded a rustic air base with two dirt runways, a five-room latrine, and a twelve-capacity shower and wash.

The officers' mess was spartan at best. The enlisted men's mess was a tarpaulin, with furniture made from planks and drums. Instead of barracks, the men were sheltered in six-man tents pitched among the trees. The men uniformly came to consider Iron Range as their worst posting of the entire war. For now, it was home to the 289 officers and 1,407 enlisted men of the 90th Bombardment Group.

On November 16, the 90th Bombardment Group undertook one of its earliest missions. Fourteen aircraft were each loaded with 2,300 gallons of fuel and six 500-pound bombs. They were scheduled to depart Iron Range at 2300. The mission was to fly 850 miles during the night to arrive at the target, Rabaul, in Papua New Guinea, in the early morning. However, the crews were not yet familiar with Iron Range, and none had taken off there at night.

The lead Liberator, *Punjab*, was piloted by the 320th squadron commander, Maj. Raymond Morse. He and his copilot, the commanding officer of the 90th Bombardment Group, Col. Arthur Meehan, took off from runway Gordon on schedule at 2300. What ensued on the ground was chaos. Poor visibility, mispositioned runway lights, confusion, and inexperienced crews led to a collision between *Big Emma*, a parked B-24, and Lt. Paul Larson's *Bombs to Nippon*. Larson lost control of the Liberator on takeoff, clipping *Big Emma*, and then crashing into two parked Liberators and a B-17. Larson's plane caught fire, with gasoline and bombs exploding into a massive fireball. The flames were blown in all directions, with fuel dumps exploding. All eleven men died in the blaze, and four aircraft were destroyed. The four remaining Liberators in the lineup aborted the mission.

The nine airborne Liberators continued toward Rabaul. Only five made it to the target, inflicting minimal to no damage on the enemy. Lt. Robert N. McWilliams Jr., in *Patches*, could not even locate the target. The Liberators began to return to Iron Range at 0900 on June 17. Several Liberators were missing. *Tear-Ass*, which had lost an engine to enemy fire, was eventually located at Port Moresby, but *Punjab* was never heard from again. It was a demoralizing start for the 90th Bombardment Group in the South Pacific.

A seven-day cessation of operations ensued as Gen. George Kenney ordered the 90th Bombardment Group removed from combat to undergo additional training.[1] Col. Ralph Koon took over command of the group.

The first replacement crews for the 90th Bombardment Group began to arrive in late November, just in time for the start of the wet season.[2] Daytime highs approached 90°F, making it hot, wet, and humid. Afternoon thunderstorms in December would give way to monsoon rains by late January.

Regan's crew departed Hickam Field on November 17 and was fortunate to have missed the first few days, which had been a fiasco. When Regan's B-24 arrived at Iron Range, morale was at rock bottom, and the debris of four destroyed planes still littered the airfield.[3]

Surveying the airfield, Crane observed, "Well, this looks like a war zone all right."

* * *

For Regan's crew, Iron Range was a lonely substitute for home. Conditions were indeed primitive. The men lived in six-man tents pitched in the trees along the edge of the two dirt runways, Claudie and Gordon. It was a constant battle to keep the local snakes and scorpions at bay. Fighting the loneliness was an even bigger battle.

"You know, I saw one of those pythons curled up in the Marston matting at the end of Gordon," Vinni reported. "It must have been twelve feet long!"

"Keep that sucker out of our tent," Earl said, "or I'll shoot him with my Colt .45!"

"You should have been a cowboy, Early Bird." Stan laughed.

"It's the damn scorpions that I hate. Those nasty critters will sneak up and sting you," Albert remarked.

---

1   Missions resumed on November 22 and 23 with attacks on the Lae Airdrome.

2   Early replacement crews arriving the third week of November included Lt. Scott L. Regan, Lt. Jack M. Berkovitz, and Lt. Archie B. Browning.

3   Due to the rocky start of operations for the 90th Bombardment Group at Iron Range, only four missions had been flown before Regan and his crew arrived in the third week of November 1942.

"Let's go on a scorpion and snake hunt in our tent before we turn out the lights," Stan suggested.

"I wonder if the lieutenants do the same critter hunt every night," Francis said as they tore apart the tent, looking for unwanted wildlife.

"They probably just let Jerome stab them with his saber!"

"Jeez, this place is the pits!"

90th Bombardment Group six-man tents pitched among the trees at Iron Range. Courtesy of Bob Livingstone.

CHAPTER 15

FIRST MISSION

NOVEMBER 25, 1942

From 1942 until it was liberated in September 1943, the Lae airfield, along the eastern coast of Papua New Guinea, was heavily bombed and strafed by American air forces. More than a hundred missions were flown against Lae over eighteen months.[1]

In the 400th Squadron operations tent, the chalkboard told the day's story, listing combat crews and planes on missions. For the first time, Regan's B-24 was scheduled to take part in an attack on the Lae airfield the next day, on November 25, 1942.

Ordnance began the process of transporting the bombs to the hardstands, loading them onto the planes, and installing fuses. The wooden boxes containing the .50-caliber ammunition were placed throughout the ship for the gunners to set up when they arrived. Regan's crew had cleaned and oiled the .50-caliber machine guns, which they kept mounted on the Liberator.

Three hours before takeoff, the ground crews began the task of preparing the plane. The crew chief performed the preflight inspection. He primed the four engines, sequentially starting and running them up to maximum revolutions to check oil pressure, turbosupercharger, and magneto performance.[2]

---

1 Regan's first mission on November 25, 1942, was only the sixth mission flown by the 90th Bombardment Group.

2 Full ground echelon did not arrive until November 29. These early missions were with limited ground support.

Ordnance crews fusing bombs for the 90th Bombardment Group. Courtesy of Bob Livingstone.

Finally, it was time to wake Regan's crew.

It was pitch-black outside when the corporal in charge of quarters[3] entered the six-man tent, flashlight in hand.

"Sergeants, rise and shine! Make sure you shave and put on lots of clothes," he advised them, knowing this was their first combat mission. He went from cot to cot until the tent was full of the groans of still sleepy airmen.

Stan hadn't slept much that night. He was sitting up on the edge of his cot before the corporal completed his rounds.

"Kind of eager, aren't we, Sergeant?"

"Yeah, but I won't need to shave."

"Better shave. Otherwise, your oxygen mask will rub your face raw by the end of the mission."

"I'm not hairy like my Neanderthal friends." Stan laughed.

---

3   CQ, or charge of quarters, is a tasked duty to guard the front entrance to the barracks. It is usually a twenty-four-hour shift.

"Suit yourself. Breakfast is waiting," the corporal replied as he headed for Regan's tent.

Breakfast was corn willie (canned corn beef), hardtack (survival bread), and coffee with an unhealthy dose of flies. The briefing was a blur. Stan could barely remember what he had eaten or what was said. But moving was an even bigger problem.

"I can barely move with all these layers of clothes on! How am I going to be able to shoot straight? I've got on my regular shirt and pants, heavy underwear, extra socks, my electric jacket and pants, electric gloves, heavy shoes, sheepskin boots, a wool scarf, and, oh yes, my parachute. With my flak jacket and helmet, all this stuff must weigh seventy pounds. I look like a snowman!"

"Better than freezing your ass off when we get up to twenty-two thousand feet," Early Bird said. "Better get your machine guns mounted and loaded."

"Why am I the only one dressed like this? It's like a sauna in here!"

"Well, rookie, next time, leave your extra-heavy clothes on the plane. You won't need them until we start climbing. It's going to be 85°F and humid today," McMurria[4] said.

"Oh, OK. Thanks," Stan mumbled, as beads of sweat ran down his face.

On the flight deck, Regan and Kerby completed the preflight checklist. Regan reviewed the details from the briefing. He studied the route to the target, checkpoints, mission procedures, enemy defenses—both flak and fighters—and the weather forecast.

"Albert, do you have the code for the day?"

"Aye, aye, Cap! Radio operator is ready."

With all four engines running, Regan was given the green taxi flare and proceeded to the runway. They were the fourth of seven planes in the lineup. Angling his Liberator forty-five degrees to avoid creating a dust storm for the plane following, he and Kerby ran up the engines. The noise was deafening, and a massive cloud of dust covered the aircraft. By the time they got to the runway and were given the

---

4   Lt. James Austin McMurria (born September 13, 1917) of Columbus, Georgia, was a B-24 Liberator pilot for the 321st Bombardment Squadron.

green light to take off, visibility was zero from the Kansas-sized dust storm blown up from the dirt runway by the previous Liberator.

"Crap! I can't see a thing!" Regan hollered.

"Just keep us going straight down the runway. Man, this is bad," Kerby agreed.

Somehow, the lumbering Liberator found its way into the air through the dust and darkness.

"We're off, men. Let's have a perfect first mission. Check everything twice. We'll be stopping at Port Moresby in about an hour to refuel; then we'll head over the Owen Stanley Mountains to the target, Lae Airfield."

At ten thousand feet, the one-hour flight to Port Moresby was uneventful.

As they approached the shoreline of New Guinea, Regan called out, "We're entering enemy territory; keep a sharp lookout for Jap Zeros and bombers. Call them out loud and clear."

Through the darkness, Regan spotted the poorly lit runway lined with rows of oil-burning smudge pots. After landing and refueling at Jackson Airdrome in Port Moresby, the seven planes took off and headed west for a night crossing of the Owen Stanley Mountains. At twenty-two thousand feet, the Liberator would easily clear the pass through the mountains, but in the dead of night without any moonlight, making this flight for the first time was harrowing.[5]

"Man, it's dark out here," Crane said.

"You and Albert just keep plotting our position. I don't want to run into an unsuspected mountaintop," Regan replied.

"No problem, Scott. I got us all the way here from Hawaii, didn't I?"

"That you did, Professor. Those two other Liberators got lost just before we arrived. One ran out of fuel west of Iron Range, and the

---

5   The highest mountain in the range is just under 13,500 feet, with an average of 9,000 feet. For safety, you'd need to be at 15,000 feet, but if you were on track or visual, 10,000 feet would be OK. Trouble is, the range is usually only clear in the early morning, and back then you never really knew if you were on track or not. There are gaps through which you can fly, but if you pick the wrong one (they all look alike) and it's a dead-end, they are too narrow to turn around in. Even today aircraft come to grief there; a very unforgiving place.—Bob Livingstone

B-24 Liberators with Connell's Special taxiing at Port Moresby, at Jackson Airdrome, also known as 7-Mile Drome. Courtesy of Bob Livingstone.

other headed east and disappeared into the Coral Sea. They never heard from either crew again."

"That's not the way of the Fighting Irish," John laughed.

"All right, men, we're at twenty-two thousand feet. Make sure you plug in your heater and turn the rheostat up. It's -20°F out there. And call out your oxygen checks. Albert, you're in charge."

"How are you guys doing in the glasshouse?" Regan asked the crew in the Liberator's nose section.

"It's a bit crowded up here, Scott. We have a gunner, navigator, and bombardier all squeezed into this shower stall."

"OK. Be on the lookout for Zeros."

"No problem. Stan's giving me a crash course in gunnery tactics."

"It's easy, Jerome. Grab the gun with two hands and sight your target. Here, try moving the machine gun around. That's it."

"No sweat. It's kind of like fencing with a huge saber!"

"Here's the trick, Jerome. Sgt. Scott always said never shoot at the enemy. Instead, you want to shoot where the enemy is going to be. Lead the target and aim high because gravity will make your bullets drop."

"Got it! Lead the target and aim high."

Jerome swung the .50-caliber gun right to left, following an imaginary Zero bearing down on the Liberator. The sudden loud burst of gunfire made everyone jump.

"What the hell was that?" Regan demanded. "Call out the enemy!"

"Nothing from the tail," Vinni reported.

"Waist gunner negative."

"Top turret negative."

"Belly gunner cramped as hell, but no Zeros," Francis reported.

"Stan, what's going on up there?" Regan demanded.

"Sorry, Scott. I got carried away firing at imaginary Zeros." Jerome replied sheepishly. "This sucker's got power!"

"Stop playing around, Jerome. We'll be needing a bombardier soon."

"Aye, aye, Captain," Jerome replied, taking his seat at the Norden bombsight.

"Thanks, Stan. That was fun."

"Anytime, Jerome. That's why we have two guns up in the nose."

The sky ahead was growing lighter, and Stan could finally make out the rugged mountains and jungle below.

"Woah! Can you believe we were flying over these mountains in the dark?"

"Good thing you've got an ace navigator," Crane said, smiling.

"No way I want to crash-land down there. We'd never make it out alive," Vinni said.

"Didn't you pack the escape map?" Eldie asked.

"What escape map?" Stan asked.

"The map they gave us with the trails leading through the jungle. It's the only way we'd find our way back to Port Moresby."

"Oh, crap! I left mine in the tent," Stan muttered.

"It's OK, just stick with me. I'll get us home. No alligator or nip soldier is going to take out this backwoods boy!" Eldie replied.

Aerial view of Owen Stanley Mountains. Jonty Crane. Creative Commons.

"I'm sticking with Eldie, and next time I'm packing my own jungle map," Early Bird added.

"Enough chatter, boys. We aren't crashing in the jungle today, and we've got a mission to complete," Regan called out over the intercom. As they approached the coastline, Regan took a northerly heading, following the lead plane.

"It's 160 miles to Lae. We'll be there in forty-five minutes. Call out the Zeros."

The rugged coastline led directly to Lae, where the land turned sharply eastward. Lae Airfield was positioned right at the crook of the turn. Along the entire coast, the unforgiving, dense green jungle came right up to the edge of the deep blue Solomon Sea.

The P-38s split off, flying lower toward Lae.

"Let's take her down to fourteen thousand feet, George. John, keep plotting our position, so we'll be able to get back to Iron Range, in case we get separated," Regan said.

"No problem, Scott. I've been updating our position every ten minutes."

"Albert, are you manning the waist gun?"

"Yep. I have my headset on and my .50-caliber in hand."

"Eldie, it's time to arm the bombs," Regan instructed.

Eldon walked forward along the catwalk to the bomb bay and proceeded to remove the safety cotter pins and the serial number tags for each bomb.

"Bombs armed and ready to rock," Eldon reported as he placed the serial number tags into his flight suit pocket. *Gotta remember to turn in these tags.*

"All right, men. Test fire your machine guns and call it out."

Each gunner gave a short burst from his gun and called in the report.

"Nose gunner ready times two," Stan reported.

"Top turret gunner ready," Byrd shouted.

"Belly gunner ready," Francis confirmed.

Both waist gunners fired their weapons and reported, as did Vinni in the tail.

"OK, men. We're descending to eight thousand feet.⁶ Call out the enemy planes. Let's nail this bomb run and keep our Liberator flying."

Kerby said, "I think we lost the lead plane. Where the hell did they go?"

"Forget it. We're on our own. Jerome, she's all yours."

Peering through the Norden sight, Jerome could see the target in the distance and then noticed the puffs of black smoke.

"Scott, we've got flak ahead."

"Yeah, I can smell the black powder," Albert reported from the waist window.

"We'll have about ten minutes of flak, boys. Hang on, and do your jobs."

Jerome kept the target centered and noticed the P-38s buzzing

---

6   The Liberators were assigned different altitudes between 6,500 feet and 8,000 feet to avoid midair collisions in case one airplane overtook another.

around below them.

"Killing the drift here," he called out as he adjusted the course for a stiff onshore crosswind.

"Crap! I can see the muzzle flashes of their anti-aircraft guns!" Stan hollered.

The explosions from the shell bursts jolted the plane as they flew through the smoke toward the target.

Looking through the bombsight, Jerome calmly kept the airfield centered. Then he saw the small black specks taking off from the strip.

"We've got company coming up to greet us, boys. Three Zeros."

The gunners strained to pick up the enemy fighters.

"Where are those bastards?"

"Opening bomb bay doors."

As the sight angle narrowed, Jerome felt a surge of adrenaline course through his body.

"This is it, boys! Bombs away!"

He watched the bombs falling away from the plane. Suddenly

B-24 bombardier. National Museum of the United States Air Force. Public domain.

he spotted the P-38s directly over the target, moving to intercept the Zeros.

"Crap! We're going to bomb our own guys!" Jerome shouted.

"Don't worry, Jerome. Not even you are that accurate or unlucky. The odds of hitting your own planes are one in a million," Crane said.

"I swear we're going to hit those guys!"

The bombs were on a collision course with the P-38s directly over Lae Airfield.

Please, God, let me miss for once.

Three seconds later, the bombs exploded on the airfield as the P-38s gave chase to intercept the three Zeros.

"Jerome, get over here and man the other nose gun," Stan yelled as he pulled Jerome up from the bombardier seat and pushed him to the right nose gun.

"Zero eleven o'clock low," Stan shouted as he squeezed off a burst from his gun.

"Zero two o'clock low."

Jerome spotted the Zero on the right, climbing to intercept the Liberator. The tracer bullets from the Zero lit up the sky.

"Nail him, Jerome!" Stan yelled.

The burst of bullets from Jerome's gun trailed the Zero as he kept on firing, trying to get in front of the plane.

"Stop firing, Jerome. Short bursts, or you'll melt the barrel," Stan said. "And remember, lead the Zero and aim high."

"Come on, Scott, get us out of here!" Crane yelled.

"Bandit three o'clock high," Early Bird yelled from the top turret. He sighted and led the Zero and squeezed off a burst of firepower.

"Got him!" Byrd yelled as he watched the Zero burst into flames and spiral down toward the ocean.

"Let's climb into the clouds for cover, George," Regan yelled, and they ascended toward a fluffy white cloud bank.

The two remaining Zeros passed below them, pulled ahead approximately five miles, and then turned to attack the Liberator head-on.

"Two Zeros, one head-on and another at twelve o'clock low," said Stan. "Jerome, you take the one below, and I'll nail this guy

Top turret gunner, B-24 Liberator. Worldwarphotos. Public domain.

coming head-on."

The tracer bullets from the two Zeros crossed in front of the Liberator.

Jerome and Francis in the belly fired at the Zero attacking from below.

Stan sighted the Zero attacking head-on. They were closing at five hundred miles per hour. He had one second to react.

"This one's for you!" Stan yelled as he fired the .50-caliber machine gun into the rapidly closing Zero.

The Zero flew by in a ball of orange flame and smoke. Stan strained to see the Zero fall, but it was behind the Liberator.

"You nailed that one, Stan," Vinni called out from the tail. "Splash one, Zero!"[7]

The final, now lone Zero, hightailed it back toward the safety of Lae.

---

7   Regan's crew, credited with shooting down four enemy aircraft, was one of the top crews in the war. The 90th Bombardment Group shot down more than any other bomb group; only one fighter group shot down more.

After a moment of silence, the men took a deep breath and let out a raucous cheer that filled the interphone and lifted their spirits as the Liberator banked right, starting the journey back to Iron Range.[8]

"Boys, that was quite a day," said Regan. "What a start for our first mission! John, plot a course to take us home."

On the way back to Iron Range, Eldie intently studied the escape map, memorizing the red jungle trails as he plotted the long walk back to Port Moresby. Best to be prepared for Nips, alligators, and headhunters.

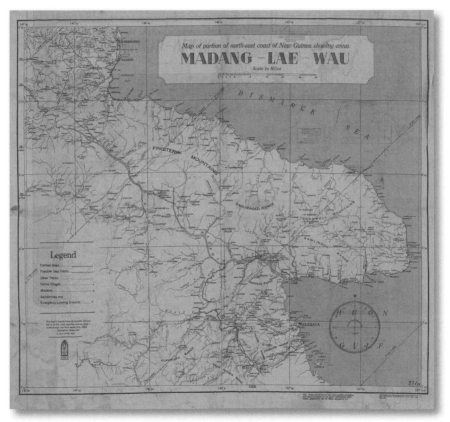

New Guinea escape map, 1943. Courtesy of Bob Livingstone.

---

8   The flight from Lae back to Iron Range was about 500 miles or 2.5 hours for a Liberator cruising at 200 miles per hour.

CHAPTER 16

BETWEEN MISSIONS

DECEMBER 1942

The Liberator crews were flying, on average, one mission every other day. The losses of aircraft and inexperienced crew mounted quickly. Between missions, the crews were clannish and stuck together. All the crews behaved the same, as no one wanted to get too close to other men, who might be gone tomorrow. The boys were horribly homesick, and while relaxing inside their tent, talk always turned toward home.

"Albert, where are you from in the Bronx?" Jerome asked.

"Northwest Bronx, up near Van Cortlandt Park in the Fieldston neighborhood. How about your family, Jerome?"

"West central Bronx in Mount Hope. We're just a couple miles north of Yankee Stadium."

"That's amazing! We live less than five miles from each other! I rode the BMT subway[1] through your neighborhood every day going to Aviation High on East Sixty-Third in Manhattan. We definitely went right by your house going to see the Yanks play!"

"Yeah! They kind of stunk last year in the World Series. I can't believe we lost to the Cardinals in five games. They're getting old. You know, Albert, we live five miles apart back home, and we had to travel

---

1 Brooklyn Manhattan Transit.

nine thousand miles to this god-
forsaken place to talk baseball!"

"Well, when this is all over,
we'll have you over for Sunday
dinner. My mom makes a great
pot roast with potatoes and gravy,"
Albert said.

"Man, what I wouldn't give for
some good home cooking."

"Terrific! And then we'll all go
watch the Yanks play."

"I can't wait to see DiMaggio
and Joe 'Flash' Gordon."

"Yeah, it's hard to believe
Flash beat out Joe for the American League MVP."

"Pot roast and baseball! What
could be more perfect?"

*Going to chow: Sgt. T. Hughes, Sgt.
K. Hinrichs, Sgt. C. McCord, Sgt.
O'Mallory, unknown friend.*

* * *

Despite the guys' good humor, conditions at Iron Range were worse
than anyone expected. Living in a jungle with snakes, mosquitoes, and
unrelenting flies was bad enough. But the empty tents and seats at the
mess hall were a somber reminder of the constant threat of death.

The men certainly needed something to cheer them up, but it
wasn't going to be the grub. The cooks, working in open tents without
screens, did their best with limited resources. They spent more time
swatting mosquitos and shooing flies than cooking. The menu rarely
varied: corned beef, dehydrated potatoes, a terrible goulash from a can,
hardtack, and hot coffee boiled in a ten-gallon container.

Dysentery was rampant.[2] Waiting in line with a mess kit in hand,

---

2   The swarms of flies were in part due to mountains of rotting garbage, left by prior
    crews and the Japanese, that were a breeding grounds for fly larvae. The 90th Bom-
    bardment Group set about drying and burning tons of accumulated garbage.

Enlisted men's mess tent at Iron Range. 90th Bombardment Group. Photograph by Russ Whitcomb. Used with permission of San Diego Air and Space Museum.

the men were literally and figuratively sick to their stomachs even before they took a bite.[3]

For other reasons, Wednesday, December 2, was a red-letter day for the 90th Bombardment Group.

"Hey, Vinni. When are you going to make that still for us?" Early Bird asked over lunch in the enlisted men's mess tent.

"I told you. I milk cows. I don't make moonshine."

"Sure, sure! But moonshine's in your Kentucky blood. Al Capone swears by the white lightning they brew in your neck of the woods."

"Maybe you should ask Mr. Capone."

"Well, I hear he's pretty handy with a semiautomatic machine gun. Maybe we need him to be our tail gunner."

"Forget you, Earl! Besides, didn't you hear about those yo-yos

---

3   Col. Arthur H. Rogers, *The Jolly Rogers.*

who brewed a batch of hooch in a forty-four-gallon drum used for leaded gas?"

"What about them?"

"There's five of them in lead-lined coffins waiting to be shipped home."

Just then, Stan burst into the mess tent and hollered, "Mail! Lieutenant Randall just arrived with a ton of mail!"

All the men jumped up from the tables and ran after Stan toward the runway.

Lt. Allan Randall was unloading sacks of mail from the hold of the twin-engine RAAF C-47 Skytrain. The two large doors behind the wing were open, and mail sacks were being loaded onto a truck.

The men cheered wildly as the mail sacks kept coming. They counted each sack, shouting in unison.

"...seven, eight, nine, ten"—and still they kept coming—"...twenty!"

When they loaded the twentieth and final sack, the men cheered and then began chanting. "Randall! Randall!"

Lt. Randall appeared in the doorway of the C-47, took a deep bow, then waved at the Yank troops.

"There's over fifteen hundred pounds of mail for you blokes, courtesy of the Royal Australian Air Force. It'll be a bit of home for you mates out here in the wilderness."

The men ran after the truck, still cheering, almost delirious with hope and expectation.

"I hope we all get mail," Stan yelled above the din.

"I've been writing Ruth every other day," Jerome replied.

"Fifteen hundred pounds of letters. There's got to be something in there for us," Vinni shouted.

Any message from home was a welcome relief from the loneliness of war, but mail from the States took two months to reach Iron Range. This batch was the first mail delivery since the squadrons had arrived in mid-November. The letters on Lt. Randall's plane had started their journeys in October.

"All the mail is mixed together. We'll be here for hours," Early

Bird complained.

"Where else do we have to be today?" Stan asked.

"Regan, Scott!"

The guys cheered when they knew the lucky stiff getting mail. "Go, Scott!"

"Sayre, Paul."

"MacDonald, Joseph."

After ten minutes, Stan pushed his way to the front and offered his help.

"Let me call out some names. Otherwise, we'll be here all night."

"Help yourself, Sergeant."

Stan grabbed a sack, pulled out a stack of letters, and started calling out names.

"Michelson, Leonard." Stan looked around at the expectant stares.

From the back, a voice called out, "Why is the Jap touching our mail?"

Stan froze, unsure of what to do. He felt his face flush. "Who said that?"

"I said it! Do you want to make something of it, you dirty Jap?"

Stan put down the sack, jumped off the truck, and headed through the crowd. Gwunde had said to stand tall and fight. Now was the time to do so.

The crowd of soldiers cleared a path. Stan had his fist balled up as he approached the soldier.

"You take that back, or I'll knock your head off, you stupid hick." Stan stood chin to chin with the soldier, who was a head taller.

"Who you calling a hick?"

The soldier had his fist balled up and was preparing to take a swing at Stan.

Stan felt the stares of a thousand eyes when suddenly there was a rush of bodies from the crowd.

"We're all calling you a hick, you dumbshit!" Jerome shouted, deftly grabbing the soldier's right wrist in midswing.

Vinni, Early Bird, and Eldie joined in restraining the soldier.

"This sergeant is no Jap," Jerome said. "He's an American warrior and a damn fine gunner. Stan has already shot down a Zero, and we just got here!"

Turning to the crowd, Earl growled, "Any of you want to give our friend a hard time had better be ready for trouble, because I guarantee we will find you. Now, does anyone have a problem with Stan delivering the mail?"

"Let the gunner back up on the mail truck. I want my letters!"

The rest of the mail call proceeded without incident. Jerome got a letter from Ruth, and Vinni received one from his wife, Emily.

"Fox, Francis."

"Who'd you get a letter from, Francis?"

"One's from my mom in Burbank, and another is from my friend Euclid Leblanc. He's that famous jockey back home. I think he's even shorter than I am." Francis laughed.

"Sorry, I couldn't fight my way through the crowd in time to defend you against that fathead, BFW.⁴"

"It's good to have friends around this place. I'm not sure the trouble is over."

"No worries, Stan. We've got your back."

On the way back to the mess tent, they passed Lt. Randall, who stopped to shoot the breeze.

"You Yanks really take care of each other. We Aussies admire that."

Stan smiled. "Thanks for bringing our mail. How long are you going to be here?"

"I'll be here for a couple of hours. I need to refuel, but it looks like I'm in line behind a group of Liberators preparing for a big mission. I have no problem waiting for those boys. I also need to have those five coffins loaded. It is going to be a morbid three-hour flight back to Townsville. I feel like a hearse."

---

4   A "fathead" is a stupid or foolish person in 1940s slang.

Randall continued: "Come by the C-47 after lunch. I have something for you, mates."

* * *

Stan and the guys crowded around the C-47, waiting for Randall to show up. The cargo door swung open, and Randall stuck out his head.

"Who wants a choccy biccy?"

"What did you say?"

"A choccy biccy, mate," Randall replied, opening a crate and handing out chocolate-covered biscuits.

The guys looked them over, and finally, Francis took a bite. "These are great! Can I have another?"

"This whole crate's for you. But there's more. Here, take this other crate, but keep it shut till you get back to your tent."

"Thanks, Randall. See you next time."

Lt. Randall gave the guys a wave. "Welcome to Straya, mates!"

Back at the tent, Vinni opened the second crate. "We just struck it rich, boys! It's a crate of XXXX Bitter longnecks!"

The guys gathered around while Vinni passed out the bottles of Australian beer. He paused, looking at Stan and Albert.

"Are you two old enough to drink beer?"

"Give 'em a beer, Vinni," Scott said. "If they're old enough to get shot at by Nips, they're old enough for a sip of XXXX Bitter."

Stan and Albert guzzled the warm beer with gusto.

"This hits the spot with my choccy biccy," Stan laughed.

"Thank you, Randall!" The guys toasted their new friend.

* * *

Later that evening, the serenade of crickets, cicadas, frogs, and other nightlife filled the air. The pulsating trill of a sooty owl and the strange wail of a bush stone-curlew sounded like they were right outside the tent. This jungle was no place to wander around at night.

Inside the officers' tent, huddled under mosquito netting, the lieutenants were busy reading and replying to the letters they'd received from home.

"I can't think with all that racket outside. That animal sounds like a woman screaming!" Jerome complained, putting down his letter.

"I know. It may be a possum in heat. This place gives me the creeps at night. What did Ruth say in her letter?" John asked.

"Well, she'd just received my letters from Honolulu. Ruth agreed we should have our honeymoon in Hawaii."

"When did you pop the question?"

"It was the day Stan took us on a tour of San Francisco. We were at Coit Tower on Telegraph Hill. I didn't have time to get a ring, but I got down on one knee and asked her anyway, and she said yes," Jerome explained, smiling.

"I remember the panoramic view from up there. It was amazing. You should take Ruth to the luau on Waikiki Beach."

"I want more of that lomi lomi salmon. How is your wife, Louise?"

"I think she's getting lonely in Dunkirk, New York. She'll probably move back to Morris, Illinois, to be with her parents. You know, we've only been married for three months. There wasn't even time for a honeymoon," John lamented, shaking his head.

As the nightlife screeched outside their tent, Jerome and John sat quietly with their thoughts of home and the girls they'd left behind, now so very far away.

"Geez, this place is the pits."

"*Terribilis est locus iste,*" John agreed.[5]

* * *

The next day at breakfast, Eldie had an idea. "Let's go on a trek through the jungle."

"Sure. We'll each take beer and a couple of choccy biccys," Stan replied.

"And I'll bring a machete to hack a trail and to protect us from

---

5   *Terribilis est locus iste* is Latin for "this place is terrible."

pythons," Jerome said, heading for the supply tent.

"This sounds like a recipe for disaster, but I'm in." Scott laughed.

"Get your gear and beer and meet outside our tent in thirty minutes," Eldie said.

Eventually, all ten guys began the trek, with Jerome and Eldie in the lead, hacking through the dense rain forest.

After thirty minutes of slashing through the jungle, they'd gone a hundred feet. Vinni stopped them.

"This is nuts! Here's a trail. Let's follow it instead of making our own."

"OK. But we'll still need the machetes to protect us from snakes," Jerome replied.

"No worries. I brought my Colt .45," Early Bird said, patting his shoulder-holstered piece.

"Who knows a song about women?" Francis asked.

"Here's a good one called 'Roll Me Over in the Clover.'

> We've tried it once or twice.
> And found it rather nice.
> Roll me over, lay me down, and do it again.
> Roll me over in the clover,
> Roll me over, lay me down, and do it again."

"Perfect! How many verses does it have?"

"As many as we want, or until we run out of beer!"

The guys sang and drank and cursed MacArthur, the war, and the damn snakes. It was a perfect day in the Queensland jungle.

"We need a new song; let's try 'Waltzing Matilda,'" Francis yelled, holding up his bottle of XXXX beer.

> Once a jolly swagman camped by a billabong,
> Under the shade of a coolabah tree.
> He sang as he watched and waited till his billy boiled,
> You'll come a-waltzing, Matilda, with me.
> Waltzing Matilda, waltzing Matilda,
> You'll come a-waltzing, Matilda, with me."

Jungle python in the Southwest Pacific. Courtesy of Bob J. Tupa.

He sang as he watched and waited till his billy boiled, "You'll come, a-Waltzing, Matilda, with me."

"What the hell is a billabong?" George asked.

"Dick Bong is a P-38 pilot.[6] Bill Bong must be his brother," Crane answered.

"OK, Professor. Then what's a swagman?"

"Beats me. Who's got another beer?"

"Let's make a toast to . . . to tomorrow, and to whatever it brings," Scott shouted as they raised their bottles to Bill Bong and the swagman. The rest of the afternoon, filled with drinking, singing, and cursing, was an effective but temporary distraction from the war's loneliness and horrors. That day, the ten men became a crew for the first time.

It was them against the war, death, the horrible food, and the damn snakes, in no particular order.[7]

---

6   Richard "Dick" Bong was America's top WWII ace and a Medal of Honor recipient, who shot down at least thirty-eight Japanese aircraft.

7   As Lt. Walter Higgins, the pilot of *Cowtown's Revenge*, summed up the plight of American aviators in the bush.

* * *

That evening, Jerome wrote a V-Mail letter to his sister, Grace, in the Bronx. He reassured the family that all was well and conveniently neglected to mention the abysmal conditions and the pythons. No sense worrying the folks back home.

> Out here, things are going along pretty well. I feel fine, and everything is OK, so don't worry. Have you heard from Ruth lately? Keep in touch with her. There is nothing much new out here.
>
> P.S. We had turkey today.[8]
>
> Love, Jerome

---

8   The Thanksgiving turkey dinner Jerome is describing was wishful thinking or another attempt to paint a rosy picture for the folks back in the States. There were no turkey dinners at Iron Range unless they came out of a can.

CHAPTER 17

IN THE HEAT OF BATTLE

DECEMBER 1942

The 90th Bombardment Group suffered heavy losses in the early days of the war. Crews were not well trained, with some first-time pilots having less than 120 flight hours. The men, straight out of training, found themselves in combat approximately eight days after leaving the United States. They learned on the job, and often fate was not kind. They flew missions in a remote location, off a dirt runway, for a new bomb group suffering from high losses and low morale. During the first three months of battle, from November 1942 through January 1943, the 90th Bombardment Group lost fourteen Liberators and 132 crewmen.[1]

On December 13, Lt. Leroy Iverson, on patrol for the 320th, spotted a convoy of five Japanese troop-carrying destroyers. A squadron of two other Liberators, flown by Lt. Archie Browning and Lt. Robert McWilliams, engaged the enemy, shooting down a Betty bomber and possibly two Zeros. These were the first enemy aircraft shot down by the 320th Squadron. The convoy, traveling from Rabaul to Buna, continued undeterred.

The next day, December 14, 1942, twenty-four Liberators left Port Moresby in hot pursuit of the Japanese convoy, which undetected

---

1   Personal communication with Bob Livingstone, June 2020.

Illustration of December 14, 1942, mission attacking Japanese troops at the mouth of the Mambare River and Japanese convoy off Cape Ward Hunt. The Tampa Tribune, *Tampa, Florida, December 17, 1943.*

had unloaded a thousand Japanese troops at the mouth of the Mambare River. The Liberators delivered damaging blows to the troops and supplies along the Mambare and Kumusi Rivers. The convoy of Japanese destroyers was located and engaged off Cape Ward Hunt. Throughout the day, swarms of Zeros attacked the Liberators. Lt. Paul Johnson shot down two of the Zeros, as did the Liberators piloted by Lt. Roy W. Olsen and Lt. Leonard E. Campbell. Lt. Charles Weber's crew claimed one Zero. The early days of the war in New Guinea were an old-fashioned shootout.

That same day, the airfields at Lae and Gasmata were attacked by B-24 heavy bombers, including the Liberator piloted by the popular Lt. Scott Regan.

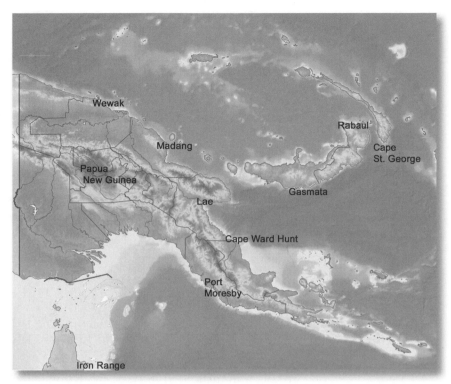

New Guinea relief map with labels. NordNordWest. Creative Commons.

The explosions of the ack-ack (anti-aircraft)[2] guns buffeted Regan's Liberator as it flew through the puffs of black smoke at eight thousand feet. Peering through the Norden bombsight, Jerome tried to focus on the target, Gasmata Airfield. His payload today was twelve five-hundred-pound bombs, armed and ready.

"Come on, Jerome, drop those bombs! I see Zekes coming up to greet us!" Stan shouted.

"Patience! OK. Opening bomb bay doors."

"I count seven Zekes, Jerome!"

"Bomb's away! OK, Scotty. Get us out of here."

---

2   "Ack-ack guns" refer to the anti-aircraft artillery designed to shoot upward at enemy airplanes.

"Take the other nose gun, Jerome. We've got a fight coming. Those Nips love head-on attacks."

"They figured out our Achilles' heel. One well-placed cannon blast directed at the nose will take out everyone in front of the waist gunner," Crane explained.

"Call out the Zeros, boys. We've got unwanted guests for dinner," Scott told his crew.

"Three Zekes at twelve o'clock," Stan reported. "They're splitting off, twelve o'clock, high, low, and straight on."

"Hold your fire, Jerome," said Stan. "You go low, and I'll take the one head-on. Early Bird, you nail the Zeke coming in high! They're closing fast. OK. Fire!"

The Zero's tracer bullets lit up the sky, while the Liberator's .50-caliber guns blazed a path of death across the heavens. A piece of one Zero's rudder flew off as it crossed right in front of the Liberator.

"Way to go, Jerome!"

"Two Zekes at nine o'clock high," Eldie called out from the left waist.

"I got a Zeke on our tail," Vinni shouted into the intercom.

The noise from the .50-caliber guns and the roar of the four 1,200-horsepower engines was deafening. Spent .50-caliber shells littered the floor.

"Got one!" Early Bird shouted from the top turret. The smoking Zero plummeted toward the sea.

"Splash one Zeke!" Francis confirmed.

"Keep calling out the enemy fighters. I'm climbing into that cloud bank ahead," Regan yelled.

The remaining five Zeros pursued the Liberator, passing it and then turning for another head-on pass.

"Crap! Here they come again," Stan yelled.

The Zeros split up, attacking from the top, bottom, and head-on. Tracer bullets lit up the sky as the planes closed at five hundred miles per hour. Stan led the Zero, aimed high, and sent a burst of the .50-caliber bullets into the air. The Zero burst into flames as it flew past on the right.

B-24 Liberator waist gunners. Early in the war, fighting was pretty basic for the gunners, who fought with rolled-up shirt sleeves and a Mae West inflatable life jacket. Courtesy of Bob Livingstone.

"Got one!" Stan shouted.

"Way to go, BFW. Confirmed kill," Albert yelled as he watched the smoking Zero spiral down toward the ocean.

The remaining Zeros pulled back and followed the Liberator northeast along the coast of New Britain.

"Looks like we're in the clear for now," Regan reported. "Keep a lookout for more enemy fighters."

"John, plot a course to take us back to Iron Range."

"Zekes at six o'clock!" Vinni called from the tail. "There's three of them giving chase!"

Regan tried to climb higher into the cloud bank, but the thin, wispy clouds did little to hide the Liberator.

Closing fast, the lead Zero fired his machine gun into the

Liberator's tail section. The bullets ripped through the rudder and vertical stabilizers.

Vinni fired a burst into the attacking Zero.

"Got one!" Vinni yelled. "A piece flew off that sucker. He'll be limping home."

"He's smoking, but still flying," Eldie reported.

The other two Zeros, circling above the Liberator, dove down on their target from a thousand feet above.

"Crap! Here they come," Early Bird yelled from the top turret. "Two Zekes, eleven and two o'clock high."

The top turret and left waist's bursts found their mark, as a flaming Zero disappeared into the clouds.

"Anyone see that one splash down?"

"Negative. Lost him in the clouds. But he looked like burnt toast!"

"Scotty, get us out of here before we run out of ammo," Jerome said.

On the way back over the Bismarck Sea, two more Zeros attacked Regan's Liberator, but he shook them off one more time.

The running battles along the coast of New Britain and far out to sea lasted three hours. When Regan finally landed his crippled Liberator at Iron Range, the men breathed a collective sigh of relief.

Inspecting the plane, Regan and Kerby marveled at their good luck.

"Look at all those bullet holes," Regan whistled. "Our tail and wings look like a sieve. There must be three hundred holes!"

"It'll take some work to patch her up," said Regan, "but she got us home safely, and we'll live to fight another day."

"By my count, we

Other Allied airmen dumped a number of 500-pound bombs on the airdrome at Lae, New Guinea, and a dozen 500-pounders on the Japanese airfield at Gasmata, New Britain. Of 12 Japanese planes which met the Gasmata attack, five were reported shot down or disabled by one four-engined B-24 "Liberator" bomber.

These reports said two Japanese planes crashed in the sea, another disappeared in flames beneath the clouds and parts flew off two others.

Newspaper account of Regan's B-24 Liberator's battle at Gasmata on December 14, 1942. The Charlotte Observer, December 17, 1942.

Jeeps mired in mud on a New Guinea road, 1942. Courtesy of Bob Livingstone.

splashed two Zekes," continued Regan, "with one probable, and damaged at least two more. Not bad for a day's work."

For their actions that day, Air Medals were awarded to Sgt. Earl Byrd and Sgt. Clifford S. Low.

Then the rains came. By mid-December, the dirt runway was a gelatinous, muddy mess. Taking off with a full load of bombs became challenging and dangerous.

Still, they flew, and they fought. The logistical challenges of flying all missions from Iron Range increased the times and distances of missions. One-way flights were up to 350 miles longer when staged out of Iron Range. This inconvenience led to a policy of basing one rotating squadron at Port Moresby each week. The returning squadron was placed on stand-down, and the other two squadrons were kept on alert for maximum-effort missions, requiring more planes. This rotating schedule continued for six weeks.

* * *

On December 19, the 90th Bombardment Group and the 43rd Bombardment Group's B-17s were in pursuit of a convoy of four Japanese warships and two merchant transport ships spotted the day before off Madang.[3] The flight included Liberators piloted by Lt. Paul E. Johnson and Lt. Elmo E. Patterson of the 319th Squadron and Capt. Dale J. Thornhill, Lt. John R. Wilson, and Lt. Scott L. Regan of the 400th Squadron. Maj. Harry J. Bullis, on board Regan's plane, led the flight. Following an 0500 departure from Port Moresby, the Liberators rendezvoused at Kerema, north of the air base along the southwest coast of New Guinea. The predawn crossing of the Owen Stanley Mountains brought them to the eastern coast of New Guinea just after sunrise. They flew north along the coast in search of the Japanese convoy. Just past Madang at 0814, they spotted the convoy between Kar Kar and Bagabag Islands.

"There they are, Major Bullis," Regan called out, pointing at the group of six Japanese ships.

"I see them. Two transport ships, two cruisers, and two destroyers. Have your radio operator report the convoy's position to the other crews," Bullis replied. "Start your bomb run, Regan. You're in the lead on this one."

"Zekes at eleven o'clock! Get 'em!" Early Bird called out from the top turret.

The streaking Zeros and the ack-ack anti-aircraft guns created havoc.

"Those damn Zekes are attacking us from the nose! Why don't they learn a new trick?"

At three hundred miles per hour, the streaking Zeros flew into the Liberators head-on, with cannons firing and machine guns blazing. They inflicted heavy damage on Lt. Patterson's plane on the very first pass. The Liberator went nose up and began to stall, falling straight down toward the sea.

---

3   On the previous day, December 18, 1942, the 90th Bombardment Group was also in pursuit of the convoy, but that mission was in shambles because of the weather. Only two of the B-24s found the convoy.—Bob Livingstone

"Patterson's in trouble!" Regan reported. "Albert, radio them to bail out!"

"It's too late," Bullis replied.

"Do you see any parachutes?"

"Negative. But I can't see where she went down," Eldie reported from the left waist.

"Lieutenant Johnson's Liberator's got two Zekes shooting up the tail turret. That tail gunner is a goner," Albert reported from the right waist gun.[4]

"Proceed with your bomb run, Regan," Bullis ordered.

"Descending to six thousand feet," Regan reported as he flew through the ack-ack and buzzing Zeros toward the Japanese convoy. "We'll make three bomb runs. Albert, go make sure the bomb bay doors stay open," Regan ordered.

Cowles left his radio operator's station and positioned himself just below the flight deck in front of the bomb bay doors. He made sure the doors didn't creep closed during the bomb run and possibly hang up the ordinance.

"Looks good from here, Scott," Albert reported.

"Stay there until we release the bombs and then get back to your waist gun."

Albert looked through the open bomb bay at the ocean six thousand feet below. The zigzagging convoy of ships left behind an irregular wake. He had his hand on the manual lever and kept a broom handy in case the doors began to shift. The five-hundred-pound bombs were armed and ready.

Suddenly, a plane with red suns painted on the wings streaked by, a few feet below the Liberator.

---

4   Cpl. Marvin E. Frandsen, the tail gunner in Lt. Paul Johnson's Liberator, was killed. Sgt. Walter Wilson, the tail gunner in Lt. John Wilson's Liberator, sustained a severe hip injury on a bomb run and later died from pneumonia on December 26, 1942.

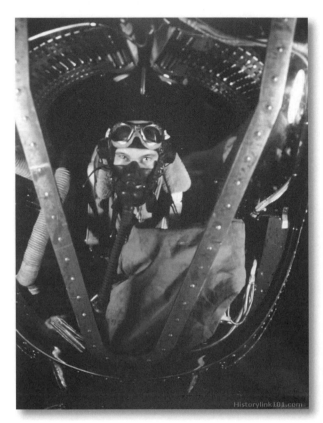

B-24 Liberator bombardier. Public domain.

"Holy crap!" Albert yelled. "We got Zekes flying right up our bomb bay, and all I got to fight them off is a broom!"

"I see 'em. His guns must have jammed," Francis called out from the belly as he sent a burst of gunfire into the Zero.

"OK, I have the convoy in my crosshairs. Those bastards are moving fast and zigzagging," Jerome reported.

"Target the average position of the zigzagging ship," Crane offered.

"Bombs away!"

The other two Liberators dropped their bombs on cue. Jerome watched as the five-hundred-pound bombs splashed into the water, missing their targets by a wide margin.

"Crap! No glory there, Scott. Let's go around and try again," Jerome reported.

The ack-ack fire followed them as they passed over the convoy.

"Those Jap gunners are better than we thought. Who said they couldn't shoot?

"OK. Let's all target the cruiser in the middle of the convoy. Aim for the midpoint of the right-to-left zigzag," Regan told the other three Liberator crews.

"We'll drop down lower to give our bombs a better chance of finding their mark."

The new approach was no more successful, as on the next pass, the Liberators' bombs splashed harmlessly into the ocean. They failed to

Allied Headquarters in Australia, Sunday, Dec. 20 (AP).—The Allied command communication:

Timor: Our attack planes strafed and sank a small cargo ship off the northeast coast.

New Guinea: Lae: Our medium and heavy bombers raided the airdrome. Madang: The enemy's naval forces are active off the northern coast. Near Vitiaz Straits, several hundred miles northwest of Buna, our heavy bombers attacked an enemy convoy of two merchant and five warships, scoring four direct hits on the deck of a light cruiser, which sank following the explosion of its powder magazine. During the attacks our planes shot down two Zero fighters. The enemy entered the harbors of Madang and Finschafen durinng the night and then departed to the northeast before morning.

News article from Sunday, December 20, 1943, describing the air war in the Southwest Pacific. Daily News. *New York.*

make a single direct hit on the convoy. The Liberator gunners did shoot down two Japanese Zeros during the attacks.

The return flight to Port Moresby by the remaining three Liberators was somber. The battle of December 19 was a costly encounter for the 90th Bombardment Group. Corp. Frandsen was dead, and the entire eleven-man crew of Lt. Elmo Patterson's B-24 was killed in action. The final casualty occurred seven days later when Sgt. Walter Wilson, the tail gunner for Lt. Wilson's Liberator, succumbed to pneumonia while hospitalized for his hip wound. The challenges of bombing fast-moving Japanese shipping targets in the open seas would require rethinking and new tactics. [5]

---

5   Shipping claims are difficult. Aircrew estimate of ship types were almost always incorrect, and claims of sinkings were almost always incorrect also, at least from high-level bombing. For morale reasons and for home consumption, claims were often either accepted blindly or inflated by higher ranks to make everyone look good. Who could challenge these claims made on an attack in the middle of nowhere?—Bob Livingstone

CHAPTER 18

HOLIDAYS IN THE BUSH

DECEMBER 1942–JANUARY 1943

C ol. Arthur H. Rogers, commanding officer of the 90th Bombardment Group, described wartime in the Australian bush in his memoirs: "As the days and weeks passed, our living conditions grew worse. The rainy season had begun, and tents were mildewing and rotting so that they leaked like a sieve, and it was impossible to keep cots and clothing dry. The entire camp smelled of mildew, and we were still eating the same diet of corn beef, dehydrated eggs, potatoes, and goulash. Many of the men were sick with dysentery and malaria."[1]

Though some bright spots lifted the men's spirits, missions did not stop for the holidays. On Christmas Eve, Maj. Cecil L. Faulkner located and sank a Japanese transport ship near Gasmata, a town located on the southern coast of New Britain. During this battle, fifteen Zeros attacked his Liberator. His crew shot down three of the enemy planes.

When they returned that night, they found the men had decorated the officers' club for a Christmas Eve party. They wore their dress uniforms and sang Christmas carols while their thoughts were of their families so far away. On Christmas morning, services were

---

1   Col. Arthur H. Rogers, *The Jolly Rogers*.

90th Bombardment Group movie night. 90the Bombardment Group Collections.
Used with permission from the San Diego Air and Space Museum.

held in the medical tent by Chaplain William Beeby. The cooks in the mess hall outdid themselves with a holiday menu not to be forgotten. They treated the men to a turkey dinner with mashed potatoes, gravy, peas, cranberry sauce, fruit salad, mince pie, pickles, bread, butter, and lemonade. Countless letters written home that night preserved the details of the holiday meal.

Another batch of mail delivered by Lt. Randall did even more to lift the men's spirits than the turkey dinner or the evening movie, the 1939 comedy *That's Right—You're Wrong*, with Kay Kyser and Lucille Ball.

Letter from Jerome Lesser to his sister, Grace Lesser, dated December 25, 1942. Courtesy of the Lesser family.

* * *

The next morning at dawn, the stillness of the camp was rudely interrupted.

"On guard! Damn the Japs!"

"Jerome, shut that bird up!" Kerby groaned. "It's too early!"

Jerome admired his pet sulfur-crested cockatoo through the mosquito netting.

Little Gracie. She's gorgeous and smart, just like the original Grace.

"Leave her alone, Kerby. Little Gracie has more brains than half the guys in this outfit, and she's a good sentry against pythons."

"She shits all over the tent, and she bit my finger the other day!"[2]

"Well, she saved your ass from that twelve-foot green tree python curled up in your bunk last week. Show some respect!"

Scott rolled over to check on the commotion. "What's the fuss about? Can't we enjoy our day off?"

"Jerome's bird is having nightmares," John explained, looking up from his book.

"I prefer that noisy cockatoo to a slithering python in my tent."

"On guard! Damn the Japs! Damn MacArthur!"

"Shut her up!"

The small bark outside the tent made all four guys and Little Gracie look up.

"Can I come in?"

"Sure, BFW. Why are you up so early?"

The tent door opened, and Stan entered with a fluffy white puppy.

"I wanted first pick from Sayre's Samoyed litter. Isn't she great!"

The white Samoyed puppy jumped out of Stan's arms and ran across the tent, nuzzling Scott's hand.

---

2   Bob Livingstone's personal recollections about cockatoos: "You mention a pet cockatoo. They are bastards of birds. I was bitten right through the fingernail by one when I was young. If you feed one, you get hundreds, so you stop. They then destroy your house in spite by chewing off every piece of timber on it. We have a dead tree in our acreage which overlooks the valley, and the 'boss cocky' sits up there and screams across the valley in the early morning, and bloody flocks of them fly up and circle around screaming back at him. They talk really well, but boy they are rotten animals!"

"Hey! I want some, too," Jerome said as the guys crowded around, petting Stan's puppy.

"She's adorable. What's her name?"

"Don't know, but she is definitely our mascot."

"Well, you'll have to get in the dog line at the mess tent to feed her. I hope she likes canned goulash and hardtack. But do not feed her that Spam in a can."

Hundreds of dogs smuggled in from every state in the Union filled the camps at Iron Range. The stowaway flying dogs had arrived in B-24 Liberators and B-17 Flying Fortresses as unlisted passengers. The brass looked the other way, knowing that these dogs were soldiers' only connection to home. Stan's puppy was from the next canine generation at Iron Range.

"Get me a beer! Damn the Japs!"

The guys laughed and spent the rest of the morning arguing about the puppy's name. They settled on Roscoe Junior.

* * *

That afternoon, the group of men in the officers' mess crowded around a table in the corner.

"The lighting is better over here. Now I can see your mug!" Don Barclay explained.

"Don't make me look silly."

"You kind of look like Donald Duck!" Jerome cracked.

"More like Li'l Abner!"

"Shut up! I'll be the judge."

After a few minutes, Don looked up from his sketch, then held it up, gazing at his model. "Not bad! I think it captures your manly side, Lieutenant. Here, have a look."

Scott laughed. "You certainly captured my curly golden locks. "Thanks, Mr. Barclay."

"My pleasure, Lieutenant."

"Sit down for lunch, Scott," Crane said. "We have pizza! Actually,

During World War II, actor, artist, and caricaturist Don Barclay (1892–1975) drew more than 10,000 caricatures of servicemen in the Pacific, Europe, North Africa, the Middle East, and China as part of a USO one-man show. 90th Bombardment Group Special Collections. Used with permission from the San Diego Air and Space Museum.

it's hardtack with tomato sauce and Spam. It's not half bad. Bring your mess kit."

* * *

After lunch, the photographer surveyed the assembled group of American aviators.

"The folks back home need a face to represent the warriors in the South Pacific," he told Maj. Bullis. "We can't sell war bonds without a poster boy to loosen up the purse strings. A photo of two hundred aviators won't do the trick. Major, I just need one young man's face, but that face has to inspire visions of hope and freedom and give the folks back home a reason to buy war bonds."

"These young men are warriors, not models. Pick the one you

Officers' mess. 90th Bombardment Group Special Collections. Used with permission from the San Diego Air and Space Museum.

want and take your photograph. We have missions to fly, so don't take all day."

He scanned the faces looking for the perfect one. Young, innocent, hopeful, a defender of freedom. The all-American boy, but a little exotic. Not white bread. A face that would tell a story if you listened with your heart.

"I said pick one! Now hurry up!"

He scanned face after face in the rows of men. And then he paused. "Who's that one in the back with the big gun? He looks too young to be in a war."

"They call him BFW. It stands for Baby-Faced Warrior."

"He's perfect! Have him come down here, and let the others go back to whatever it is they do."

"Sgt. Low, front and center," Bullis called out.

Turning back to the photographer, he growled, "What these men do is to fight wars, so you don't have to."

Stan came forward carrying his .50-caliber gun. "Yes, sir."

"Stand on this box and look up at the sky," the photographer instructed. "OK. Now turn slightly to the left. Hold your gun in both hands. No. Don't smile. Look up. Let the folks back home feel your pride."

"Perfect. Now hold that pose."

He snapped several photos, but he knew the first one was perfection.

"That's a wrap! Now tell me, Sergeant. Where are you from, anyway?"

"From the United States of America, sir. Just like you and the rest of these men."

"That's good enough for me, son."

Clifford Stanley Low, B-24 gunner. Courtesy of the Low family.

CHAPTER 19

THE LETTERS HOME

JANUARY 1943

While operating out of Iron Range, the 90th Bombardment Group found its footing as a fighting unit in a short three months. It built an impressive combat record, bombing ground and shipping targets, sinking twenty-nine Japanese ships of all types while shooting down ninety-one enemy planes.[1] The confidence of the men shone brightly in their letters home. Although censorship prohibited them from providing specific details of missions, their words were crystal clear. They were kicking butt, making life difficult for the enemy, and thoroughly enjoying their victories.

In early December 1942, Jerome wrote proudly but tentatively to his sister, Grace: "We are doing our best to bring this war to a quick end. But you'll have to read all about it in the newspaper."

By early January, after seeing the news coverage of his crew's exploits, Jerome wrote excitedly to Grace: "I don't know when it was or which one it was, but my crew and I had our names in the papers of our hometown with an article of what we had done. Maybe you saw it? My pilot's mother sent the clipping to him. What do you think of your brother now?"

By the middle of January, his crew was having tremendous success fighting the enemy in New Guinea. His letter to Grace was brimming

---

1   During World War II, the 90th Bombardment Group achieved fame as the "The Jolly Rogers," accumulating thirteen battle stars and two distinguished unit citations.

Two Transports Sunk, Third Hit

Battle Continues Off New Guinea; Defeat of Nipponese Army Complete

By The Associated Press

ALLIED HEADQUARTERS IN AUSTRALIA.—Allied planes battered furiously at the remnants of a 10-ship Japanese convoy off the New Guinea coast Friday in the violent climax to a 24-hour running battle in which they were reported officially to have sunk two big transports, one heavily loaded with troops, damaged a third and shot down 18 fighters.

An International News Service dispatch called the engagement one of the greatest sea and air battles in the southwestern Pacific area and said it still was raging Friday as the allied air force poured scores of reserves of strength into a bold attempt to smash the most powerful Japanese convoy yet sent against New Guinea.

Newspaper article from January 8, 1943, confirming the success of 90th Bomb Group in sinking a Japanese convoy. Palladium-Item Media Group. Richmond, Indiana.

with confidence and bravado: "Everything here is going along fine and dandy as you no doubt can tell from the news. We are doing a good job down here, and we get a big kick out of blasting the damn Japs out of wherever they hide. It seems that the rising sun is starting to set. The Jap son of heaven is getting slapped around, and that Nazi son of a b . . . is really getting it in the neck, so we are all happy."

Jerome wasn't alone in his confidence. On January 16, 1943, tail gunner Paul Vinson wrote to his brother and sister-in-law: "You both understand, I'm sure, but censorship regulations forbid my telling where and just what I'm doing. However, you both know what I trained for, and it is no secret that I'm in active combat. It has given me much satisfaction to know that I've helped make some Japs most uncomfortable. Believe me, I'll do my best to continue to do so."

By January, the letters home also reflected the isolation and loneliness that each man felt. Mail from home took months to arrive. Waiting and hoping for a letter from home was what kept these soldiers going day after day. While battling the enemy in the South Pacific was difficult, the loneliness of their separation from loved ones back home was an even greater battle. Their letters were filled with disappointment that there had been no word from home, tempered by the hope that the next mail call might bring them a letter or a package to connect them with their families.

By the middle of January, a few more letters began to trickle in for the few fortunate soldiers. On January 16, Paul Vinson wrote to his brother and sister-in-law. The mundane details from the home front meant so much to Paul, nine thousand miles away from the life and loved ones he left behind.

Jerome Lesser in 1942. Courtesy of the Rotenberg family.

> Yesterday was a big day for me. I got my first bunch of mail since leaving the states. You can't imagine how swell it was to hear from you. The picture of little Jenny is so grand. I'm very glad to have it. Hasn't she grown!! It's more apparent to me, I suppose, as it has been a long while since I've seen her. How many teeth has she now?
>
> As yet, no Xmas mail has arrived for me. The best I could do this year was to send wires. Next year, however, I hope things will be much different.

Well, I must close and get off some other letters. I want to answer them today because . . . Remember me. Always my best.

Sincerely,
Paul

At Iron Range, the men sent Western Union telegrams from the office of the group chaplain, Capt. William Beeby. The chaplain conducted regular church services several times a week, had a small lending library with the only books north of Townsville, and operated the EFM wireless service, allowing the men to send telegrams to loved ones.[2] While less personal, the telegrams were at least a way to let their families know they were alive and well.

On New Year's Day 1943, Stan sent a Western Union holiday greeting to his mother in Salem, Oregon. BFW Clifford S. Low was twenty years old.

---

2   The EFM, or expeditionary forces message, service provided low-cost predetermined messages that were converted into numbers and then converted to telegrams with words at the receiving end.

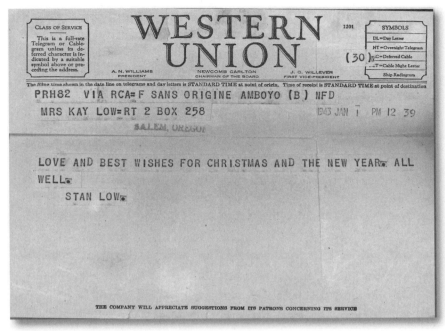

Telegram from Stan Low to his mother, dated January 1, 1943. Courtesy of the Low family.

CHAPTER 20

PORT MORESBY, NEW GUINEA

JANUARY 1943

Port Moresby is surrounded by a pretty coral reef, forming a natural protective barrier for the coastal town bordering the Gulf of Papua. The water sparkles with vibrant hues of turquoise, teal, peacock blue, and aquamarine. Tall coconut palms line the white sand beaches. Hills rise sharply from the coast, and a series of narrow valleys extends into the surrounding jungle. Early in the war, Port Moresby was the Allies' foothold in New Guinea and was under constant attack by Japanese ground and air forces.

There was little around Port Moresby. The surrounding dry forest country gave way to the dense jungle once you left the coastal plain.

The adjacent airstrips were named by their distance from Port Moresby: 3-Mile (Kila), 5-Mile (Ward), 7-Mile (Jackson), 12-Mile (Durand), and 14-Mile (Schwimmer). The heavy bombers flew out of 7-Mile airstrip; 3-Mile was for the Havocs and Kittyhawks; 5-Mile was given over to the Aussies and their Beaufighters, Kittyhawks, and Dakotas; 12-Mile was for Airacobras and P-40s; 14-Mile for P-3s and B-26s; and 17-Mile for B-25s and more P-40s.

It was the middle of January, and it was hot and sticky in Port Moresby. The daytime high temperature was headed for 90°F, with

Port Moresby, New Guinea, in the 1940s. Courtesy of the Low family.

80 percent humidity. It was always hot in New Guinea. The seasonal variation in daytime high temperature between winter and summer was only five degrees.

Regan brought his Liberator into 7-Mile for a smooth landing on the surprisingly dry, three-thousand-foot Marston matting airstrip. Dense undergrowth and trees surrounded 7-Mile, or Jackson Drome. Along one side of the runway was a conveniently located deep ditch that men could dive into when the Japanese bombs began to fall.

Regan's crew, who had arrived as rookie replacements a mere seven weeks ago, were now seasoned old-timers. *The All-American Crew* had flown fifteen missions with strikes against airfields, troop encampments, supply depots, and shipping convoys. They could expect at least five more missions during the next seven-day stretch, when the 400th would serve as the primary squadron at Port Moresby.

B-17s parked in protective revetments at 7-Mile Drome, Port Moresby. United States Army Air Force. Courtesy of Bob Livingstone.

The Liberator slowed as it rumbled down the runway, lined by the smudge pots used to light the strip at night. A speeding jeep passed them and cut in front of them. With one hand on the wheel, the driver waved a checkered black-and-white flag.

"Howell[1] is a crazy man." Regan laughed.

"Yeah, but you better follow him if you want a good parking spot," Kerby advised. "He's the parking boss at 7-Mile and a good guy to have as our friend."

Howell led Regan to a prime spot at the front of the lineup, surrounded by a protective horseshoe-shaped earth revetment. They passed a dozen newly arrived C-47 transports clustered on the edge of the runway without protection.

After shutting down the Liberator, the crew scrambled out through the bomb bay. Roscoe Junior was the first one off the plane.

---

1   Sgt. Alonzo Howell.

Control tower at 7-Mile Airfield, Port Moresby, New Guinea. Courtesy of Bob Livingstone.

"Hey, Alonzo! Nice parking spot!" Regan called out. "Thanks. We have a little something for you."

"Hey, thanks, Lieutenant. You shouldn't have. You know we enlisted guys love the Aussies' XXXX Bitter longnecks!"

"Sure thing, Alonzo. Here, take a couple to Glenn and Travis in the control hut. Just be sure they don't drink it until they're off duty."[2]

The men clambered onto the jeep sent to take them to Hotel de Gink in Tent City, southeast of 7-Mile. De Gink was a row of tents assigned to the visiting crew.

Regan looked around at the men in his crew and smiled at their attire.

---

2   Glenn Stuck and Travis Rogers manned the control tower in six-hour shifts, day and night. An exposed platform above the thatched hut in the middle of the runway served as the control tower. Using three flags and colored flashlights, they maintained order and safety for the landing and departing bombers.

Tents at Port Moresby, New Guinea. Courtesy of Bob Livingstone.

"You guys look like buccaneers."

"Well, we are the Black Pirate squadron, Scotty," Early Bird replied. "We just need eye patches!"

They were uniquely dressed, each in a different uniform with various head coverings. Each carried a Colt .45 in a shoulder or hip holster for protection, although Early Bird had his Colt .45 strapped to his right leg. A long jungle knife or a short hunting knife tucked into a belt and a canteen completed the outfit.

"If we go down in the jungle, I want to be ready," Vinni said.

The men had stuffed their pockets with survival gear, including a compass, matches, trail maps, a first aid kit, fishhooks, iodine, quinine, and morphine. Many of them were more afraid of crocodiles and headhunters than they were of Zeros.

"But if I do go down, I'm taking my girl with me," Jerome boasted, holding up his Colt .45. "See, I modified the grip. It's clear plexiglass with a picture of Ruth on both sides!"

"Hey! I want to do that," Vinni chimed in. "I have a picture of Emmy that would be perfect."

"It's easy. We just need the shop guys to make the new clear grips. I'll show you how," Jerome offered.

Changing the subject, Eldie lamented, "I hope we don't have any more moonlight Jap raids on 7-Mile. Last time it was constant air raids every night."

"They put in more ack-ack guns since we were here last," Jerome noted. "But the Betty bombers do love 7-Mile."

"Those guys in the C-47s parked out in the open had better watch out for air raids tonight," Eldie advised.

With a growling stomach, Albert suggested, "Let's go to Sloppy Joe's for dinner. Remember to bring your mess kit and utensils."[3]

Junior's puppy yap of approval made Stan smile.

* * *

At Sloppy Joe's, with mess kits in hand, the soldiers and airmen stood shoulder to shoulder, waiting for the best food at Port Moresby. It wasn't fine dining, but it was plentiful, and the company was excellent, as was the latest gossip.

Jerome and Stan arrived early. Fighting side by side in the Liberator's nose, they had grown close. Jerome's intervention against the redneck who called Stan a Jap had pretty much cemented their friendship. Each man trusted the other with his life.

Thousands of American men were stationed in the South Pacific. Once in a great while, the odds were that a soldier would unexpectedly bump into a friend from back home. However, it seemed like fate when both Jerome and Stan ran into a friend from home on the same day in January 1943.

Fiddling with his mess kit, Jerome was surprised when he heard

---

3   Sloppy Joe's, at the end of 7-Mile, provided passable food in plentiful amounts. Buck privates and majors stood shoulder to shoulder in the small makeshift diner with three tables, a counter, and a field kitchen.

his name called out over the din of the crowded room.

"Jerome Lesser! Is that really you?"

"Coach Sieja! What are you doing out here?"

"Captain Sieja now. I'm a C-47 pilot. Not much use for a fencing coach out here!"[4]

"Those must be your C-47s we saw parked on the edge of 7-Mile."

"Yes, but I sure wish we had a few revetments for protection from the Jap bombers."

Turning to BFW, Jerome explained, "Stan Sieja was my fencing coach at Textile High in New York City."

"Coach, this is Stan Low, or BFW; he's the gunner that protects this bombardier's ass."

"Nice to meet you, Stan. I like your name. What's a BFW?"

"We call him that for short. It means . . ."

"It means Big Fat Weenie!" Stan interrupted.

"No. It means Baby-Faced Warrior." Turning back to Stan, he explained, "We guys called Sieja the Fencing Pole."

"Well, Lesser was the best fencer on the team. City champion, no less. I have to go to a briefing, Jerome. Good to see you. Let's meet later and catch up on old times."

"Great, Coach—I mean, Captain Sieja!" Jerome said with a mock salute.

Later, as Jerome and Stan walked past the operations shack, Stan called out, "Jack Wu! What are you doing here? You're supposed to be in Portland!"

"Stan, my man! Wow! I can't believe I finally ran into you."

"What squadron are you with, and what's your job?"

"I'm in the 320th on *Sky Lady*, but we're being transferred to the 400th. I'm a gunner like you. Who's your friend, Stan?" Jack asked,

---

4   Maj. Stanley S. Sieja became a squadron commander for the Air Transport Command. He was awarded the Distinguished Flying Cross with Clusters. After a brief postwar stint as a test pilot, he joined Princeton University, where he coached the Princeton Tigers fencing team from 1946 to 1982. He was named Coach of the Year by the National Fencing Coaches Association in 1964, 1968, and 1976, and was inducted into the Helms Athletic Foundation Hall of Fame in 1967.

petting the pup's head.

"That's Junior. But I can't believe you're another Chinese gunner!" Stan laughed. "How can they stand it?" Stan turned to make introductions. "Jerome, this is Stan Wu. He's from Portland, Oregon, near Salem, where I grew up. Our families are close."

Before Jerome could respond, Jack said, "I heard about how this guy saved your ass from that redneck hick who called you a Jap back at Iron Range."

"Yep, Jerome and the other guys have my back, and I take care of Jerome in battle. He's a pretty good gunner himself."

"Shoot where they're not. Lead the Zeke and aim high!" Jerome parroted.

"That's it! You know, Stan. You shouldn't be worried about the redneck flyboys. It's the headhunters in New Guinea that are the real problem. They hate the Japs. If we have to bail out and the natives find us, they'll think we're Japs and put our heads on a stick for a trophy!"

"That's not a pretty thought." Stan winced.

"If I ever have to bail out, I'm sticking with our pilot, Warren Smeltzer. No head-on-a-stick fate for me," Jack replied.[5]

"Don't worry, Stan. If we ever have to bail out and join the Caterpillar Club, you just stick with me," Jerome advised. "I'll make sure you keep your head on straight."[6]

---

5   On October 18, 1943, *Sky Lady* crashed into the jungles of New Guinea. The crew bailed out. When Jack Wu reached the ground, he was surrounded by natives, who mistook him for a Japanese airman. His prospects looked dismal until Jack was rescued by a crewmember. The men used their parachutes to make the skull-and-crossbones insignia of the 90th Bombardment Group. They were assisted by friendly natives, who took them to a Catholic mission. All ten men survived their ordeal and returned to combat.

6   The Caterpillar Club was composed of men who were forced to bail out in the jungles of New Guinea. Fending off the jungle, crocodiles, and headhunters, some made it back to Port Moresby.

CHAPTER 21

TWENTIETH MISSION: LIGHTHOUSES AND CARGO SHIPS

JANUARY 19, 1943

Regan's twentieth mission on January 19 was a solo attack on Cape St. George, at the southern tip of the island of New Ireland. It was strategically important, as it guarded the entrance to Saint George's Channel used by Imperial Japanese naval ships departing Rabaul for the open sea. The lighthouse and concrete bunker at Cape St. George also provided the Japanese with an early lookout for American bombers sent from Guadalcanal to bomb Rabaul.

"Looks like we're going solo again, boys," Regan reported.

"Too many missions and not enough Liberators to fly them," Crane observed.

Of the 90th Bombardment Group's sixty Liberators, on average, only fifteen were typically available for missions on any given day. The challenges of keeping the Liberators flying, coupled with mounting losses due to enemy attacks and accidents, made solo Liberator missions the order of the day in January 1943.

"It's been a couple of weeks since we had any company on a mission," Kerby noted.

B-24 Liberator 90th Bombardment Group over Salamaua, New Guinea, 1943. Public domain.

"Who needs company? These boys have the blood of Pirate Calico Jack coursing through their veins!" Crane laughed.

"I want to be Genghis Khan," Stan complained.

"So long as you keep shooting down Zekes, you can be anyone you like, BFW," Regan replied.

The five-hundred-mile trip from Port Moresby across the Owen Stanley Mountains and then on to New Ireland was uneventful. As they approached New Ireland from the south, Kerby spotted a Japanese cargo ship headed through the channel toward Rabaul.

"Let's drop our load on that ship!" Kerby suggested.

"We're pretty close to Rabaul. We could be stirring up a hornet's nest," Regan replied.

"A few Jap Zeros don't scare this crew!" Eldie called out over the interphone.

"OK, but first, let's take out the lighthouse and the bunker so they can't contact Rabaul."

Regan descended to four thousand feet and headed for Cape St. George.

At the very southern tip of New Ireland, it was an easy target.

"Jerome, take us in. She's all yours."

"We have ten five-hundred-pounders. I'll save five for the

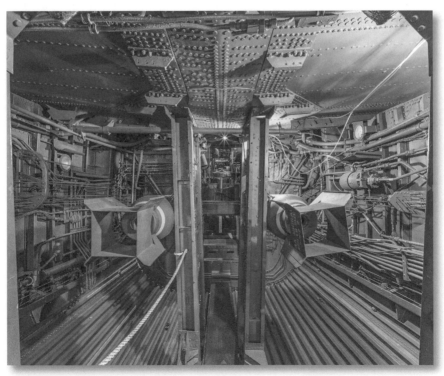

B-24 Liberator bomb bay area. National Museum of the United States Air Force.

transport. Eldie, go ahead and arm the bombs."

Lesser peered through his bombsight, entered the elevation and airspeed, and adjusted for the drift.

"Target sighted, opening bomb bay doors. Let's see if we can take out both with one drop."

"They see us coming, Jerome. We have some ack-ack fire coming from the lighthouse," Stan reported, looking over Jerome's shoulder.

"Keep a lookout for Zekes, boys. We're over enemy territory. Call 'em out. You know the drill," Regan ordered.

"Aye, aye, Captain Blackbeard!" Early Bird laughed. "Bombs away!" Come on! Make this a pretty bomb run!"

All the guys watched the five bombs fall away toward the cape.

Fifteen seconds later, Jerome shouted, "Nailed the bunker, missed the lighthouse."

"Guys, man your guns. We're going to buzz the lighthouse!" Scott shouted as he descended, circling to the right, taking them out over the Solomon Sea.

Flying in just above sea level, the Liberator roared on toward the lighthouse at two hundred miles per hour.[1]

"The lighthouse will be on the starboard side, just like target practice, boys. Stan and Jerome, you lead from the nose, Early Bird and Eldie next from the top turret and waist, and Vinni, you finish it off from the tail. Oh, and Francis, you fire whenever you like from the belly," Scott instructed.

"Let's go strafing boys," Albert sang out from the waist.

The orchestration of the strafing pass was perfection.

With .50-caliber guns blazing, Scott brought the Liberator in fast and low at three hundred feet above the deck. The roaring machine guns slammed bullets into the lighthouse for twenty seconds as they made their pass.

"All right! That was fun!" Vinni called out from the tail. Let's do it again!"

"No, we have a rendezvous with a Jap cargo ship," Scott replied.

---

1   The lighthouse at Cape St. George was 341 feet tall.

Waist Gunner Cpl. Evan B. Smith, 320th Bomb Squadron, December 9, 1942. Courtesy of Bob Livingstone.

"Jerome, we're going to make a low-altitude pass at a thousand feet. Be ready."

"Let's make two passes, Scotty," Jerome suggested.

"You got it, Jerome. Now, pickle-barrel this bomb run!"

The cargo ship saw them coming and began a weak zigzag course.

"Not enough zig or zag for those Nips," Jerome called out. "I have the cargo ship sighted. Bombs away!"

The thousand-foot drop was over in a few seconds.

"Splash two! Damn! Let's go around and do it again," Jerome reported.

On the next pass, Jerome was intent on nailing the cargo ship. Come on, boys! Nail that Jap ship!"

"Bombs away!"

Jerome held his breath and then yelled out, "Nailed it! Two strikes on the navigation deck and forecastle."

The guys cheered.

"Way to go, Lesser," Vinni called out from the tail. She's smoking but still afloat."

"Man your guns. We're going hunting for a Jap cargo ship. She'll be on your starboard side."

Regan circled around and brought the Liberator in just above sea level at two hundred miles per hour. The roaring Pratt and Whitney engines kicked up an ocean spray that flew in through the waist windows.

"You know the drill, boys! Fire at will!" Scott yelled as they bore down on the transport ship.

The combined firepower of the Liberator's .50-caliber guns created a path of destruction along the entire length of the transport ship. The gunners emptied a thousand rounds of .50-caliber bullets into the transport in a few seconds.

"She's really messed up and smoking," Vinni reported from the tail as Scott pulled up to regain altitude.

"Can we do it again?" Stan asked.

"Negative. Let's get the hell out of here before the little nasties give chase from Rabaul," Scott replied. "John, plot us a course back to Port Moresby."

"Roger. I'm on it, Scott. Heading two-two-zero. I'll adjust for wind in a minute."

Later Crane instructed, "Course two-two-five will correct for a twenty-three-mile-per-hour cross tailwind from 90 degrees. Ground speed 216 miles per hour gives a flight time of 2:18 back to Port Moresby."

* * *

After a few minutes, Vinni called out, "We got company, boys! A squadron of Zekes is hot on our tail."

"Man your guns. Make sure you're wearing your flak jacket. Call out the Zekes," Regan ordered.

B-24 glasshouse with nose gunner and bombard B-24 glasshouse with nose gunner and bombardier, who worked side by side in very cramped quarters. Courtesy of Bob Livingstone.

"Let's find some cover in those clouds," Kerby advised.

At ten thousand feet, the clouds were too scattered to offer much protection from the enemy fighters.

The ten Zeros streaked by Regan's Liberator and then turned back.

"Crap! Another head-on attack," Jerome groaned.

"Why do we always have to be in the glasshouse?"

"Take up your gun, Jerome. This way, we get the first crack at the Nips," Stan said.

"They're splitting up," Regan called out as four of the Zekes dove to attack from below.

"Three Zekes one o'clock high; three Zekes twelve o'clock head-on," Stan called out over the interphone.

"Zekes from below three o'clock and nine o'clock!" Francis reported. "I need some help here, guys!"

Stan fired a burst into the Zeros attacking head-on, sending one down in flames. At the last second, the other two rolled over and split S'ed out, barely clearing the Liberator. Jerome led the two Zekes attacking from above at one o'clock and sent a blast in their direction.

Suddenly, the nose's plexiglass shattered as 7.7-mm gunfire from an attacking Zeke found its mark.

"Shit! That was close. Are you OK, Stan?"

"Yeah, I nailed one of' em."

Francis and the waist gunners, Eldie and Albert, fought off the four Zeros attacking from below.

"Take that, you little nasties!" Albert shouted.

The roar of the .50-caliber guns was deafening. Hundreds of spent casings littered the floor in the waist.

As the Zekes passed by the waist window from below, Early Bird

Mitsubishi A6M Zero, WWII. Wikimedia Commons.

was poised at the top turret, waiting for the enemy planes to come into his view.

At that instant, the Zeke flew up over the Liberator. Byrd pounced, pouring lead into the streaking plane.

"Nailed him!" Byrd shouted as the smoking Zeke fell toward the ocean.

"That still leaves eight of those bastards," Kerby yelled. "I hope we have enough ammo after our strafing passes."

"No worries. Your armorer had them load extra boxes of ammo just in case. Nothing like being prepared," Francis replied.

"Good thinking, Francis," Scott responded.

The Zekes kept their distance, planning the next assault on the lone Liberator.

"Keep tracking our position, John. After we shake these guys, we'll want to make a beeline back to Port Moresby," Regan ordered. "How are you guys doing in the glasshouse?"

"It's a bit breezy up here with the plexiglass shot out, but we're OK," Jerome answered.

The Zeros again split up on the next pass, attacking the Liberator from the tail, both waists, and the front. The roar of the machine guns made it impossible to hear anyone speaking on the interphone.

"Number two engine is smoking," Kerby called out.

"We're going to have to shut it down before it catches fire," Regan replied as he feathered the prop. "OK, men, we're down to three engines. Damage report."

"We've got hydraulic fluid leaking in the waist," Eldie replied.

"Watch out for fires, men. We don't want to blow up our Liberator. Early Bird, go and see if you can patch that leak."

A few minutes later, Byrd reported, "The Nip bullet put a hole in our hydraulic line on the port side of the waist. I slowed it down, but it's still leaking."

"OK, get back to your turret. We'll deal with that later. We still have plenty of fight left, men. Call out the Zekes."

The battle had been raging for forty-five minutes along the coast

B-24 Liberator with smoking number 2 engine. Public domain.

of New Britain and far out to sea. Three more Zekes were damaged and put out of commission.

"We have five more Zekes on our tail. They know we're flying on three engines, so shoot straight, boys. We still have a long way to get home."

"At least we aren't leaking gas yet," Kerby observed.

"That's because I'm protecting your top side and the wing fuel cells," Byrd replied.

"Here come the little nasties!" Vinni shouted. "Six o'clock high."

"Three o'clock high and low," Albert yelled.

The Zeros' bullets stuck home, riddling the wings and tail. The tail, waist, and top turret .50-caliber guns blazed away in response.

"Nailed one," Vinni shouted.

"He's smoking and heading for a splashdown!" Eldie yelled. The remaining Zeros pulled back and retreated toward Rabaul.

"They're going home, boys!" Albert shouted.

"Hallelujah!" Scott replied. "Keep a lookout for more Zekes. I think we're heading for home, boys."

"Early Bird, go and check on the hydraulic fluid leak. Also, review with Jerome and BFW how to manually lower the gear and flaps."

"She's still leaking hydraulic fluid pretty bad," Byrd reported. "John, how much longer back to Port Moresby?"

"With three engines, at least another forty-five minutes. Heading two-four-five."

"Roger, heading two-four-five."

"We may be landing without brakes, even if we can manually lower the gear and flaps," Kerby said.

"Let me try something, Scott. I heard about a guy who drained the hydraulic fluid out of the tail turret," Byrd suggested.

"OK, check it out, but don't put it in the reservoir until we get closer to home."

"Vinni, Eldie, and Albert, I want you to rig parachutes at the tail and waist windows to slow us down. Secure them to the gun mounts and have them ready to deploy just in case," Regan ordered. "John, plot us a course for 5-mile Drome. Without brakes, we're going to need their longer six-thousand-foot runway. Early Byrd, how are you doing draining the hydraulic fluid from the tail turret?"

"I collected as much as I could get. Let me know when you want to add it to the reservoir."

"Albert, call in to 5-Mile control. Let them know we're making an emergency landing and advise them to have the fire trucks and ambulances ready. Early Byrd, can you slow the leak down anymore?"

"Doing my best, Scott. The reservoir is almost empty."

"ETA twenty minutes to 5-Mile," Crane reported.

"Stan, Jerome, and John, get down there and start lowering the landing gear and be ready to lower the flaps."

They began to turn the cranks furiously, manually lowering the tricycle landing gear.

"Crap! My arms are going to fall off!"

"We have plenty of time. Keep cranking!"

"OK, Scott, 5-Mile is standing by with emergency crews and fire trucks," Albert reported.

"Early Bird, add your hydraulic fluid to the reservoir now!"

"Roger that, Cap!"

"I see the strip," Kerby called out. "It's nice and long!"

On final approach, Scott ordered, "Lower the flaps manually."

"Engine 1 is sputtering," Kerby called out.

"We're close, boys," Regan said as they crossed over the runway threshold. "Deploy the parachutes! All three of them. Now!"

From the control tower, the men watched as the Liberator, with its three billowing white parachutes, touched down.[2]

Regan jumped on the brakes. "Not much in the way of brakes, George."

"Keep her going straight down the runway, Scott. I hope those parachutes hold."

The Liberator roared down the runway. "It's not working!"

"Give it a second," Regan replied.

The plane gradually slowed down, finally coming to a stop just before the end of the six-thousand-foot runway.

"Let's get out of here before she blows up!" Regan ordered.

The men escaped from the Liberator and ran off the runway as the fire trucks circled, waiting for the explosion.

The All-American Crew was stopped dead in her tracks. She did not explode that day, but one engine was shot, and bullet holes riddled her body, tail, and wings. Somehow, on their twentieth mission, the crew's ingenuity and Regan's leadership brought them home in one piece.

* * *

That evening outside Sloppy Joe's, a reporter with notepad and pencil in hand approached Regan, who was eating his dinner on the top of an empty oil drum.

---

2 The parachute-assisted landing was first performed by Lt. Charlie Pratee, pilot of *Belle of Texas*, during an emergency landing at Tarawa without brakes in December 1943, for which he was awarded the Distinguished Flying Cross.

B-24 Pegasus after emergency parachute-assisted landing at Norfolk, England, 1944. United States Air Force. Public domain.

"Scuttlebutt is that you boys had quite a day out there," the reporter said.

"Yes. The Zekes were coming at us pretty fast and furious, but we fought off the Japs, and we're here to tell the story. Who are you, anyway?"

"Pat Robinson. I'm an INS correspondent writing a book about you boys here in New Guinea. You're all heroes in my book."[3]

"Well, Mr. Robinson, there aren't any heroes out here. We're just men doing our jobs."

"How are your new Liberators going to stack up against the established Fortresses?"

"The Libs fly faster, farther, and higher and carry a much larger

---

3   Pat Robinson, author of *Fight for New Guinea*, 1943, was the first American correspondent to set foot in New Guinea, where he spent ten months, from June 1942 through March 1943. The International News Service (INS) was a US-based news agency founded by newspaper publisher William Randolph Hearst in 1909. In May 1958, it merged with rival United Press to become United Press International.

payload. There's no comparison. She may not be pretty, but the Liberator will win this war. The days of the B-17 are numbered."

"I know you can't talk about today's mission. Tell me about that battle you had last month out near Gasmata in New Britain."

"I thought our missions were classified. How do you know about it?"

"Son, I've been out here for so long that if it flies, I know about it."

Scott proceeded to describe their solo mission to Gasmata in mid-December.

"Yes, it was a running battle that went on for almost three hours. Three different squadrons of Zekes jumped us, and my guys fought them off each time," Scott reported proudly. "Our shot-up tail and wings looked like Swiss cheese."

"Who else can I interview about that mission?"

"Hey, BFW, come on over here and set Mr. Robinson straight about the importance of the nose gunner."

Stan came over, listened intently to Pat Robinson, and then described what it was like to have a Zero on a head-on collision course, closing at five hundred miles per hour.

"The Zero is closing at eight hundred feet every second. They start firing at a thousand feet out. I have about two seconds to react, get off a burst from the .50-caliber machine gun, and then he's gone. If I miss, we're burnt toast."

"How many Zeros did your crew shoot down that day?"

"We had two definite kills, one probable, and two smoking Zekes that were headed for home with pieces missing."

"Who shot down the Zeros that day?"

"Well, it was a team effort."

"Who on your team got credit for the kills?"

"I shot down one from the nose, and Early Bird took out a Zeke from the top turret."

"Where are you from, Stan?"

"Salem, Oregon."

"That's where you live. Where are you from?"

"Salem, Oregon. But if you mean am I Hungarian, then the answer is my father came to America from China a really long time ago."

"So, you're Chinese?"

"No, Mr. Robinson. I'm Chinese American. I live and breathe red, white, and blue. Make sure you put that in your book!"

"I'll remember, and I'll be sure to send a copy of my book to your mother in Salem, Oregon."

"That would be swell, Mr. Robinson. And please don't call me BFW. That's just for the guys. I'm Clifford Stanley Low, the all-American gunner."

B-24 Liberator Sky Lady *of the 90th Bombardment Group at Port Moresby, 1943. Courtesy of Bob Livingstone.*

CHAPTER 22

ONE MORE "REKKY": THE SEARCH FOR MCMURRIA

JANUARY 22, 1943

Regan and Crane exited the six-man tent at Hotel de Gink and headed for the palm-frond-thatched line engineering and operations shack at 7-Mile Drome.

Remarkably, their Liberator had been patched up at Ward Drome. The ground crew replaced the No. 2 engine and repaired the hydraulic system. She was deemed airworthy, fit to fly the men back to Iron Range for a week of rest and relaxation. After twenty missions, they had earned a break. If they were lucky, they could hitch a ride to Brisbane or maybe even Sydney for some real time off, away from the war.

As they entered the operations shack, Maj. Bullis intercepted them: "I need a volunteer, Regan. We have a reconnaissance mission up toward Wewak. The Japs are up to something, and we need to get eyes on their airfield. Yesterday, McMurria reported seeing twenty-seven Zeros at Wewak Field and a convoy of two transport ships and three

Lt. James A. McMurria, Iron Range, Australia, 1942–1943. Courtesy of Bob Livingstone.

destroyers in the harbor.[1] Now he's been missing for over twenty-four hours. You are the only airworthy Liberator that isn't committed to some other mission."

"Have any other crews gone out searching for McMurria's plane?"

"Yes, Lieutenants Haviland Smith and George Schaffer from the 321st went out earlier today. They searched every island from Finschhafen to Wewak but didn't find a thing. Listen, Regan, I know your crew is supposed to rotate back to Iron Range. This is a volunteer mission. It's your call."

"When do we leave, Major?"

"First light tomorrow. Talk to your crew first. You know where to find me."

* * *

---

1   James A. McMurria. *Trial and Triumph*. McMurria reported twenty-seven Zeros at Wewak. Waist gunner Patsy Grandolfo and nose gunner Tom Doyle each shot down one of the attacking Zeros.

"Well, that's about it, men. We can go back to Iron Range tomorrow, or we can volunteer for one more 'rekky' and maybe find McMurria's crew."

The silence of the nine men gathered around Scott was deafening. Vinni was looking down at his picture of Emmy through the clear pistol grip of his Colt .45.

"There's no one else?" he asked softly. "I was hoping to make it to my thirtieth birthday."

"There's no pressure here, guys. Either we all agree to go, or it's back to Iron Range."

Jerome stood. "We're all in this together. If I didn't go, I'd never be able to look in a mirror again—ever."

"Hell, I never expected to go home anyway," Eldie added. "I already told my mom I wasn't coming back."

"I got your back, Eldie," Early Bird replied. "We'll get you home to Evart, Michigan, and your dog, Zeke. How'd you pick that name, anyway?"

"If we went down, some other crews would come looking for us. You know they would," Francis added.

One by one, the men spoke and found courage in each other's words.

"How about the two youngsters, BFW and Albert? You two aren't even old enough to drink or vote, but you get to vote in this," Crane said.

Stan and Albert looked at each other, and then both smiled and nodded.

"We grew up on this plane with you guys. We're a crew, and we won't let you down," Stan replied.

All eyes turned to Vinni, still looking at his photo of Emmy.

He looked up, put the gun in his shoulder holster, and said, "There's only one way home, boys, and it's through Wewak. This Black Pirate has one more mission to fly, and then maybe I'll build you that still, Jerome!"

* * *

Lt. Randall showed up with the mail that afternoon to a cheering mob of aviators and ground crew.

"Hey, Stan. I have something for you!" Randall called out.

Stan took one whiff of the pink envelope and smiled. Lilacs in spring perfume. The message "Cheek to Cheek" on the back made his heart soar.

Afterward, Randall offered to take Regan's crew to dinner at the Aussie mess in Bomb Happy Valley. It was a good change of scenery, and for unexpected reasons, the food was a little better than their usual fare.

"Hey, mates. Let me show you some real Aussie cuisine."

"Thanks, Randall. Do they serve choccy biccys?" Stan asked.

"For you, BFW, we just might be able to rustle one up."

Inside the Aussie mess, Randall offered, "For your dining pleasure tonight, we are serving bully beef, rice, jam, cocoa, tea, and ANZAC wafers!"[2]

"Hey! That's the same old menu we've had for months!"

"Aye, mate, except I brought the choccy biccys and XXXX bitter ale!"

"Let's eat!" Kerby laughed, digging into the bully beef. "You know why they call this place Bomb Happy Valley?"

He smiled at the puzzled looks and explained, "Because the Betty bombers drop their bombs here first on their way to 7-Mile Drome."

"Let's eat a little faster." Francis laughed. "Pass me a bottle of beer, please."

* * *

That evening, the rain turned the roads outside into a muddy mess. In their tents, the men huddled under their mosquito nets were shirtless and sweating. It was another perfect evening in New Guinea, 85°F and humid.

---

2   ANZAC wafers is another name for hardtack.

Kerby paused as he stared at the blank sheet of paper, a letter to his mom in Charlotte, North Carolina. He was startled by a familiar squawk.

"Damn the rain. I need a beer!"

"Shut up! Let me think, you, stupid bird!" George exclaimed as he began to write.

January 21, 1943

Dear Mom,

It's raining cats and dogs outside the tent, and our bombardier's bird is talking nonstop. There's not much new here. We're staying nice and warm and have plenty to eat. We've even developed a taste for Australian cuisine and drink.

Our crew was assigned to go on leave, but we volunteered for one more recon mission first. A B-24 is missing, and we will continue the search. You'd be proud of the men out here, Mom. They are brave to a fault and unassuming. I doubt you could find a bad one in the lot of them. We're all just doing our jobs.

Please give my love to Juanita and Aunt Georgia, and send my regards to my friends at the *Charlotte News*. Tell them I expect them to save my job at the proof desk. Well, that's all for now.

With all my love,
George

* * *

Wewak is located along the northwest coast of New Guinea. The territory of New Guinea and the Catholic mission built the single-runway airfield in 1937, positioning it along the water's edge, running parallel to Wirui Beach. The Imperial Japanese Army took over Wewak on

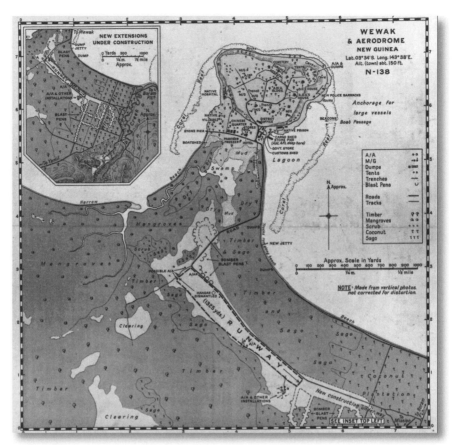

Map of Wewak. Courtesy of Bob Livingstone.

December 18, 1942, and began improvements on the airfield. A small U-shaped harbor protected the Japanese ships, and the adjacent garrison housed the soldiers.

There had been little activity at Wewak Airfield in late December 1942 and early January 1943. However, the situation changed rapidly. On January 17, 1943, a detachment of twenty-three A6M2 Zeros and six B5N2 Kates commanded by Lt. Cmdr. Takashi Hashiguchi took off from the carrier *Jun'yō* and flew via Rabaul to Wewak Airfield. They were the first Japanese aircraft to operate from the captured civilian airfield.[3]

On January 20, 1943, Lt. McMurria, on a solo "rekky," spotted twenty-seven Japanese Zeros at Wewak Airfield. Three minutes later, he encountered and reported a Japanese convoy of three transport ships and two destroyers off Wewak.

His last radio message was that three Zeros were attacking them. This sighting was the Allies' first knowledge of the Japanese military buildup. In response, five Liberators from Port Moresby immediately took off in search of the convoy.[4]

They did not locate the Japanese ships, but twenty-five Zeros intercepted them. In a running battle lasting forty-five minutes, the American planes sustained substantial damage while reportedly shooting down twelve of the Zeros and damaging six.

Two days later, on January 22, 1943, Regan's daylight reconnaissance mission was to confirm and photograph the Japanese air and naval buildup and to look for signs of McMurria.

As with all "rekky" missions, they would be flying solo. To avoid detection, Regan had instructions to fly off to the side of the target at high altitude and to keep near cloud cover so they could duck in if intercepted by the enemy. Even with these precautions, one of every ten reconnaissance planes was lost. Given the events of January 20, the odds were much worse for a solo Liberator entering a hornet's nest loaded with Zeros.

* * *

Staying near the cloud cover at fourteen thousand feet, Regan looked down at the coast as they approached the small finger of land protruding into the Bismarck Sea.

---

3   The Zeros from the carrier *Jun'yō* stayed at Wewak Airfield until January 24, 1943, flying to Kavieng Airfield and then on to Truk before returning to the *Jun'yō*. During this one week, they claimed to have shot down four B-24 Liberators—one damaged and three probables.

4   Five Liberators were flown by Maj. Faulkner, Lt. Dowie, and Lt. Cook of the 321st Squadron and Lt. Olsen of the 319th Squadron.

B-24 waist gunner with movie camera. Courtesy of Bob Livingstone.

"Coming up to Wewak, Albert. Do you have your camera ready?"

"Roger, Cap. I'm ready to play Cecil B. DeMille," Albert laughed.

"Get your film, and then let's get out of here!" Eldie answered. "There's been way too much Zeke activity around here lately."

In the glasshouse, Stan opened a paper bag, pulled out its contents, and offered them to Jerome and John.

"You guys want a little snack? I brought Randall's choccy biccys."

"Don't mind if I do, Stan." Jerome smiled, munching on the chocolate-covered biscuit.

"Thanks, BFW. I don't imagine you remembered to bring the XXXX beer."

"I saved some in the tent so we can celebrate later tonight when we get back," Stan replied.

"Yeah! And then it's going to be a week of leave!"

"There are only five Zeros on the airfield. I got my film. Now

Aerial view of Wewak, 1943. Courtesy of Bob Livingstone.

let's look for the convoy in the harbor, and then get out of here," Albert reported.

The harbor was empty. In search of the Japanese convoy, Regan flew northeast from Wewak over the expansive Pacific Ocean.

"Nothing out here but ocean, Scott. Let's head back," Kerby advised.

"John, what's that speck of an island up ahead, just under the clouds?" Regan asked.

"Should be Wageo Island."[5]

"Let's make a low-level pass. Keep your eyes peeled for our missing Liberator, boys," Regan called out.

Roaring over the tiny mountainous island at six hundred feet, the Liberator came in above the treetops.

"I think I saw a flare!" Jerome yelled from the glasshouse. "It's got to be McMurria! Make another pass, Scott!"

---

5   Wageo Island is also known as Vokeo Island and is located forty miles east of Wewak with an area of 16 km².

Wageo Island, aka Vokeo Island. Wikimedia Commons.

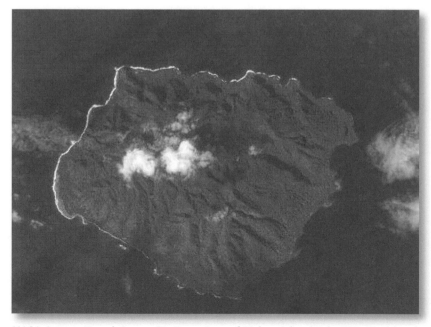

NASA International Space Station view of Vokeo Island, aka Wageo Island. Wikipedia.

Hiroyoshi Nishizawa, Japan's highest-scoring Zero pilot, leads a flight of A6M3 model 22s of the 251st "Kokutai" from Rabaul in 1943. National Archives. Public domain.

Regan made a wide turn to the south, preparing for another pass over the island.

Scanning the horizon as they continued out over the ocean, Scott and Jerome both saw it in the same instant.

"Oh, shit. Here they come," Jerome exclaimed, dropping his choccy biccy to the deck. "I have never seen so many Zeros."

In the chaos of the ensuing battle, Regan's last order was chilling: "Jerome, destroy the bombsight."

* * *

Three days later, on January 25, 1943, two Liberators, piloted by Lt. Paul Johnson and Lt. Lark Martin, took off from Port Moresby on an armed reconnaissance mission to Wewak in search of Regan's plane and crew. Regan's last coded message, "Intercpted by Zeros," had been followed by silence.

Two and a half hours into the flight, Johnson and Martin sighted the convoy, consisting of three transport ships, one light cruiser, and one destroyer. After reporting the position of the convoy, eighteen Zeros intercepted them.[6] In the ensuing running battle, the Zeros severely damaged Lt. Martin's Liberator, which lost engines 3 and 4. Five men were wounded. When they limped back into Ward's Drome at Port Moresby, Lt. Martin found four hundred bullet and cannon holes in his "flying sieve" of a Liberator. Lt. Johnson's plane was in only slightly better condition, with the tail turret destroyed, one engine smoking badly, ailerons ripped, and holes all over the ship. While the fate of the two missing Liberators was unknown, a single plane would not have survived a coordinated, overwhelming attack by so many enemy Zeros.

---

6   McMurria reported twenty-seven Zeros at Wewak on January 20, 1943, and that his crew shot down two enemy planes.

CHAPTER 23

THE ANNIVERSARY

MARCH 1943

The flickering glow of the single candle lit Emily's face as she peered out from behind the white veil. Wearing the veil brought her closer to Paul. The candle rested on the dining room table she and Paul had picked out together for their new home. The room was now quiet, with the warm glow of the setting sun filtering through the house's curtains on Lancaster Road. Her parents, worried about her as always, had wanted to come over. But this day was hers to spend with Paul and Paul alone. It was hard to imagine that one year had passed since their hurried wedding. Then he'd left, and now here she was alone with a candle and her thoughts of Paul. Emily held her diamond wedding ring up to the flame and watched the reflections dance around the room.

"Well, Paul, I love you. Happy anniversary. We'll have that life together that we always planned," Emily whispered. "Oh, and happy thirtieth birthday, Paul.[1] Please, Paul, come home safe, my dearest."

The knock at the door startled her. *Knock! Knock! Knock!*

She glanced through the curtains into the semidarkened yard.

Who could be bothering me today of all days?

Knock! Knock!

---

1   Paul and Emily's wedding anniversary was March 14, one day after Paul's birthday on March 13.

*Emily Vinson. Courtesy of
the Davidson family.*

"Oh, all right!"

Emily slowly opened the door and peered out. She gasped when she saw the vague outline of a man in uniform and then let out a sigh of relief when she spotted the bicycle and her friend.

"Bill, what are you doing here at this hour? Why aren't you working at the dairy?"

"It's my other job, Emily," he replied without smiling.

Emily looked at her childhood friend with a puzzled expression. "What's going on, Bill?"

"Just this." Bill handed her the envelope. "You have to sign for it here."

Emily's heart was pounding, and her hands shook as she took the envelope, "No!" she sobbed. "Not today!"

"No, Emily. It's not what you think. Just read it," Bill said, as he picked up his bicycle and hurried off into the darkness.

Inside, her hands were still shaking as she opened the telegram. Emily sank to the floor, and she struggled to read the words. Tears streamed down her face, and her deep sobbing filled the empty home.

Variations on this event were playing out in the homes of ten families across America.

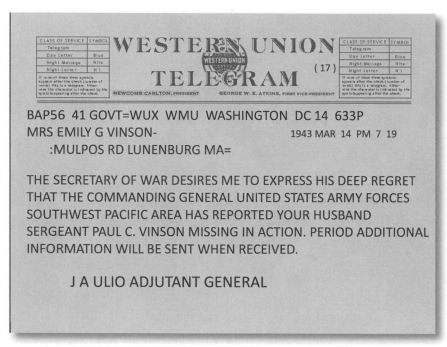

Western Union telegram, dated March 14, 1943. Courtesy of Robert Prescott.

Two hundred miles south in the Bronx, the Lesser family had just settled down for dinner at their apartment on Walton Avenue when the doorbell rang. Grace jumped up and ran to the parlor. Opening the door, she was face-to-face with a young boy dressed in a black tie, gray button-down coat, and flat-topped hat with a badge announcing *Western Union*.

"Telegram for Mr. and Mrs. Alfred Lesser."

Reaching for the envelope, Grace pulled her hand back. She was silent.

"You have to sign for it here."

Signing quickly, Grace gingerly carried the unopened envelope inside and placed it on the table in front of her parents.

The entire family stared at the envelope. No one spoke, and the silence was deafening. Finally, after what seemed like an eternity, Alfred and Martha Lesser stood, took the telegram in hand, and went into the bedroom, shutting the door behind them.

When her parents emerged from the bedroom, they never spoke of the telegram or its contents, not that day or any other day. The possible loss of their beloved Jerome was a pain they bore in silence. Because of the slow mail delivery in 1943, Jerome's letters continued to arrive for several months, giving them hope that he was alive.

In Evart, Michigan, the family of Floyd McCallum refused to believe that there was any situation Eldon could not overcome. Eldon was simply too tough and too much of an outdoorsman to die. MIA telegram or not, they all knew in their hearts that Eldon would come walking out of the jungle any day now.

In private, Edna May kept hearing her son's last words when he snuck home from Willow Run: "I don't think I'm coming back, Mom." But the old-timers in Evart knew better. There was no way some crocodile-infested jungle could keep Eldon down. He'd be showing up in town soon enough. They all knew, and they held out hope.

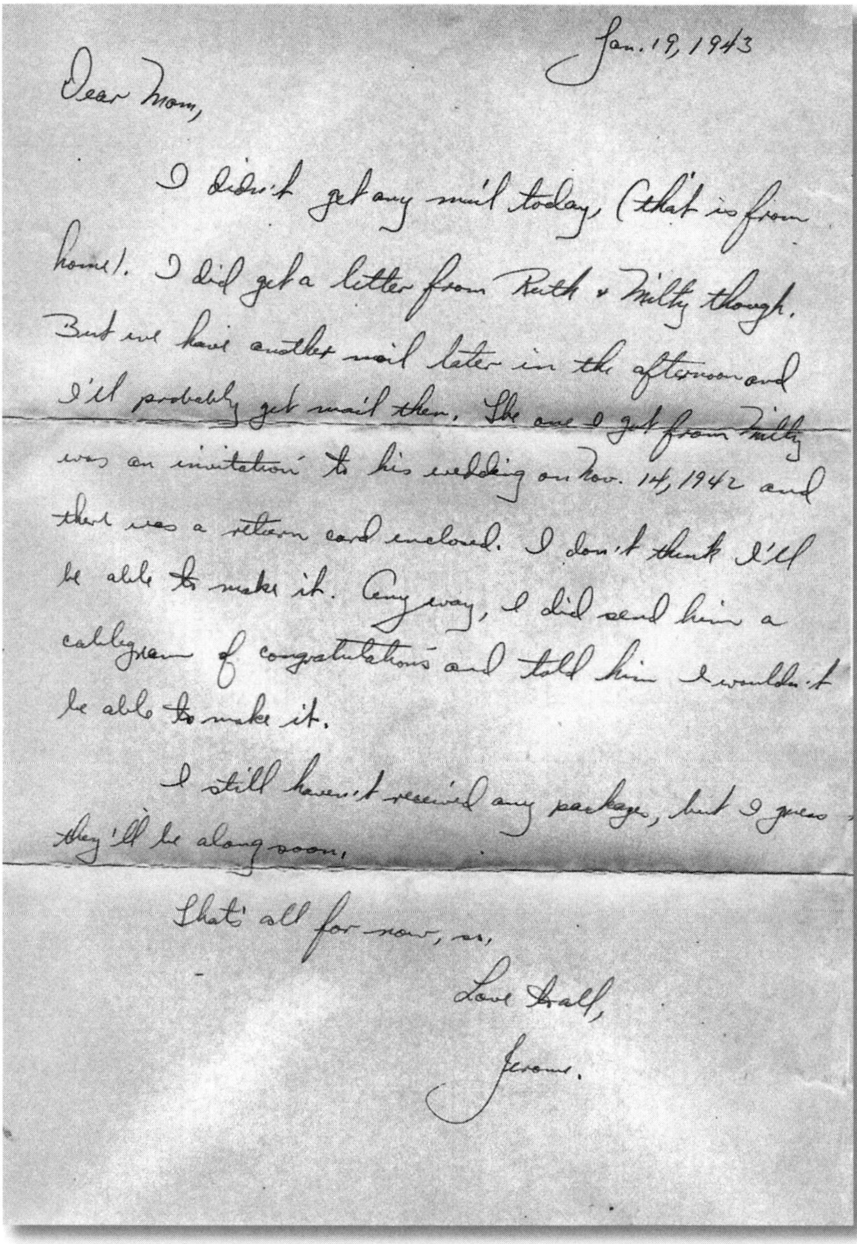

Jan. 19, 1943

Dear Mom,

I didn't get any mail today, (that is from home). I did get a letter from Ruth + Milty though. But we have another mail later in the afternoon and I'll probably get mail then. The one I got from Milty was an invitation to his wedding on Nov. 14, 1942 and there was a return card enclosed. I don't think I'll be able to make it. Anyway, I did send him a cablegram of congratulations and told him I wouldn't be able to make it.

I still haven't received any package, but I guess they'll be along soon.

That's all for now, so,

Love to all,

Jerome.

Letter from Jerome Lesser to his mother, dated January 9, 1943. Courtesy of the Lesser family.

PART II

SAIPAN: AVIATION ENGINEERS AND FLYING LEATHERNECKS

The war in the Pacific proceeded as the United States invaded island after island in their relentless drive toward Japan. In June 1944, Clifford Stanley Low's brother, Loren, was about to invade Saipan in the Central Pacific as part of Operation Forager. He carried with him a photograph of his kid brother, the B-24 nose gunner, who he knew would be emerging from the jungles of New Guinea any day now.

CHAPTER 24

SCHOFIELD BARRACKS

APRIL 1943

Loren stopped his D8 bulldozer, shut off the engine, and jumped down from the cab. There was still plenty of work to be done, repairing and improving the field, hangars, and surrounding roads. Loren watched the replacement B-24 Liberator crews fly in and out of Hickam on the way to their deployment in the South Pacific. He wondered if any of them would run into his kid brother, Stan.

"Corporal, report to the CO's office at HQ," Lt. Flatbrush called out, interrupting his thoughts.

Now why am I in hot water? They took my stripes after my trip to see Stan. Isn't that enough?

"Yes, sir."

Inside the CO's office, Loren stood at attention. He'd never been in here.

"At ease, Corporal. This notice arrived for you," the major said as he held out the telegram.

"Thank you, sir."

Outside, Loren sat and opened the telegram. His hands were shaking. He recalled the last time he saw Stan, the night of the luau on Waikiki Beach. He tried to picture Stan surrounded by his crew, enjoying the food and the warm tropical Hawaiian evening. Stan was so proud.

Clifford S. Low in 1942.
Courtesy of the Low family.

As he read the telegram, he let out a sigh. *Well, it could be worse. Stan's just missing.*

Still, he hated picturing Stan on some Pacific island trying to survive the Japanese, alligators, and headhunting natives.

At least he's not alone. He'll be OK. I better write to Mom and MeiMei.

That night after chow, Loren sat down on his bunk and pulled out a sheet of paper and the new pen from the base commissary. He gazed at the photo Stan had given him when they last met. He was dressed in battle gear with his .50-caliber machine gun slung over his right shoulder. Loren smiled when he recalled Stan's worried request: "Don't ever show this to Mom or MeiMei or Elsie. It will drive them nuts with worry."

Well, little brother, you be tough out there.

He thought about Stan growing up in Salem, Oregon, and then in Stockton, in Central California. Stan was always the baby. Loren worked hard to make sure his brother was tougher than the other kids.

Remember, Stan. Keep fighting and never give up hope.

Loren grew up with those words. He didn't know their origin. His mom used to whisper them to him when he was small, and then he'd taught Stan the same lesson on the hop farm.

Loren picked up the pen and began to write his letter to his mother, searching for words of reassurance.

Clifford S. Low, aka BFW, in 1940, weighing hops on the farm in Keizer, Oregon. His older brother, Loren, looks on. Yellow Fox, the Nez Perce who worked on the farm, is in the foreground. Courtesy of the Low family.

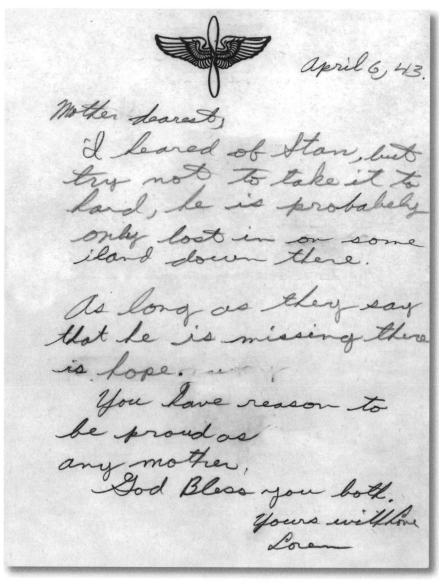

Letter from Loren Low to his mother, dated April 6, 1943. Courtesy of the Low family.

CHAPTER 25

FLYING LEATHERNECKS AND AVIATION ENGINEERS

SAIPAN

JUNE 1944

The decades-old photographs of the two warriors only hinted at the confidence and bravado of the two men from very different worlds. Fate and a world at war crossed their paths on a tiny island in the South Pacific. History would reveal how these two men's actions in June 1944 played a pivotal role in the invasion of Saipan. Taking Aslito Airfield on the southern tip of the island was a crucial strategic step in the Japanese empire's defeat. Without the daring of these two Americans, the outcome might have been vastly different.

The American invasion of Saipan occurred on June 15, 1944. It was preceded by the largest mobilization of American forces in history, with an armada of 535 ships carrying 127,570 US military personnel, all converging on the island of Saipan, 3,800 miles from Pearl Harbor.[1]

First Lt. Leonard Wollman, an aviator for the United States

---

1   Rex Gunn, "Aviation Engineers Battalion," *BRIEF, 7th Army Air Force Magazine*, October 17, 1944.

Marine Corps,[2] was attached to the VMO-4 artillery-spotting squadron of the 4th Marine Division. Flying small, high-wing Stinson OY-1 monoplanes, Lt. Wollman and his copilot provided essential tactical reconnaissance, spotting enemy artillery emplacements on Saipan and directing naval, air, and land artillery strikes against the enemy. The men of VMO-4 were based on the carrier USS *White Plains*,[3] which had departed San Diego, California, on April 24, 1944. They left Pearl Harbor for their first combat mission and were now headed for Saipan as part of Operation Forager.

World War II Marine pilot Leonard Wollman. Courtesy of the Wollman family.

Wollman grew up in Brooklyn in the 1920s and 1930s in an immigrant neighborhood where Yiddish, Polish, and Italian were more commonly heard than the English spoken in his home. His father, Samuel, an investigator for the Metropolitan News Company

---

2   Shore-based aircraft for the invasion of the Marianas totaled 879 planes; 52 belonging to the Marine Corps, 269 to the US Army, and 258 to the Navy. Marine aircraft consisted of 172 fighters, 36 night fighters, 72 dive bombers, 36 torpedo bombers, and 36 transport aircraft.

3   The USS *White Plains* escort carrier was commissioned on November 15, 1943, assigned air unit Composite Squadron 4 (VC-4), with 16 Grumman F4F Wildcat fighters and 12 General Motors TBM Avenger torpedo planes, and VMO-4 Observation Squadron with 8 Stinson OY-1 planes.

on Canal Street,[4] was born in Brooklyn to Russian and Austrian parents. Leonard's mother, Clara, was born in England. Clara lit the Shabbat candles on Friday evenings, and the family celebrated some of the High Holidays but were not strict observers of Jewish religious traditions. Leonard attended public schools and the Brooklyn Hebrew School.

The family's two-story brick home at 1464 East Third Street was semi-attached and was a mirror image of the neighbors' house. The boys spent evenings and weekends playing stickball in the Brooklyn streets. There were always the fallback games,

Photograph of Leonard Wollman from the yearbook of Abraham Lincoln High School, located 2.5 miles south of the Wollman home on Third Avenue.

punchball and stoop ball, when a stick was lacking. The competition was fierce, but the Wollman brothers held their own. Even as a youngster, Len was famous for his iron will and determination. Quitting was simply not an option. Throughout his life, Len's constant companion on the streets was his younger brother, Bob, who went on to become a track star as the New York City hurdles champion.

An outstanding student and natural athlete at Abraham Lincoln High School, Len sought out other young men from his community with similar inclinations, including Jerome Lesser. Jerome was three years older but shared Len's interest in sports, math, and science. Leonard had watched in awe as Jerome Lesser, a young Jewish boy

4   Metropolitan News Company president Morris Eisenman was a longtime supporter of Jewish community causes. The company distributed the morning newspapers of New York City for decades and was purchased by the *New York Times* in 1992.

from the Bronx, was crowned the New York City fencing champion. Wollman recalled meeting up with Jerome Lesser when he was fifteen years old, approaching him after the Rosh Hashanah service at the Hebrew Institute of University Heights.[5] Both boys were relieved to be out in the sun after Rabbi Simon Kramer's service.

"Hey, Jerome! That's something about your fencing title!"

"Thanks, Len. You should take up the sport. You're a good athlete, and I could show you some moves."

"What's it like being in a fencing competition?"

"It's kind of like a dance or a chess match. Moves and coun-

Leonard Wollman in 1942. Courtesy of the Wollman family.

termoves. You have to react, but also anticipate your opponent's moves and weaknesses."

"I don't see you here very often," Len observed.

"I came today to hear Abe Veroba sing.[6] That guy has a voice. It's hard to believe we're the same age," Jerome replied.

"Yeah, he'll probably be a cantor someday. Where are you going next year after high school?"

---

5   The Hebrew Institute of University Heights, at 1835 University at West Tremont, was founded in 1925. Rabbi Simon Kramer came from Chicago. On the High Holidays, the congregation numbered up to 1,500.

6   Abraham Veroba (1917–1996) was from Brooklyn. He became a decorated aerial gunner in WWII and, as Len Wollman predicted, became the famous and beloved Cantor Abraham Veroba.

"Probably headed for City College. They have a fencing team and pretty good math and science departments. How about you? I'll bet you'll end up at NYU with your grades."

"Who knows? Right now, I'm pretty focused on my studies and track. We'll see what happens. I want to be a teacher, but I like sports and dancing."[7]

"Do you still play that violin? I remember the photo of your elementary school orchestra in the newspapers. You guys were famous!"

"Hardly! But I still play once in a while. Anyway, congratulations on the fencing championship. You're the famous one, Jerome."

"See you around, Len. Don't forget my offer to teach you my best fencing moves," Jerome laughed as he tousled Len's hair like an older brother.

* * *

Leonard Wollman did attend Brooklyn College and New York University, where he excelled academically.

Twenty-one-year-old Leonard enlisted in the Marine Corps in March 1942. He chose the Marines because he "liked a tough outfit." By July, PFC Wollman was in Officer Candidates School in Quantico, Virginia, graduating as a second lieutenant in October. In 1943 he underwent training at Camp Lejeune in New River, North Carolina, before being assigned to Camp Pendleton in Oceanside, California, in the fall. A fateful training accident at Camp Pendleton brought him back to Brooklyn on leave.

On December 2, 1943, 1st Lt. Leonard Wollman married his childhood sweetheart, June Rick. Having grown up on the same street in Brooklyn, they believed their marriage and romance had been destined since they met when they were ten years old. The newlywed couple moved into their apartment at 522 Ocean Avenue in Brooklyn. Within a month, Leonard was preparing to go overseas with the 3rd

---

7   Len Wollman was on the dance committee in high school and later taught square dancing in school and at the Ocala Camp in Florida.

Battalion, 14th Regiment, 4th Marine Division of the United States Marines.

* * *

Loren Low's path to the island of Saipan was considerably longer, having enlisted in January 1941. In his own words, he "got his flag a-waving" and couldn't wait to get into the fight.

Loren Low in 1942. Courtesy of the Low family.

Loren enlisted in the Army Air Corps a full eleven months before the Japanese attack on Pearl Harbor set in motion the events that changed the world and the lives of millions of young men. Sgt. Low was part of the "regular Army," composed of patriotic men who felt the calling to enlist and fight for their country before the draft made service compulsory.

Loren, born in 1917, was the seventh of ten children. His father, Low Sun Fook, was a Chinese laundryman and hop farmer in Salem, Oregon. He had immigrated to America in 1877 with little more than the shirt on his back. As a trusted merchant and entrepreneur, he quickly learned how to make money and friends in the white community of Salem.

Loren Low in 1941. Courtesy of the Low family.

Loren, tall, good-looking, and strong as an ox, was encouraged by the Chinese on the farm to sign up for the Flying Tigers, to protect China from the invading Japanese. Loren's emphatic reply still rings loud and clear: "There is only one country I will fight for, and that's the United States of America!" Following enlistment, he was the first to raise his hand when they asked for volunteers to go to Hawaii to join the 804th Aviation Engineers of the 7th Army Air Force.

Loren Low writing a letter home. Courtesy of the Low family.

In 1941, twenty-three-year-old Loren was one of the first of Salem's young men to ship out. Before he did, he penned a letter to his mother and kid sister that expressed the world's uncertainty and his love and longing for his family. Loren's intense pride in being an American was evident in his parting words.

To his mother, he wrote: "I love you, mother, more than you'll ever know. I have never said much to you about this before, but when a fellow goes away as far as I am going, he will think more about those things. Don't worry about me, for I'll be all right. Uncle Sammy will take care of me."

He ended his letter with a message to his kid sister, MeiMei, saying, "With everything in this wide world the way it is, it's great to be an American."

In the war against Japan, American forces engaged in an island-hopping campaign as they invaded island after island in the South and Central Pacific. At each island, aviation engineers were a critical component of the invasion force, quickly turning sand, coral,

USS White Plains *in San Diego Harbor. US Navy Photograph 80-G-302258, National Archives and Records Administration, Still Pictures Division, College Park, Maryland.*

and mud into fighter- and bomber-ready runways.

In three years, the 804th Aviation Engineers fought at Pearl Harbor and built airfields on Canton Island, Christmas Island, Baker Island, Makin Island, and Saipan.

In January 1944, Loren was on Funafuti Atoll on his way back to Oahu after the campaign on Makin Island. One rainy afternoon, Loren witnessed a shiny silver B-24 Liberator make an emergency landing with three sputtering engines.

Wow! That was close. Maybe someone on that Liberator knows Stan.[8]

* * *

In June 1944, the Allies designed Operation Forager to capture the Central Pacific islands of Saipan, Tinian, Guam in the Marianas, and Palau in Micronesia. The fleet departed Pearl Harbor on June 5, 1944.

---

8   The B-24 *Silver Streak* was being flown by Col. Art Rogers, CO of the Jolly Rogers, on his way home after seventeen months of active combat. Rogers indeed knew Stan and his B-24 crew from his early days at Iron Range, Australia.

Loren Low and the battle-tested 7th Army Air Force Aviation Engineers fought their third major engagement in six months.

In the three weeks leading up to the embarkation, the engineers worked around the clock to prepare their battle-zone construction equipment. The men overhauled the equipment by waterproofing the motors and raising the exhaust pipes above the cabs of the tractors, bulldozers, and other vehicles.

Loading the LSTs was a feat of engineering and planning, as each square foot of space was accounted for in detailed maps of equipment measured down to the inch. They backed up the equipment onto the LST,[9] with lighter trucks and jeeps on the main deck and the heavy equipment, like bulldozers, below on the tank deck. The men loaded two hundred tons of Marston matting, perforated steel planking used to construct runways. On the loading docks of Pearl Harbor, their unit's heavy construction equipment filled three LSTs.

Simultaneously, the sailors and aviators of the USS *White Plains* were preparing to set sail for their first active engagement. The *White Plains*, a Casablanca-class escort carrier, had sailed to Tarawa in February and then on the Kwajalein Atoll, but they arrived after the action had subsided.

This time would be different, and the USS *White Plains* would be in the thick of battle. The aviators and ground crew prepared the Composite Squadron 4 (VC-4), sixteen Grumman FM-2 Wildcat fighters, and twelve General Motors TBM 1C Avenger torpedo bombers for the voyage. The VMO-4 observation squadron, under the command of Capt. Nathan D. Blaha, boxed and placed into wooden crates the eight Stinson OY-1 observation planes.

---

9   An LST, or landing ship tank, was a flat-bottom vehicle used in World War II to support amphibious operations by carrying tanks, vehicles, and cargo, and by landing troops directly onto shore without docks or piers.

CHAPTER 26

SAIPAN INVASION

JUNE 15, 1944

T
he USS *White Plains* arrived at Saipan before dawn on June 15, 1944, the day of the Marine and Army invasion of the Japanese-held island. Naval aviators and a handful of Marine leathernecks packed the squadron ready room.

Wollman had celebrated his twenty-fourth birthday on board the *White Plains* as she steamed from Pearl Harbor toward the Marianas. Leonard looked around the ready room from his cushioned leather seat. The Navy Wildcat and Avenger torpedo bomber pilots were all the same: young, confident, and white. Laughter, yelling, and good-natured grousing filled the room. A few men were dozing. Most, like Wollman, were feeling the butterflies, but none would admit it.

"Hey, Wollman! You flyin' with me again today?"

Leonard felt the poke before he heard McLean's words. Lt. Col. "Red" McLean, a TBM Avenger pilot, could have been Leonard's brother, or at least a close cousin, with the same sandy curly hair, piercing eyes, and slight build.[1]

"Sure thing, Red. You going to let me fly the Avenger today?"

McLean laughed. "Sure. Once you're done spottin' the enemy, and we drop our torpedo on a Jap cruiser, you can fly us back to Pearl!"[2]

---

1   Coll McLean was from Wisconsin but now lived in Marshfield, Oregon, near Coos Bay.
2   McLean was joking since there were no flight controls in the second seat compartment.

Aircraft carrier squadron ready room, World War II. Library of Congress. Public domain.

Leonard smiled as McLean took the seat next to him. Like Leonard, he wore his leather helmet, flight goggles, a Mae West inflatable life jacket, and parachute. After the preflight briefing, they were headed straight for the flight deck and Saipan. The third member of their crew, radioman Melvin Tigner, was missing.

"Hey, Winnegar! You seen Tigner?" McLean yelled across the room.

"No, the old man is running late. You need a radioman?" Andy Winnegar asked, grinning.

"Yeah! If Tigner doesn't show, you can fly with me any day, Andy." McLean laughed.

"Hands off my guy, Red! Andy flies with me!" Pat Owens, another Avenger pilot, protested. "The kid's the best radioman, bombardier, and gunner in the squadron."

Lt. Cmdr. Robert C. Evins, the commanding officer of Composite Squadron VC-4, entered late, stood at the front of the briefing room, and waited. The bantering stopped immediately.

"Men, we have twenty thousand Marines going ashore this morning along with southwest Saipan at Red, Green, Blue, and Yellow Beaches," Evins said, pointing at a map of Saipan. "VC-4 will be flying a CAP/Strike mission.[3] We will patrol the air over the invasion armada and beaches and engage any Jap aircraft intent on harming our leatherneck and grunt brothers. The Zeros will be coming from

Eighteen-year-old Andrew J. Winnegar, ARM2/c in VC-4, was a radio operator who flew in a TBM Avenger with pilot Ltjg Walter P. Owens. Capt. Grady Gatlin was the Marine Observer. Courtesy of Andy Winnegar.

the Aslito Airfield along the southern end of the island. We also have reports of carrier-based enemy fighters, so watch your backs."

"We'll fly at different assigned altitudes to shorten the response time to engaging the enemy. Those Marines have a rough day ahead of them. Your job is to neutralize the enemy airpower. All of it. Do you understand?"

"Yes, sir!" came a raucous reply. "Let's go!"

"Not so fast, boys. Your secondary role today is to strike the enemy gun emplacements and Jap troops wherever you find them. We need to soften them up, so strafe and bomb the enemy at will. They have some big-time artillery down there, and we want to silence those cannons if we can."

The men let out another raucous cheer.

---

3 CAP: Combat Air Patrol

"The three TBM Avengers will be flying with Marine spotters from VMO-4. Your mission is to patrol for Jap submarines and to locate Jap artillery emplacements. Call in the coordinates to direct naval strikes against these targets. Make sure you know where our guys are before you start raining down the firepower from our naval artillery. Any questions? No? Well, then Godspeed and happy hunting, men!"

* * *

Nicknamed "the Turkey," the TBM Avenger was neither pretty nor sleek, but she was a brute that could pack a punch with a torpedo, five-inch rockets, bombs, three .50-caliber machine guns, and a single .30-caliber gun. With a top speed of 275 miles per hour, the Avenger could almost keep up with the more agile fighters. The Avenger had a crew of three: pilot, radioman bombardier, and turret gunner.

On the flight deck, Wollman climbed up into the gun turret positioned at the back of the cockpit, grasping the .50-caliber machine gun. Carrying the K-20 camera, radioman Melvin Tigner entered the cramped tunnel running from the plane's rear forward to just behind the pilot.

"I got the cheap seats on this flight," Tigner yelled. "Noisy, smelly, and cramped as hell!"

"Yeah, my view's a lot better from up here in the turret," Wollman replied.

"And all the bullets rip through my part of the plane." Tigner laughed nervously, sticking his finger through a two-inch hole in the fuselage from the last flight. The metalsmiths had missed it.

McLean started and warmed up the Avenger's Wright Twin Cyclone engine. Taking their position on the *White Plains* catapult, McLean called out, "Hang on to your hats, boys."

The catapult officer gave McLean the one-finger turn-up signal.

McLean nodded, advancing the throttle to full takeoff power. The engine roared, straining against the restraining hook. With the final launch signal, the Avenger catapulted down the deck and off the end of the flight deck. Wollman's head snapped forward. They were airborne in two seconds as the plane dipped down, passing over the carrier's bow, and then ascended, heading toward Saipan.

Thirty minutes later, Wollman spotted the thirty-four LSTs that had already unloaded 719 Higgins boats and LVT amphibious tractors in four lines headed for the eight assault beaches along southwest Saipan. The landing craft formed up in lines four thousand yards from the beach.

"I'm glad we're up here," McLean muttered over the radio. "The view's a lot better, and there's fewer people shootin' at us."

Precisely at 0630, the naval bombardment ceased as the big fourteen-inch guns on the USS *Tennessee* and USS *California* fell silent in preparation for the next phase of the landing.

Immediately, twenty-four gunboats went in first, sweeping the beaches with 4.5-inch rockets and 40-mm cannons, turning aside at the reef.

TBM Avenger torpedo plane on an aircraft carrier flight deck. Wikimedia Commons. Public domain.

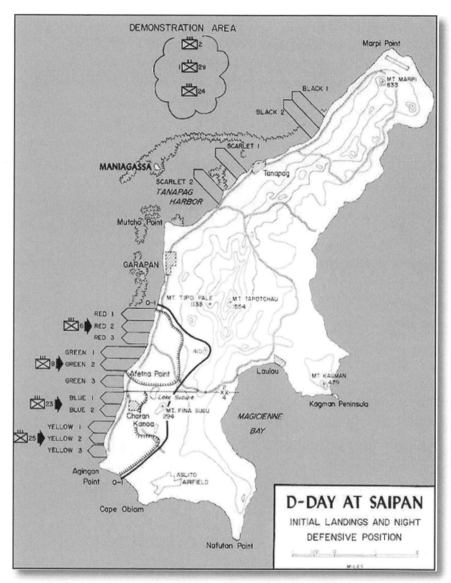

Map of D-Day at Saipan, from Breaching the Marianas: The Battle for Saipan *by Capt. John C. Chapin. US Department of Defense, Marine Corps History Division. Public domain.*

"OK, now it's our turn," McLean called out as the carrier-based fighters and Avengers lined up to make strafing and bombing runs at the Japanese troops dug in beyond the beaches.

As the Avenger dove toward the target from three thousand feet, Wollman felt his body pushed back into the seat by the 4-g force as the plane accelerated toward the enemy.

Over the next thirty minutes, the strafing and one-hundred-pound bombs and rockets made an impressive display of airpower but did little harm to the dug-in enemy.

"Keep a sharp lookout for enemy planes and artillery, Leonard," Tigner said.

Wollman looked back at the lines of advancing amtraks. It was a twenty-seven-minute gut-wrenching ride from the departure point to the beaches. He pictured his Marine brothers huddled inside the amphibious vehicles, headed for an uncertain fate. For some, it would be their last ride.

"Semper Fi," Leonard whispered.

"Man, you got that right," McLean replied. "You Marines have guts."

The quiet was eerie as the 31,000 Japanese held their fire until the Americans passed over the coral reef and entered the lagoon. Then, all hell cut loose as the deafening barrage from the concealed coastal artillery commenced. Three amphibs were hit almost immediately, stranding two near shore and leaving the third smoking a hundred yards offshore. The beaches' congestion and chaos made the Marines an easy target for Japanese mortar and machine-gun fire. The fighting was fiercest on the southern Yellow beaches, where after a full hour of battle, the 1st Battalion of the 21st Marines had succeeded in pushing in just twelve yards from the beach. Nevertheless, by nightfall, twenty thousand combat-ready soldiers had landed on Saipan at the cost of up to 3,500 American lives.

During the assault on Saipan, air squadron VC-4 from USS *White Plains* provided cover for the fleet against enemy torpedo and air attacks, strafed the beaches, and spotted enemy shellfire, helping to

Landing craft waiting to go in, Saipan invasion, June 15, 1944. Coast Guard photo 222-19. Public domain.

repulse three major enemy attacks.

Directing the K-20 aerial camera out the side windows of the tunnel, Tigner photographed the area ahead of the advancing Marines while Wollman kept his eyes peeled for enemy pillboxes and artillery emplacements.

It was a spectacle of death and destruction that Leonard never forgot for the rest of his life, though he seldom mentioned it.

As they skirted the coastline looking for Japanese submarines, Wollman called out, "Looks like we got some action up ahead!"

"Whoa! That ack-ack is thick as a swarm of angry wasps," McLean replied, noting the black puffs of smoke filling the sky. "Think I'll change our altitude before they get us bracketed in."

In no time, they were surrounded by the smoke and explosions from the Japanese artillery fire.

Marines crawling into position on Saipan beach after their LVT was disabled by Japanese mortar fire. Public domain.

"Flying low and slow so you guys can play Cecil B. DeMille makes us sitting ducks up here!" McLean called out.

"You got that right! Six hundred to a thousand feet at 150 knots is perfect for us observers, but it guarantees lots of bullet holes in our Avenger," Wollman replied as he reported the action to Cherokee.[4]

"That's a bit too close," Tigner yelled from the tunnel as the plane shook from an explosion just below the Avenger.

"I think they got us dialed in, boys," McLean replied. "Damn. Those Japs are puttin' holes in my plane!"

Seconds later, the Avenger shook as she took a direct hit to the fuselage behind the right wing.

"I'm hit!" Tigner screamed.

"How bad are you?" McLean came back.

---

4   "Cherokee" was the code name for the ship-based command center that coordinated the artillery and naval firing, with information supplied by the observer planes.

Ack-ack artillery fire, Saipan invasion, June 15, 1944. Coast Guard photo 222-18. Public domain.

"Lots of blood from my right arm. Those bastards blew a hole in the rear fuselage. The seat took most of the impact."

"Put on a tourniquet," McLean instructed. "Len, crawl down into the tunnel and give him a hand."

"It's too far back to the *White Plains*," Wollman replied. "We need to get Tigner some help soon."

They were headed north along the coastline when McLean turned southeast.

"I'm heading for Aslito Airfield. I just hope the Marines have taken it. It's the only place we can put down. Leonard, call in our position and let them know we're dropping in with wounded."

Looking down, McLean saw the bombed-out Japanese runway and destroyed Zeros.

Aslito Airfield with destroyed Mitsubishi A6M Zeros, June 15, 1944. Courtesy of Bob Livingstone.

"Cherokee, this is LEO 2.[5] We've taken heavy ground fire with badly wounded radio operator. Executing emergency landing on Aslito," McLean reported.

"LEO 2, Cherokee advises Aslito Field too hot. Recommend setting course for Charan Kanoa for emergency landing."

"OK, boys, you heard it. Let's head for the coast and Charan Kanoa," McLean directed. "What a mess! I'll have to land between all those bomb craters. Here we go," McLean called out as he descended toward the single runway.

The landing on the dirt strip was a bit rough, but he got them down in one piece. An amtrak full of Marines rushed over to greet them with carbines in hand.

---

5   LEO 2 was the radio call sign used to identify McLean's observation TBM Avenger.

McLean taxied to a stop. Wollman crawled out of the turret and helped Tigner out of the tunnel.

"You flyboys are the first to land on Charan Kanoa," the Marine greeted them. "Welcome to our little hellhole."

"Thanks, Sergeant. We got a wounded man who needs medical attention."

"Medic is on the way. In the meantime, keep your heads down. We'll post sentries, but this place is still thick with Jap snipers."

While bloody, Tigner's deep wound responded to basic first aid delivered by the Marine medic.

As they prepared to taxi down the dirt runway, McLean waved. "Thanks for the hospitality, boys. Hope to see you all back home!"

On the way back to the *White Plains*, Leonard observed, "This will probably be my last ride with you, Red. Our Stinson OY-1 planes are

TBM Avenger at Charan Kanoa airstrip, June 15, 1944. The wounded radio operator is leaning against the wing while Lt. Leonard Wollman confers with pilot Lt. Coll McLean. Marine sentries guard the first American plane to land on Saipan. National Archives 80G-234708.

ready to be deployed in a day or so."

"It's been swell having you on board, Len."

"I'm going to miss the power of this beast," Leonard replied.

"Well, Len, Marine spotter pilots have balls as big as a Texas longhorn bull. You guys are flying those unarmed Stinsons through the same enemy hellfire with the same Zekes and ack-ack that were shootin' at us today. Unreal!"

Leonard smiled, looking back toward the smoking Saipan beaches.

"Now, which way to Pearl Harbor?" McLean asked, grinning. "It's time to head on home."

* * *

On the morning of June 17, two days after the initial invasion of the beaches along western Saipan, events began to unfold that put the

TBM Avenger torpedo planes during the invasion. Courtesy of Bob Livingstone.

lives of 1st Lt. Leonard Wollman and Sgt. Loren Low on a collision course.

The Japanese task force had also steamed to the Philippine Sea in anticipation of a showdown. The eighty-eight-ship convoy included the Japanese carrier *Jun'yō*, "Peregrine Falcon," with its squadron of Mitsubishi Zeros. The *Jun'yō* had sailed from its port in Rabaul, where it had seen action in the South Pacific in New Guinea, Guadalcanal, and the Solomon Islands.

The first two planes of VMO-4 left the *White Plains* 150 miles off-shore on June 17, heading for Saipan. The Navy aviators humorously referred to the small, unarmed Marine spotter planes as the "Cricket Circuit." The first Stinson, piloted by Lt. Thomas Rozga, landed on a thick, sandy road opposite Yellow Beach 1, about a half mile from the front line. First Lt. Leonard Wollman and his second pilot, Captain George E. Hooper, landed their Stinson OY-1 on the dirt strip at Charan Kanoa, between Green Beach and Blue Beach. Both planes

Stinson OY-1 taking off from USS White Plains *and landing on Saipan at Charan Kanoa, June 1, 1944, with Lt. Leonard Wollman. www.historyofwar.org/Pictures/pictures_USS_White_Plains_CVE66_OY1_grasshopper.html. Public domain.*

immediately began their mission to provide tactical reconnaissance for the 4th Marine Division. Lt. Wollman switched to the pilot's seat and took off over the beaches. In the back seat, Capt. Hooper gazed inland, away from the devastation and smoke-filled beachheads.

"Len, look at the farmland. It's so lush. From up here, you'd never know there's a deadly war going on down there."

"Save it, George. Let's go hunting for Jap gun emplacements so our guys can take them out."

"Roger that, Lieutenant," Hooper replied as they headed north along the coastline. They flew at about 500 feet, constantly changing altitude to confuse the Japanese artillery below.

As they headed out to sea, turning southward for another pass along the coast, Mount Tapochau dominated the landscape. At 474

Saipan western coastline, 1944. Wikimedia Commons. Public domain.

meters, it was the highest point on the island and commanded a striking 360-degree view of Saipan.

Suddenly, the air was filled with explosions as the Japanese artillery at Mount Tapochau began firing their 120-mm cannons.

"Shit! Are those guys shooting at us?" Hooper yelled. "Those must be their big 120-mm cannons."

Lt. Wollman looked down the coast to Yellow Beach and saw the target. There were three LSTs about to unload, approaching the beach—one with its ramp down.

"Who are those guys? I thought the Marine 4th Division was all on the beach or had moved inland."

Approaching Yellow Beach, Wollman called out, "Those aren't Marines. That's a battalion of engineers with bulldozers! Those guys are about to be creamed!"

Capt. Hooper grabbed the radio and called in an artillery strike from the USS *Tennessee*, directed at Mount Tapochau.

"Cherokee, this is Marine Spotter 1. Adjust fire. Over."

"Marine Spotter 1, this is Cherokee. Adjust fire. Out."

"The is Marine Spotter 1. Grid 7 Bravo, Mount Tapochau. Over."[6]

"This is Cherokee. Grid 7 Bravo. Out."

"Two 120-mm howitzers, targeting three LSTs in the open at Yellow 1. Over."

"Two 120-mm howitzers. Out."

"Shot. Over," Cherokee called out, indicating a round was en route.

"Shot. Out," Marine Spotter 1 replied.

"Splash. Over."

"Splash. Out," Marine Spotter 1 called, indicating the round had landed with adjustments to follow.

The first artillery strike was beyond the target fifty yards and to the right fifty yards. Hooper called in the report.

"Direction 90 degrees magnetic, subtract 50, left 50. Over."

---

6   In WWII, a basic alphanumeric grid system overlay was used, with each location representing 100 yards x 100 yards. 7 Bravo is one grid location.

Stinson OY-1 Marine squadron VMO-4 over western Saipan coastline following invasion, June 1944. www.historyofwar.org/Pictures/pictures_stinson_L-5_saipan. html. Public domain.

"Direction 90 degrees, subtract 50, left 50. Out."

As they waited for the next naval artillery barrage, the 120-mm cannons on Mount Tapochau continued firing toward the approaching LSTs.

"Cherokee, Marine Spotter 1, three LSTs off Yellow 1 under fire from Mount Tapochau. Condition critical."

"Those guys are riding into a death trap. They won't even have armored amtraks like the Marines. Those engineers are going to drive their equipment across four thousand yards of open beach!"

"They'll never make it!"

Just as he uttered the grim prediction, Wollman looked out to sea and spotted a small black dot above the horizon, approaching from the west.

"I hope that's one of our guys!"

"Can't tell from here. We have to do something."

"It's a Zero!" Wollman called out. "Those guys don't see him coming."

Without hesitating, Lt. Wollman placed his small spotter plane into a steep dive and banked to the right, aiming his aircraft directly at the LST.

Come on, look up!

The ramp was down on the lead LST, and an engineer was guiding his bulldozer toward the surf, black smoke coming from the exhaust pipe as he revved the diesel motor.

Wollman buzzed the bulldozer, rocking his wings back and forth. "Come on. Look up!"

The explosions of the shells fired from the cannons on Mount Tapochau were deafening. Smoke filled the air, and the shock waves jolted the small plane. The rounds struck to the right of the convoy of LSTs. The next volley would bracket them to the left, and then all hell would break loose.

Wollman flew his Stinson through the smoke breaking out two hundred yards above the LST. At that moment, the helmeted engineer,

LST landing, WWII. US government photograph. Public domain.

stripped down to his T-shirt, looked up.

"He sees us! My God, I hope he spots the Zero!" Hooper yelled as he pulled out of the dive and banked to the right, just above the surf.

In the next second, the naval artillery volley struck the gun emplacement on Mount Tapochau, silencing the big guns.

The Japanese Zero went into a dive straight at the lead LST. It was too late. The engineer's fate was sealed as bullets rained down from the sky, ripping a path of destruction across the bow of the ship.

.

CHAPTER 27

SAIPAN ARRIVAL: 804ᵀᴴ AVIATION ENGINEERS

1944

The LST, or landing ship tank, was designed to carry tanks, other equipment, and personnel into battle for amphibious assaults in WWII. At 328 feet long with a beam of fifty feet, the LST comprised an upper main deck and a lower tank deck, which could accommodate twenty Sherman tanks. Although affectionately referred to as "Large Slow Targets," only twenty-six of the 10,520 LSTs built during World War II were lost to enemy action. When at sea, an LST took on water for stability, and during landing operations, the water was pumped out to produce a shallow-draft vessel. The bow was equipped with two massive doors, opening to a width of fourteen feet, and a steel ramp, which was lowered to allow vehicles to be driven off the flat-bottomed LST directly onto the beach.

For the engineers aboard the three LSTs, the two-week trip from Pearl Harbor was tense boredom. Powered by two 900-horsepower Jimmy diesel engines, the LST had a flank speed of eleven knots. The engineers passed the time playing cards, smoking, exercising, and watching the scenery from the main deck. Drills and duty were an almost welcome relief. The men knew they were going to war but had not been told their destination.

A brief stop for staging at the Funafuti Atoll required passing through the protective submarine gates. When the 804th Aviation Engineers departed, they were traveling in a flotilla of sixteen LSTs. One of the LSTs had trouble steering, so it would blast its horn, and the other ships scattered to avoid a collision. Eventually, they put the wayward LST far behind on the starboard stern of the convoy.[1]

Loren Low, WWII. Courtesy of the Low family.

At Eniwetok Atoll, they joined up with the rest of the massive American convoy, composed of hundreds of ships, headed for Saipan.

On deck, Fred Kossow looked out to sea. No matter where he looked, there were ships all the way to the horizon.

My God! We're in the middle of an armada. I have never seen so many ships.

Sgt. Loren Low was on the lower tank deck checking his bulldozer. He had started the auxiliary motor every day since they'd left Pearl Harbor. Starting the engine every third day was recommended to prevent the motor from freezing up in the salt air. But for Loren, it was always better to be safe than sorry.

Always be prepared, Loren recited, recalling his ever-handy Boy Scout motto.

---

1 Story told by Fred Kossow, 804th Aviation Engineers, September 2008.

His D8 Caterpillar bull-
dozer had taken him into battle
on Baker and Makin Islands
and had never let him down,
protecting him from falling
coconuts and enemy fire.

*Don't you worry, Li'l Abner.
We'll get through this one and
build our guys another runway.*

Loren secured Li'l Abner
at the bow of the LST, directly
behind the ramp. Loren would
be the first to drive off the ship.

*That's just the way I like it.
Best not to be late for dinner!*

Loren's musings were interrupted by a voice from the side
of the tank deck where the men
were quartered.

*Fred Kossow, c. 1940. Courtesy of the
Kossow family.*

"Loren, did you hear where we're headed?" Fred Kossow called out.

"Nope. What's the dope, Fred?"

"Saipan, my man! And we got lots of company. It's going to be
a really hot battle zone. I hear fifteen thousand Japs are dug in and
waiting for us!"[2]

"No problems here," Loren replied, "We'll just do our job. The
Marines will take care of the Japanese."

"You mean Japs. Right?" Fred replied as he approached Loren.

"Japanese, Fred. Growing up, too many people called me things I
didn't like, but I always made sure they didn't do it twice."

"Suit yourself, Loren. But get yourself and Li'l Abner ready. We'll
be landing in a few days."

"We better go up on the main deck to watch out for Zeros. I want

---

2   Allied intelligence was incorrect. In fact, 30,000 Japanese soldiers were dug into the
    cliffs and caves of Saipan.

to check out those .50-caliber machine guns. They look like the guns my kid brother used on his B-24."

"You heard any news about your brother?"

"No, Stan's still MIA, but it's been over a year since they went missing in New Guinea."

"You never know. They may come walking out of the jungle some-day and surprise us all."

Loren smiled at Fred's optimism but felt the same knot in the pit of his stomach that gnawed at him whenever he thought about his kid brother.

"OK, Fred. You have Daisy Mae ready to go so we can be the first to drive off this ship."

"No way I'm going to be first! I'll be right behind you."

* * *

Two days later, June 17, D plus 2, the aviation engineers' convoy of three LSTs approached mountainous Saipan from the west. The for-ty-four-square-mile island was the largest in the Northern Marianas, about twice the size of Manhattan. Even at this distance, the smoke from the smoldering wreckage and devastation on the beaches was still evident two days after the initial invasion by the 2nd and 4th Marine Divisions.

In the mess hall early that morning, Loren called out to Fred Kos-sow, "Hey Fred! Have you ever seen so much food?"

"No, and it's probably not a good sign," Kossow replied. "Kind of like a last meal."

"Well, no point in wasting a spread like this," Loren replied as he piled his plate sky-high with eggs, sausages, pancakes, and waffles.

"Slow down, Loren. You're going to need sideboards on that thing to pile up any more grub."

"A growing boy's gotta eat, Fred!" Loren laughed.

"I just hope you don't end up barfing it up in some foxhole on the beach." Fred smiled at his always hungry friend.

"It shouldn't be that bad. Our boys softened them up with artillery barrages, and the Marines should have cleaned house two days ago. What could go wrong?"

"You're the one who's always saying to be prepared. I'm just saying be ready to drive your Cat really fast across the coral reef and landing beach, in case some Jap's firing at us."

"I'll be ready, Fred. I just won't be hungry." Loren laughed, downing another cup of coffee with his second stack of pancakes.

*　*　*

Later that morning, below deck, the smell of diesel fuel and oil was thick as Loren prepared Li'l Abner for the landing on Saipan. The tank deck was dimly lit, but he could make out the other engineers preparing their heavy equipment. It would take most of the day to unload the bulldozers, trucks, graders, rollers, supplies, and the hundred barrels of diesel and fuel.

In the seat of Li'l Abner, Loren gazed ahead at the massive doors of the LST that would soon open up into another world. He felt his pulse quicken as he inhaled deeply and then let the air out slowly.

His thoughts were interrupted. "Put your helmet on, soldier, unless you want to get your head shot off!"

"Yes, sir!" Loren replied, reaching for his helmet behind the dozer's seat.

"You're first in line, so be ready to roll as soon as these doors open. We don't want you holding things up. And put on your shirt!"

"I figured we're going swimming during this landing. So, I put it in a plastic bag with some dry socks," Loren explained, pulling out a bag wrapped with rubber bands.

"You probably put some breakfast in there, too," Fred called out from the dozer right behind Li'l Abner.

"Suit yourself. Just be ready to roll as soon as we land, the doors open, and the ramp lowers onto the beach."

An awful scraping sound filled the hold as the bottom of the LST passed over the coral reef.

Fred covered his ears. "Geez, those guys are going to tear the bottom off this LST!"

"Don't worry, Fred. These Navy guys know what they're doing. They got the tide timed just right so we can pass over the reef without drowning in the lagoon," Loren called out.

As the LST's stern passed over the coral reef, the noise subsided, and they entered the lagoon. Loren listened to the twin diesel motors rev up as they accelerated the craft toward the beach.

"Here we go, Fred!"

"God, help us!"

With a grinding jolt, the LST hit the beach and came to a stop. After traveling 4,600 miles from Pearl Harbor, they had finally arrived. The men waited and then waited some more.

"Jeez, this is killing me. Let's get this show on the road," Jimmy, another engineer, called out from the adjacent dozer.

"I gotta pee," Fred reported.

"Me too!"

"Hold it until we get in the water."

Suddenly, the hydraulic motors came to life as the two massive doors opened. Daylight streamed through the growing crack between the doors. The warm breeze filled the LST, clearing out the smell of diesel.

"The sky's blue, Fred. It's a pretty day on Saipan."

"It won't be so pretty once they start shooting at us!"

The sailors lowered the ramp right onto the coral. It was a perfect landing.

"Piece of cake, Fred," Loren reported. "We can drive right onto the beach. The water's shallow."

Loren started the auxiliary and then the main diesel motors and drove Li'l Abner at an angle onto the ramp. The grating sound of the dozer's treads on the steel ramp filled the air. Loren got to the end of the ramp, put the dozer in reverse, and backed up a few feet. He then straightened it out and drove forward.

"Geez, Loren. What are you doing? Get off the ramp!" Fred called out.

"Trying to straighten it out so I don't drive off the edge of the ramp."

"You're wasting time, soldier. Let's go!"

From behind him, Fred called out, "What's that guy doing?"

"Don't bother me now, Fred. What are you talking about?"

"Look up!" Fred shouted, pointing at the sky.

Loren turned forward, looked up, and saw the spotter plane diving at the LST.

"Shit! He's going to crash into us!" Fred called out.

"No, he's signaling us. Look, he's rocking his wings at us!"

"What the hell is he doing?" Fred asked.

Loren squinted at the plane from his dozer on the ramp and then picked out the growing dark spot behind it.

"It's a Zero! He's going to strafe us!"

The deafening explosion to the left of the LST rocked the ship. The men behind Loren jumped off their bulldozers and took shelter. With Li'l Abner on the edge of the ramp, Loren was exposed.

"Jump, Loren!"

"No cover here! Sorry, Li'l Abner. I gotta leave you!"

Loren jumped off the dozer and dove into the shallow water, taking cover beneath the ramp. As he dove, he glanced up and saw the Zero's red rising sun and, for a split second, was sure he saw the pilot's face.

The Zero's 7.7-mm machine guns ripped a path of destruction across the beach and the LST's ramp. The ricocheting noise of bullets on metal filled the air.

From beneath the ramp, Loren stuck his head out and looked up as the Zero pulled up and circled to the right.

"He's coming back around!"

Suddenly, the anti-aircraft guns and .50-caliber machine guns on the main deck of all three LSTs came to life, firing at the circling Zero.

* * *

Looking down from the banking Zero, Lt. Hyoshi assessed the scene below. *No damage. Too many sailors with machine guns spoiling for a trophy. Better return to the* Jun'yō. *Where is that little spotter plane? I can take him out.*

* * *

In the confusion of the brief attack, the Stinson had flown just above the surf, heading back toward the strip at Charan Kanoa.

"You saved their bacon, Len."

"Yeah, let's get out of here before that Zeke spots us!"

"Roger, Lieutenant. Take us home. That's enough action for our first day."

* * *

After the run-in with the Japanese Zero, the convoy of three LSTs pulled up anchor and used the winch and cable to pull the LST back out to sea. They positioned themselves offshore from Charan Kanoa, beyond the reach of the big artillery guns. The ships were placed on high alert, with sailors and aviation engineers operating the seven 40-mm and twelve 20-mm anti-aircraft guns.

Loren and Fred were stationed along the LST port side, feeding the ammo into the .50-caliber machine guns.

"Keep your eyes peeled, Fred. That Zero's coming back, and he may not be alone next time."

"Don't worry. We'll be ready for 'em," Fred replied as the Navy gunner swept the machine gun across the sky.

* * *

The next morning, the piercing two-pitched tone sent the men scrambling. "General quarters! General quarters! All hands on deck! Man your battle stations!" The clanging alarm and flashing red "general quarters" alert had the men's pulses racing.

On the main deck, sailors and engineers manned every gun. The men were poised for the attack. Loren and Fred stood next to the .50-caliber machine guns with hearts racing.

Fred wiped beads of sweat out of his eyes. "Where are those guys?" he shouted above the din of the general quarters alert.

"Over there!" Loren shouted, pointing to a spot just above the horizon. "They're coming in low and fast!"

The men on all three LSTs opened fire simultaneously, sending bursts of machine-gun fire at the rapidly approaching Zeros.

At 350 miles per hour, the three Zeros were on them in no time with guns blazing. The pinging of the bullets ricocheting off the metal deck filled the air. The roar of the fourteen-cylinder, 1,100-horsepower engines was deafening as they passed right over the LSTs and then split off in different directions, preparing for another pass.

"Come on! Let's get those suckers!"

"Fred, did you see that guy's face? He was so close I could have touched his wing! I swear, it's the same pilot who strafed me yesterday!"

"Bullshit! How can you be so sure?"

"The pilot was grinning while he strafed us! And he's got this gold tooth in the front. I could see it plain as day!"

"Evil little bastard!"

The attacks lasted more than an hour, but the Zeros kept their distance after the first pass, knowing the LSTs' gunners would be locked and loaded and spoiling for a fight.

"Come on, you chickenshits! Bring the fight on! We're ready for you!" Fred shouted.

* * *

From the lead Zero, Hyoshi called over his radio, "Squadron, return to *Jun'yō*."

"Lieutenant Hyoshi, is that the ship you attacked yesterday?"

"Hai![3] I recognize the one with the gun. Tall, dark skin. He looks like a Chugokujin.[4] He was on the bulldozer. Don't know how I missed him yesterday."

"Hai, Lieutenant. We can hunt them tomorrow."

---

3 Hai: "Yes" in Japanese.

4 Chugokujin: Japanese for "Chinese man."

"We fight for the glory of Emperor Hirohito," Hyoshi admonished as the three Zeros headed back to the *Jun'yō*.

* * *

The next day, June 19, started slowly with clear and serene blue skies. A few wispy white clouds floated low on the horizon. Most of the engineers were below deck.

From the back of the tank deck, Loren called out, "You guys gotta come up on the main deck and see this air battle! It's incredible! We're kicking their butts!"

The remaining men of Headquarters Battalion jumped up from their bunks along the deck's sides and ran up the stairs to the main deck. A blast of moist salt air greeted them as they crowded the railing. All eyes were turned to the sky, filled with the crisscrossing contrails of American and Japanese planes.

"Whoa! Did you see that? Our guy just took out that Jap plane!"

The battle had started just after 1000 hours when the first wave of sixty Japanese planes attacked the American fleet. They scored only one bomb strike on USS *South Dakota*, while the Americans downed forty-two of the enemy aircraft.

The wildly cheering sailors and aviation engineers kept score. Over and over again, the American Hellcats, Avenger torpedo bombers, and old reliable Dauntless dive bombers shot down the attacking Japanese planes.

The second wave of 128 Japanese planes fared no better. Ninety-seven of them were lost without significantly damaging the American ships.

Japanese Zeros, D4Y1 Judys, Val dive bombers, Jakes, Kates, Jills, and a few twin-engine Mitsubishi G4M2 Betty bombers were no match for the Americans. They quickly went down in flames, crashing into the Philippine Sea.

Around 1400 in the afternoon, the Japanese sent the fourth attack wave of eighty-two planes. The Americans shot down fifty-four of them. On June 19, 1944, the Americans shot down 429 Japanese aircraft, with only twenty-nine American aircraft lost.

That day, the sailors and 804th Aviation Engineers had front-row seats, witnessing the most significant American aviation victory in the Pacific War, commonly referred to as the Great Mariana Turkey Shoot.

"That was some kind of shooting today. Our guys really put on a show!" Loren said.

"Tomorrow, it's our turn. Let's hope the Marines have those beaches secure," Fred mused. "It'll be damn hard to unload our equipment with guys shooting at us!"

Fighter plane contrails mark the sky over Task Force 58, during the Great Marianas Turkey Shoot phase of the battle, June 19, 1944. Photographed the deck of the light cruiser Birmingham. *National Archives.*

CHAPTER 28

SAIPAN LANDING, D PLUS 5

JUNE 20, 1944

After a fitful night's rest and another big breakfast, the men of the 804th Aviation Engineers were ready for a second attempt at landing on Saipan. By moonlight, the men had watched the flashes of the big naval artillery guns firing away, and now, in the early morning light, they could see the still-smoldering wreckage on the beaches. It was clear that the battle for control of Saipan was still raging.

"Looks like we get a second 'last meal.'" Fred laughed.

"I'm glad they invited me to the party," Loren replied, piling his mess kit high with pancakes, eggs, potatoes, and bacon. "This boy's got a hollow leg!"

"The harbor captain has us going in third, so we have time to go up on the main deck to watch the two other LSTs land," Fred replied.

"Let me finish my breakfast, Fred."

"You can bring a doggie bag, Loren."

***

From just outside the coral reef, the men of HQ Company watched the landing of the other two LSTs. They heard the harbor captain yelling instructions at the LST captains over his megaphone. "Get some speed up and hit the reef. Now go!" he shouted to the first LST.

"They're never going to make it onto the beach. Going way too slow," Fred yelled with the warm morning offshore breeze blowing into his face.

The first LST hit the reef and came to a grinding halt. Then after a few minutes, they opened the wing doors and dropped the ramp.

"See! I told you. They're a mile high above the beach. They'll never be able to unload their equipment."

"You, next LST! Hit it harder! You gotta get over the reef!" the harbor captain called out over his megaphone.

The second LST revved up its twin 900-horsepower diesel engines and charged for the beach. They came in right next to the high-centered first LST, but the result was just as bad. They landed way short of the beach.

"Goddammit! You guys came six thousand miles, and you can't make a beach landing! You, the last LST, back off out into the ocean and come in at flight speed! We need you over the coral reef and onto the beach! Now go!"

The final LST, carrying HQ Company and the heavy equipment, backed off and came in at top speed. They hit the coral reef with a tremendous impact and scraping noise.

"Man, they're going the tear off the bottom of this boat!"

Heading toward the beach at flight speed, they flew by the other two LSTs. The LST ground to a halt, and everyone waited. Finally, the moment of truth came when they opened the doors and dropped the ramp.

"Still too high!" Loren observed, "It's six feet down to the beach."

"Now what? We can't unload these eighteen-ton dozers from up here," Fred observed, scratching his head. "Looks like we screwed the pooch on this one."

"We're high and dry for now."

"Actually, we're high and wet!"

A few minutes later, the men spotted a cruiser going full speed just outside the reef.

"He's trying to knock us off the reef with his wake," Loren yelled. The men watched as the wake approached the LST, growing smaller as the coral reef robbed it of its energy. By the time it reached the LST, it barely rocked the ship.

"Nice try, but no gold on that one," Fred commented.

"Looks like we're going to have to wait for high tide to float us off the reef," Loren said.

In the meantime, the company commander told the men to unload fifty-gallon drums of gas and diesel. The challenge was figuring out how to wrestle them through the surf and onto the beach.

"These suckers must weigh 450 pounds each! How are we supposed to get them through the surf?" Fred yelled as Loren jumped off the ramp into the warm water.

"Come on, Fred. We got a job to do."

Jumping into the water, Fred popped up, yelling, "Get away from those drums. They're going to break an arm or a leg."

"All right, just let the tide wash them onto the beach, and then we'll round 'em up."

Later that afternoon, the incoming high tide did float the LSTs off the reef, and they made a landing in about two feet of water.

Loren, first in line on the tank deck, called out, "Li'l Abner can handle that drop no problem."

Driving his D8 dozer off the edge of the ramp, Li'l Abner took a header and hit the beach at a forty-five-degree angle.

"No sweat, Fred. Follow me!" he yelled as he revved up the diesel engine and drove Li'l Abner into the surf.

"Keep your eyes peeled for Jap Zeros. We don't want those guys using us as target practice again."

The men used the D8 dozers to pull other equipment off the LST. What they didn't plan on was the rapidly rising tide.

804th Aviation Engineers landing on Saipan. June 20, 1944. Pubst Guard Photo. Public domain.

"It's getting pretty deep out here!" Loren called out, sitting on Li'l Abner with the water coming up to the cab level. "We better get the other heavy equipment off before it gets any deeper."

The two-foot water depth when they hit the beach rapidly rose to five feet.

Swimming around his dozer, Loren hooked a chain to the back of Li'l Abner and then attached it to the next piece of equipment to unload.

Back on the seat of his D8, he revved the engine. "Let's go, boys! Follow me!" he yelled over the noise of the straining 177-horsepower engine.

Putting the dozer in gear, he pulled the equipment to shore. They repeated the process multiple times that afternoon until the LSTs were empty, and the aviation engineers, wet and tired, were on the beach with their mountain of gear and equipment.

Looking across the reef, Loren spotted a couple of dozers high-centered on a submerged pinnacle of coral.

"Those guys stuck out there are in a bit of a pickle," Loren observed. "Maybe we should go out there and give 'em a hand."

"Naw. We can push those stuck dozers off the pinnacles in the morning when the tide goes out. But they'll have to keep their diesel motors running in neutral all night."

"Speaking of night, it looks like we're spending the night on the beach," Loren observed, looking at the darkening sky.

Resting next to Li'l Abner, Loren was soaked, tired, and happy to be ashore. He didn't notice the Marine approaching him.

"Hey, soldier, how about a cup of Joe?" he asked, holding out a cup of steaming hot coffee.

"Thanks," Loren smiled, taking a big gulp of the warm coffee. "That hits the spot!"

"Here. I got more," the Marine replied, refilling the cup.

"Thanks. How long you been here?"

"We landed on June 15. My platoon is fighting inland, but I was sent back with wounded buddies."

"How bad was it?"

"It got really bad. Lots of guys didn't make it off the beach. But we made the Japs pay a high price."

"Well, thanks for the coffee. I'll remember you," Loren replied, handing the now-empty cup back to the Marine.

The sun was setting, and the soaking-wet aviation engineers had little choice but to make do. Crawling up onto a truck carrying their tents, Fred stripped off his clothes and tried to snooze on the warm hood. Loren parked Li'l Abner in front of a ridge and attempted to get some shut-eye.

* * *

In the middle of the night, the sound of a dive-bombing plane awakened Fred.

"Crap! It's going to hit us!"

Grabbing his helmet, Fred jumped off the truck, diving for cover. But, unfortunately, his helmet flew off as he struck the ground.

"Ouch!" Fred yelled as his bare head struck the edge of the running board.

Blood streamed down his face, running into his eyes. Outside it was chaos, with exploding bombs, gunfire, and men yelling. Fred replaced his helmet and waited for things to settle down.

Later, he looked out and spotted an ambulance parked right next to his truck. In the darkness, he went over to get his head patched up. What he encountered made him laugh decades later.

In the dark, he could make out the bottom half of a corpulent soldier sticking out from under the ambulance.

"Hey! Come out from under there and patch up my head!"

"No! Go away!"

Fred grabbed the soldier's legs and heaved him out. "I said, you patch up my head!"

At that moment, Fred realized the fat soldier was a lieutenant. "Well, sir, I need you to patch me up."

"All right!"

They entered the ambulance's cab, where he switched on the light and proceeded to clean and dress Fred's forehead wound. For the next two weeks, Fred worked and slept in a turban-like head dressing.

A couple of hundred yards away, Loren's nighttime snooze was interrupted by a monstrous, deafening *Bam! Bam! Bam!* as the US heavy artillery on the rise just behind his dozer began its nighttime bombardment of enemy positions.

"Guess we're not getting much sleep tonight, Li'l Abner."

* * *

Early the next morning, the aviation engineers' work began in earnest. Their goal was to reach Aslito Airfield on southern Saipan. The 105th Infantry took control of the airfield on June 18, but the area was still a hotbed of enemy resistance. The wide, sandy beach terminated abruptly at the base of a fifty-foot bluff. The fearless Maj. Edward A. Flanders led the men, directing them to bulldoze a roadway through the shallow waters to the cliff at the water's edge. Blasting crews set off

7th Army Air Force 804th Aviation Engineers' D8 Caterpillar bulldozer leads the way off the beach on Saipan, June 20, 1944. Public Domain. Coast Guard photo.

explosive charges and thus began the task of carving a cut through the bluff. Dozers and carryalls removed several thousand yards of blasted-out rock as they continued the road up to the plateau overlooking the beach.

On June 21, a platoon of men and a grader arrived at Aslito Field. They commandeered a Japanese roller and began the process of repairing the heavily damaged Japanese 3,700-foot runway and taxiways, filling in craters and shell holes, and removing shrapnel and debris.

On June 22, the rest of the battalion arrived, and work on Aslito Field began in earnest. The existing 3,700-foot runway was immediately extended by laying 800 feet of Marston matting. Surveying delineated the planned 8,500 ft. by 200 ft. first runway. Eventually, the engineers would carve out two crossing runways with a second 7,300 ft. by 200 ft. strip. Each runway was thirty inches thick to accommodate the massive B-29 Superfortress, weighing more than fifty tons.

Contrary to scouting reports, the topsoil was only a few inches deep. Immediately below was a dense coral rock that required blasting to remove and reshape. In some areas, the men had to blast away fifteen feet of coral. Up to twenty-two feet of coral was added from a nearby pit to serve as a runway base in other areas. It was grueling work.

During the first few weeks, work was performed under constant harassment by enemy snipers, strafing Zeros by day, and Japanese bombing attacks at night. As a result, the engineers carried rifles behind their dozer seats and wore helmets when they didn't interfere with their work.

Almost immediately, the men began work on a Japanese aviation gas sys-

Loren Low driving an 804th Aviation Engineer jeep on Saipan in 1944. Courtesy of the Low family.

tem. Unfortunately, the Japanese aviation fuel was useless, as it was not suitable for the American planes. Nevertheless, the men repaired and repurposed the maze of steel tanks and piping to store and transport American fuel piped in from offshore tankers for their fighters and bombers. The Japanese fuel stored in huge tanks was a dangerous target during the nightly Japanese bomb raids.

The men worked around the clock in twelve-hour shifts. The work was hot and dusty. They lived in tents and made the best of a miserable situation. The temperatures in the mideighties did not tell the whole story. The 100 percent humidity and the bugs were the real battle. A thick carpet of flies covered everything, and the mosquitoes were relentless. Malaria and dengue fever afflicted most of the men at one time or another.

The men faced a host of war-time challenges that required ingenious solutions.

"Crap! That's the third flat tire I've had this week," the driver complained.

Fred looked over at the exasperated driver trying to haul coral up from the mine. "Too much shrapnel on the field. It's going to keep puncturing your tires."

"Well, I can't get my job done, so neither can you. Flanders keeps on us about delays."

Fred Kossow. Courtesy of the Kossow family.

"Maybe I can help you," Fred replied. "Let me work on this a spell."

The corporal walked off, searching for someone to fix his flat tire, and Fred paused, deep in thought.

After a few minutes, Fred went over to the shop and explained the predicament and his proposed solution.

"Just rig me up a huge electromagnet that we can mount on the arm in front of a vehicle. Wrap copper wire around a hunk of scrap iron and attach it to a battery. It should pick that shrapnel right up."

The master sergeant smiled and then started in on Fred's invention. The next day he appeared with the contraption mounted in front of a tractor.

"Here you go, Fred. Let's see if this invention works."

The men watched the tractor make pass after pass over the road. Then, when it stopped, and they shut off the current to the magnet, a colossal load of shrapnel and every imaginable type of metallic junk fell to the ground. The men cheered wildly in appreciation.

"Hey! We're finally done with flat tires!"

"We better get to work cleaning up the runway. It's full of the same shrapnel," Loren noted.

They swept the runway with their electromagnetic tractor and dumped all the metal in a pile.

Fred called out, "Hey, look! There's one of those little spotter planes that saved your ass last week!"

Loren looked up at the Stinson OY-1 Marine spotter plane on approach to the airstrip. It was the first plane to land at the new and improved Isley Field, aka Aslito Airfield.[1]

"Let's go and see if he knows the crazy pilot that buzzed our LST."

The Stinson taxied off the runway and came to a stop in front of the curious engineers. The pilot and spotter hopped out.

"You leathernecks are the first to land on our runway! The Air Force flyboys have been buzzing around here in their P-47s, but you beat them to the punch," Fred called out.

"Thanks for getting the runway ready for us," the Marine pilot replied, looking over the engineers crowding around. "Actually, I almost landed here last week in an Avenger torpedo plane. There was lots more shooting back then."

"You guys have any guns on that plane?" Loren asked.

"No, we're a spotter reconnaissance squadron from the USS *White Plains*."

"Say, did you guys hear about someone in your squadron who buzzed our LST last week?" Fred asked.

The pilot paused, smiled, and looked at Loren. "That was me! I know you. You're the engineer on the bulldozer."

"Man! You saved our bacon that day! I can't believe it was you! What's your name?"

Smiling at the attention, the man introduced himself. "I'm Lieutenant Leonard Wollman, and this is Captain Hooper."

"Well, you boys have a lot of friends in the 804th Aviation Engineers. That Zero was about to wipe us out! If you hadn't signaled us, there would have been some dead engineers that day."

---

1   Aslito Airfield was renamed Isley Airfield in honor of an American pilot who died there in the early days of the invasion.

Leonard Wollman on Saipan, June 1944. Courtesy of the Wollman family.

"We were happy to help you out."

The men gathered around, clapping Wollman and Hooper on the back, treating the Marines like long-lost brothers and heroes.

"What's that contraption you have over there?" Wollman asked, pointing at the tractor.

"That's Fred's invention. It's an electromagnet that picks up all the shrapnel on the field, so you guys don't end up with flat tires."

"That's pretty ingenious, guys. Nice thinking. You keep the runway clear, and we'll have our squadron use this as our base."

"Consider it done! Hey! Are you guys hungry? Loren here makes a mean pot of homemade chili beans. Hot and spicy!"

The two Marines followed the engineers into their makeshift mess tent and spent the next hour shooting the breeze and stuffing themselves with Loren's chili beans.

"We should open a restaurant in Brooklyn. You could sell a ton of your chili beans to New Yorkers. Chili beans with pastrami on rye. It'd be a culinary delight!"

* * *

The following day Wollman was in his tent preparing for another long day spotting enemy positions and directing Marine artillery strikes when he heard someone calling his name over a rumbling diesel engine.

"Wollman, are you in there? Come on out, Leonard. We need your help."

Leonard stuck his head outside the tent and came face-to-face with a monstrous D8 bulldozer. He squinted, looking up into the morning sun.

"Loren, is that you? We have to stop running into each other like this."

"Yep, it's me, and Fred's here, too. We almost ran over your tent."

"Who's your friend with the camera?"

"This is Peter. He's a photographer for some magazine," Loren explained.

"He found this little fella wandering around the end of the runway," Fred said as he jumped down from the bulldozer with a small child in tow.

"His right arm is pretty messed up," Loren added. "He needs to see a doctor, maybe a surgeon."

"The medics in our dispensary are too busy and can't help him."

"Where are his parents?"

"No idea. They could be dead. A bunch of the locals jumped off the cliffs into the ocean yesterday. It was a gruesome scene."

Wollman looked at the boy. His right arm was bandaged but still bleeding.

"He can't be more than three years old," Leonard noted. "Poor kid must be hungry."

"No, we took care of that. We fed him a big bowl of Loren's chili beans!" Fred laughed. "He dove right in and got more chili beans on his face than in his mouth!"

"OK. But what am I supposed to do with the kid?"

"Take him in your plane. Get him patched up and then deliver him to the refugee camp near Charan Kanoa."

Hooper stuck his head out of the tent. "What's going on with this kid?"

"Our crazy chili-bean-eating engineer friends want us to medevac this boy."

"No problem there. You fly, and I'll hold the kid still in the back."

"You guys ready? We'll give you a ride to the field on our bulldozer."

The Marine pilots hung on to the boy as the noisy D8 rumbled out to the airstrip. Once inside the Stinson, Hooper held the boy in his lap in the back while Wollman performed the preflight checks upfront.

As they were preparing to taxi out to the runway, Peter held up his camera.

"Have the kid look at me, and Hooper, you look ahead. Perfect!"

Crouching down, Fred jostled for position, holding the new camera his wife, Bernie, had sent him.

"Leonard! Look this way!"

Leonard turned, looked back at Fred's raised camera, and replied, "This is an evacuation flight. Now stand clear so that we can get this kid to the hospital."

"So long, Leonard. See you soon!" Loren and Fred waved as the Stinson picked up speed, heading down the taxiway.

Evacuation of injured boy in Stinson OY-1 Marine spotter plane, 1944. World War Photos. Public domain.

CHAPTER 29

MARINE OBSERVATION SQUADRON VMO-4

1944

After Lts. Rozga and Wollman landed the first two Stinson OY-1 spotter planes on Saipan on June 17, the remaining aircraft were brought ashore in wooden crates two days later. By June 22, all eight Stinson planes were in operation, providing vital spotting for the artillery strikes. However, from the outset, bad luck seemed to plague the VMO-4 squadron. This black cloud continued throughout its deployment in Saipan. Within days, they lost four of the eight Stinsons, destroyed by enemy fire or accidents. The unarmed, fabric-covered Cricket was agile but was no match for Japanese Zeros and ack-ack guns.

Aslito Airfield was liberated from the Japanese on June 18 by the US Army 27th Infantry Division. The Army immediately renamed the airstrip Isley Field. However, stubborn pockets of Japanese ground resistance persisted around Naftuan Point in southern Saipan. On June 24, 1944, Lt. Wollman and Capt. Hooper were engaged in an observation mission near Naftuan Point, where the Japanese forces were holed up in caves lining the cliffs along the seashore. The naval bombardment had so far been ineffective in rooting out the enemy resistance.

View from inside Naftuan Point Cave. Courtesy of Tiffany Lucas.

"OK, Leonard. Let's see if we can call in artillery strikes on these Jap caves," Hooper said from the pilot's seat.

"Get me in close so that I can make out the caves' openings." Hooper dropped the spotter plane down to the cliff level and flew parallel to the bluff.

With binoculars in hand, Wollman called out, "OK, there's a group of caves. Let's call in a strike."

"Cherokee, this is Marine Spotter 1. Adjust fire. Over."

"Marine Spotter 1, this is Cherokee. Adjust fire. Out."

"This is Marine Spotter 1. Grid 10 Echo. Over."

"This is Cherokee. Grid 10 Echo. Out," Cherokee called out, indicating round en route.

"Shot. Out," Marine Spotter 1 replied.

"Splash. Over."

"Splash. Out," Wollman reported, indicating the round had landed with adjustments to follow.

Wollman called in adjustments to the naval artillery and observed the next strike from a safe distance.

They directed the naval guns at the entrenched Japanese forces throughout the morning until, running low on fuel, Hooper headed back toward Isley Field.

Suddenly, a lone Japanese Zero appeared low on the horizon over the Pacific. Wollman saw the Zeke streaking toward them at three hundred miles per hour.

"Let's get the hell out of here, George. That Zeke's got us in his sights."

"Roger. It's only four miles to Isley Field," Hooper called out, advancing the throttle and climbing toward the clouds for cover.

They could make out Isley Field in the distance when the Zero struck with a hail of 7.7-mm bullets and tracers lighting up the sky around the Stinson. As the Zero streaked past the slow-moving spotter plane, it laced the Stinson's left wing and tail with bullet holes.

"He's coming back around, George! We'll never make it to the field!"

The Zero assaulted the Stinson head-on, guns blazing. A hail of bullets ripped through the windshield and engine cowling. Smoke filled the cockpit.

"George, you're losing altitude. Pull up!"

Wollman looked ahead at Hooper, who was slumped forward, blood streaming down his face.

The Zero streaked past, so close that Wollman could make out the pilot's grinning face and a single gold front tooth.

Everything was spinning as the Stinson plummeted toward the ground. Wollman desperately grabbed the stick, struggling to pull the plane out of the steep dive. Smoke poured from the engine, leaving a black streak behind the dying plane.[1]

---

1   Convair Stinson OY-1 60498 (VMO-4) was lost off Saipan on June 24, 1944.

* * *

From Li'l Abner, Loren watched the lopsided battle unfold. *He'll never make it. This is going to be bad!*

"That looks like Wollman's spotter plane," Fred called out.

The plane started to pull up, but it was too late: it smashed into the ground just beyond Isley Field near the Japanese fuel dump.

"Come on, Fred. Let's get over there. Maybe we can pull him out of the wreckage."

The engineers put their D8s in gear and charged their eighteen-ton dozers toward the smoking crash site. When they arrived at the fuel dump, the spotter plane was a crumpled mess. Its fabric fuselage was torn to shreds. The impact had pushed the engine back into the front pilot's seat.

"Someone's moving in back!"

Engineers and Marines rushed over to the wreckage and ripped open the door to the tandem back seat.

"It is Wollman! Let's get him out of here before this whole fuel dump blows up!"

The men pulled on Wollman, but his legs were pinned beneath the front seat, shoved backward by the impact.

"What about the pilot?"

"He's a goner."

"Wollman's legs are a mess. It's a good thing he's unconscious."

Using prybars, the men gently moved the front seat off Wollman's legs. The ambulance arrived, and the medics transported Wollman to a makeshift dispensary.

"God! I hope he makes it," Fred said.

"Wollman's a tough cookie. He'll make it," Loren replied.

Lt. Leonard Wollman, still unconscious, was rapidly transferred to a naval ship just offshore. His fractured legs were in splints. One way or the other, the war was over for this boy from Brooklyn.

CHAPTER 30

JAPANESE COUNTERATTACK ON ASLITO AIRFIELD

JUNE 26, 1944

By the second week, the 804th Aviation Engineers had settled down into a routine. The battalion of 750 men was organized into four companies: HQ, and Service A, B, and C. The letter companies did labor, like laying the Marston matting. HQ Company ran the heavy equipment: the bulldozer, graters, and carryalls. The men worked around the clock in twelve-hour shifts and slept in pup tents.

"We're sitting ducks out there," Fred complained. "We got a rifle, but it's behind the seat, and anyway, we can't hear the snipers' firing over the noise of the diesel motor."

"Rifles wouldn't be much use against a strafing Zero or those Betty bombers," Loren said.

"Scuttlebutt is that those Japs holed up in the caves at Naftuan Point are up to something."

"Well, I don't want to be in front of some crazy Japanese banzai attack."

Six hundred Japanese soldiers of the 47th Brigade's 317th Infantry Battalion were holed up in the caves at Naftuan Point[1] along

---

1   After World War II, Naftuan Point was renamed Naftan Point.

Loren Low on Saipan with tractor, 1944. Courtesy of the Low family.

Saipan's southern tip. American warships offshore and the artillery of the 105th Infantry pounded them relentlessly, blocking their escape. Finally, on June 26, 1942, the men had consumed the last of their food and drunk the little remaining water.

In a moment of desperation, Capt. Sasaki issued the final order: "Wounded will remain in their present position and defend Naftuan Point. Those who cannot participate in combat must commit suicide. The password for tonight is Shichisei Hokoku."[2]

After midnight, Sasaki's men, crazed with thirst, used the cover of darkness to slip out of the caves. They were determined to destroy Aslito Airfield before the Americans could use it to attack Japanese soil. By 2:00 a.m., they stumbled upon the 2nd Battalion 105th Infantry and engaged in brutal hand-to-hand combat, inflicting twenty-four casualties on the Americans while losing twenty-seven of their own men.

By 3:00 a.m., Sasaki's men had swarmed onto Aslito Airfield.

---

2   Shichisei Hokoku is Japanese for "Seven lives to repay our country."

P-47 Hed Up 'N Locked, *destroyed by Japanese attack June 27, 1944, on Aslito Field.
US government photograph. Public domain.*

Three hundred Japanese soldiers wielding axes and automatic weapons broke through the lines. Aviation engineers and a few hurriedly assembled Marines fought through one desperate night against the enemy, who had seized one-third of the airfield. The Japanese bayonetted the belly tanks and tires of parked Thunderbolts, destroying the P-47 *Hed Up 'N Locked*. Hand grenades ignited the gasoline streaming onto the runway. In the chaos, Sgt. Raymond Murphy ran through a hail of fire and taxied the adjacent plane to safety.

The engineers dropped their construction tools, picking up carbines, rifles, and handguns. Some jumped onto half-tracks with mounted machine guns and pursued the enemy.

The engineers in HQ Company and ground crew opened fire on the invading Japanese, while the lettered companies swept through the surrounding fields on armored half-tracks in search of the enemy.

Loren, with a rifle in hand, ran after an armored half-track and jumped onto the hood.

"Mind if I come along? I don't want to miss this action."

"Hang on, soldier. Here we go," the sergeant called out as he revved the motor and sped off into the night.

Loren Low with rifle, WWII.
Courtesy of the Low family.

Back at the camp, Fred watched the scene unfold from his foxhole. Lt. McCoy's carbine jammed as a Japanese soldier stormed out of the cane field and approached him with bayonet drawn.

"Crap!" McCoy screamed, throwing down the carbine. In the next moment, McCoy jumped in his jeep with its motor running, put it in gear, took off after the now-fleeing enemy, and ran him down.

"Guess we'll have to call him Killer McCoy after tonight. Just don't stand in front of the lieutenant's jeep."

"Look at Lieutenant Flatbrush over there! He's such an arrogant, cocky little rooster with his .30-caliber machine gun."

"Yeah! He needs poor Snus[3] to carry ammo for him and two other guys to carry the tripod and barrel. What a wuss!"

The men could see the Zero's tracer bullets striking the ground and dove for their foxholes. But with his back to the action, Lt. Flatbrush didn't have a clue. He just stood out in the open, ordering Snus and the other two men around.

---

3   "Snus" is a nickname for a member of the 804th Aviation Engineers.

"Take the tripod and gun over to that hill! No, I said set it up behind the ridge! No, I meant over there!"

Lt. Flatbrush had the three men running all over the camp looking for the perfect place to set up his machine gun.

Snus was packing the ammunition while chewing tobacco with saliva running from the corner of his mouth into his beard. Snus didn't shave and only took a shower occasionally, so it got pretty rank when he started sweating. Finally, Snus pooped out from all the running around, sat down in the middle of the road on an ammunition can, pulled out some tobacco, and waited.

Lt. Flatbrush was furious. "What are you doing? Get up and follow my orders!"

"Sir, when you make up your mind where you're going to set up that machine gun, tell me, and I'll bring the ammo up to you!"

Fred and the other engineers had watched the scene unfold and roared with laughter at Snus's reply.

By the time the lieutenant chose the perfect spot for his machine gun, the action was pretty much over.

Although the engineers knew little about warfare, when the sun came up, the Japanese had fallen back and had destroyed only one plane. Combat engineers, Marines, and ground crews had defeated the enemy.

* * *

That evening, on June 27, Loren and Andrew Hughes[4] began the night shift. Loren climbed up onto the dozer's massive mud-encrusted treads and took over the controls as Jimmy jumped off, finishing his twelve-hour shift.

"How's Li'l Abner running today, Jimmy?"

"Dependable as ever, Loren. I had a little trouble shifting it into gear at first, but she's fine now."

"Probably that's what's left of my watch. I dropped it into the

---

4   Andrew Hughes (1914–1978) from Stamford, Connecticut, was a bulldozer operator for the 804th Aviation Engineers.

gearbox yesterday and couldn't fish it out."

"Well, it's a bunch of crunched-up pieces now." Jimmy laughed.

"I'll have my mom send me a new watch. Where'd you leave off?"

"We've been working on that nasty section of the runway near the Jap fuel dump."

"OK, Jimmy. Get some shut-eye."

"I filled the fuel tank for you. Li'l Abner's topped off with fifty-seven gallons of diesel."

"Thanks, Jimmy." Loren waved as he put the dozer in gear and headed for the fuel dump.

Working at night was preferable to the day shift. The night air was cooler, and the strafing Zeros weren't a problem after sunset. The Betty bombers were another matter as they liked the cover of darkness to drop their sticks of bombs.

Andrew Hughes joined Loren as they headed over to the fuel dump. The airfield was taking shape after just over a week, but it would be months before she was ready for the massive B-29 Superfortress bombers.

Loren and Andrew found the spot where the day crew had left off, lowered the dozer's blades, and began the job of shaping the new runway. The dust and noise of the D8s' 177-horsepower diesel motors filled the air.

Operating the D8 was like a choreographed dance in constant motion. The manual transmission had ten gears, five forward and five in reverse. Coordinating the left-hand clutch lever, the two right-hand transmission levers, the right-handed throttle lever, and the brake pedal was enough to keep anyone busy. A horizontal handle on the right operated the dozer's large blade. Steering the bulldozer was accomplished by slowing one track compared to the other, using separate brake and steering clutch release levers for each track. By now, this intricate dance was second nature for these experienced "Catskinners."

* * *

Just before midnight, the explosion from the fuel dump shook the

*Mitsubishi Betty
bomber, World
War II. Public
domain.*

ground. Loren looked over and saw the fireball and then spotted the Betty bomber high overhead.

"We've been bombed! They're going to blow up the fuel dump!" Loren shouted to Andrew, who had also stopped his bulldozer.

Loren and Andrew looked over at the rapidly spreading fire just beyond the edge of the runway. The flames had engulfed the entire fuel dump, creating an orange glow in the sky. Billowing black smoke filled the night air.

"Those guys are in trouble," Loren called out as a series of blasts from exploding gasoline drums shook the air.

"That tank must have five hundred thousand gallons of Jap fuel. It's loaded to the brim!" Andrew shouted.

A few men were fleeing from the inferno.

"Where's the rest of the company?"

"They must be pinned down or dead! Come on! Let's go!" Loren called out as he revved his diesel engine and charged toward the huge fire.

Both bulldozers quickly arrived at the inferno, but the intense heat from the flames stopped them momentarily.

Loren Low and Andrew Hughes on Saipan, June 1944. Courtesy of the Low family.

"Raise your dozer blade to shield yourself from the flames and douse your head and clothes with water," Loren called out to Hughes.

The two men walked their Cats into the inferno with blades raised as flames came up through the bulldozers. Meanwhile, the Betty bomber circled overhead, preparing to strike again.

"We gotta hurry! I think that bomber's coming back!"

Loren dropped the bulldozer's blade to scoop up dirt, but the intense blast of heat blew back into his face. He raised his hand to block it.

Maybe this will help.

Loren wrapped a wet T-shirt around his head to cover his face but had to drop his shielding hand to operate the controls.

Scooping up dirt and coral as they advanced, they dropped load after load onto the flames, smothering the fire. The dozers worked in tandem, moving through the fuel dump.

As bad as the heat was, the thick black smoke made breathing unbearable.

"Come on, Li'l Abner. Let's put out this fire," Loren said, coughing again and again as he raised the blade and advanced deeper into the flames.

Over and over, the two Cats scooped up blades of dirt and coral, extinguishing the fire and scooping flaming debris away from the men pinned down by the fire.

"We gotta protect the tank of Jap fuel," Andrew yelled. "If it ignites, we're all goners."

Maneuvering their bulldozers to the five-hundred-thousand-gallon tank, they found flames lapping at the base. Loren pushed the flaming debris aside and, looking down, saw the smoking remains of Leonard Wollman's Stinson plane in the pile of rubble.

Within minutes, the two engineers had beaten back the fire and averted disaster. The men of Company A were alive, and the vital Isley Airfield was preserved.

Loren and Andrew paused and looked at the smoldering debris.

The men of Company A were slowly coming out from their shelters. "You guys saved our butts."

"No problem," Loren replied. Time to get back to work."

"Keep a lookout for that Betty bomber," Andrew called out as they headed back to the airfield.[5]

***

The work on the airfield continued night and day. The tropical rains came by mid-July, turning the airfield into a gelatinous, muddy mess. The rains dampened spirits and made the job even more difficult, but the nonstop labor continued.

---

5   The same night, June 27–28, 1944, Japanese bombs dropped on Aslito Airfield struck Lt. Wollman's Marine VMO-4 spotter squadron, causing four casualties to ground crew. The June 26 air raid killed three enlisted men and injured nine, including three officers and six enlisted men.

804th Aviation Engineer bulldozer fighting fire 1944. Public domain.

Blasting mountains of coral used tons of explosives. Initially, the "fire in the hole!" calls got every worker's attention but soon became routine.

Loren had been operating Li'l Abner near the end of the runway. The job was to pile up mountains of dirt and coral. Without this barrier, brakeless bombers, with their shot-out hydraulics, would plunge 213 feet into the Pacific Ocean.

"Fire in the hole!"

Loren looked up in time to see the explosion. What happened next was retold in stories for decades. The blast was so massive it blew a car-sized boulder into the air.

No place to go! Loren watched as the boulder bore down on him. *Boy, that rock is huge! It's as big as a car! I'm going to have to dodge this thing!*

Loren stood his ground as the boulder and debris flew past,

missing him by a few yards.

"Well, Li'l Abner. We dodged another one. It's time to get back to work."

* * *

Saipan was declared secured on July 9, although bombing attacks continued for months. In the fall of 1944, the Army brass arrived to present medals to the soldiers. These presentations were good for morale and even better for the folks back home.

It was another perfect "80–80" day in the Marianas: a balmy 80°F and 80 percent humidity. A few fluffy white clouds drifted over the horizon, breaking up the clear blue tropical sky and carrying thundershowers that would reach them by the afternoon.

Maj. Gen. Sanford Jarman, commander of the 27th Infantry Division, presented Silver Stars for gallantry in action to Sgts. Loren I. Low and Andrew Hughes, for their actions on June 27, 1944.

"That was one hell of a fire you put out, son. You saved a lot of lives."

"Thank you, sir. Just doing my job," Loren mumbled, looking down, as Jarman fumbled, pinning the medal on this shirt.

Jarman paused, looking Loren in the eye. "This war will be won by men like you, doing their jobs. Our B-29s will begin attacking Japan any day now from the airfield you and Sgt. Hughes preserved."

After the ceremony, the Army photojournalist approached Loren.

"Let me get a few more shots for the folks back home."

He looked around, searching for the perfect backdrop.

"Stand over here in front of those mountains. OK. Hold still. Don't smile. Give me the look of a proud warrior. That's it!"

Loren let out a sigh. "Did I keep my eyes open?"

"You were perfect. Now, where is that bulldozer of yours? What do you call it? Big Emma?"

Loren laughed. "Nope. That's Li'l Abner. You know, from the comics."

"OK. Take your helmet off and place your left arm on Li'l Abner. Perfect! Give me your address back home, soldier. Your mom's going

Maj. Gen. Sanford Jarman presenting Silver Star to Loren Low, 1944. Courtesy of the Low family.

to love these."

Walking away, the photojournalist reviewed the day's events. *I can picture the headline: "They Smothered Death with Bulldozer Treads!"*

Loren wore the medal and his helmet for the rest of the day, just in case Maj. Gen. Jarman stayed around. Loren's thoughts turned to home as he drove his bulldozer across the dusty airfield.

I wish Mom and Sis could see me now.

But as his dozer rumbled across Aslito Airfield, it was his brother Stan he pictured, smiling and surrounded by his nine friends and their ten-course Hawaiian luau dinner.

Enough daydreaming. Time to get back to work.

Loren Low on Saipan with D8 bulldozer, Li'l Abner, 1944. Courtesy of the Low family.

* * *

Construction of the massive Saipan airfield, completed in less than four months, was a resounding success. This modern-day miracle, later known as "Flanders' Fields," is today recognized as one of World War II's incredible engineering feats.

The B-29 Superfortresses arrived on October 12, 1944. From the airfields on Saipan, Guam, and Tinian, these long-range heavy bombers struck directly at the heart of the Japanese empire. By the following summer, the Pacific

Loren Low with Silver Star in Saipan, 1944. Courtesy of the Low family.

War came to an end with the surrender of Japan on August 15, 1945.

Thousands of B-29s flew out of the Marianas, including this one passing directly over the head of Loren Low and the 804th Aviation Engineers.

B-29 Superfortress taking off from Isley Field. Sgt. Loren Low, second from right, looks up at the B-29 passing directly overhead. Loren often told the story of the monstrous B-29s roaring overhead on their way to Japan.

PART III

THE AFTERMATH

While the war in the Pacific ended in August 1945, the story of Regan's B-24 Liberator and its crew of ten men did not end on January 22, 1943. These men are connected to those who returned from the war and to the families and nation who preserved their memory. Their story continued in unexpected ways.

CHAPTER 31

DRAWN HOME

1986

The 2,200-mile trip from Mexico City to San Francisco was a six-hour journey back to another world.

Ruth had spent most of the past four decades living in the vibrant and colorful world of Mexico City. She'd watched it grow from a manageable three million inhabitants to a sprawling metropolis of fifteen million people. Ruth's beloved streetcars had always reminded her of San Francisco. They had now all but vanished, a relic of the past.

As she left the terminal at SFO, the blast of cool air shocked her senses, as did the lack of bright color. Gone were the vibrant reds, oranges, and yellow hues of her adopted home, replaced with the grays and pastel colors adorning the row upon row of ticky-tacky, little box houses lined up on the hillside.

Her one bag was all she had in the world. It contained a couple of blouses, skirts, sensible shoes, and a single photograph of a World War II bombardier: not much to show for four decades away from home. But Ruth was not one to accumulate possessions or people. It was better that way, with nothing to tie her down to any place or anyone.

Yet, something had drawn her back to this City by the Bay. Looking out the window of the yellow cab, Ruth shook her head.

What am I doing here? It's been such a long time. This place was never my home.

View of Hillside neighborhood in Daly City from San Bruno Mountain State Park.
Tim Adams. Wikimedia Commons.

"Where to, ma'am?"

"Nob Hill."

"I need an address, ma'am."

"Just take me there. I'll tell you where to stop."

"It's your dime, lady."

The cab ride north on Highway 101, along the bay, was spectacular. They passed through the Mission District and took the exit for the Bay Bridge.

"I don't want to go over the Bay Bridge!"

"Don't worry, ma'am. We're getting off at Third Street, before the bridge."

Recalling the streets and landmarks from almost fifty years before, Ruth instructed the driver, "Take me to Sacramento Street."

"You been here before?"

"A lifetime ago."

The views of San Francisco were just as she remembered. The city was full of people and traffic, but it was nothing like Mexico City or the Bronx. At Market Street, she looked to the right and remembered seeing the Ferry Building. Turning left on Sacramento, they passed Grant Avenue and the Dragon Gate into Chinatown.

After the cab passed Stockton Street, Ruth recognized the brick building on the right with the funny bricks sticking out.

"What's that dark brick building?"

"That's Cameron House. You know it?"

"A friend showed it to me a very long time ago."

"Well, if you stay around here, go and check them out. They're good people."

"What was that odd, tall ,pointed building? It's new from when I visited."

"Oh, that's the Transamerica Pyramid. It's been here for two decades. When did you say you were here?"

"Didn't say."

They passed the Fairmont Hotel on the left. No money to stay there.

And then she saw her destination. "Stop there!"

"Where?"

"At that big church!"

"That's Grace Cathedral. But this is the backside. Let me drop you off around front on California Street."

Ruth got out of the cab, collected her one bag, and took a big breath. The cathedral was magnificent. She was home.

Ruth wasn't particularly religious, not really an observant Jew and certainly not Episcopalian. But something about this place was famil-iar and felt like home. She entered the large doors to the cathedral and sat, admiring the magnificent Gothic arches. After an hour, she rose and turned to leave.

"Are you in need?"

Ruth turned toward the voice and found a kindly face. "I was resting."

"I know. I've been waiting. Go across the street and tell them Reverend Alan Jones sent you. They'll find a place for you to stay. And then, if you wish, come back to pray."

"How did you know?"

"It wasn't hard. Someone led you here. A person sitting alone in

Grace Cathedral San Francisco. Daderot. Creative Commons CCO 1.0 Universal Public Domain. Wikimedia Commons.

God's house for one hour with a single bag is one of God's children looking for the way home."

Ruth found her new home, at 1177 California Street: a high-rise building with fourteen floors and magnificent views of Grace Cathedral and the bay. Her studio apartment in the back of the building was viewless, but she was happy.

She returned to the cathedral the next day and found Rev. Jones. He was not surprised to see her, nor was he surprised by her greeting.

"I'm not Christian, you know. I was born Jewish, so maybe I shouldn't be here."

"You are here, and I knew yesterday, but it does not matter."

Grace Cathedral, San Francisco. CaliforniaThroughMyLens.com. Courtesy of Josh McNair.

"How did you know?"

"The tag on your bag says, 'Ruth Hirshfield.'"

"You don't mind?"

"Of course not. You are always welcome as a friend or a person in search of the light."

"Maybe I should go to a synagogue."

"You should go where your heart takes you."

"I came by to thank you for helping me find a place to stay."

Rev. Jones smiled and motioned for Ruth to sit and rest.[1]

***

---

1   The welcoming attitude of Rev. Alan Jones and Grace Cathedral was extended to all, including those afflicted with HIV during the AIDS crisis in the 1980s and '90s. They welcomed HIV-positive people into the church at a time when they faced stigma and discrimination. Grace Cathedral offered funerals for anyone who had died of AIDS, whether the person was a member of the congregation or not. The cathedral was burying up to thirty-five people a week at the height of the crisis in the early '90s.

That afternoon, Ruth found herself in front of the dark brick building with the funny bricks sticking out. She knocked on the large oak doors.

When the door opened, a young Chinese girl peered out expectantly, without uttering a word.

"I am here to ask a question. Is Miss Cameron available?"

The young girl ushered Ruth into the parlor. "Wait here."

She disappeared up an oak staircase that led to the second floor.

As she sat in the lobby, Ruth turned at the sound of footsteps running on the stairs and girls giggling. She looked up the stairs. They were empty.

"Doreen can see you now."

Who's Doreen? I came to see Miss Cameron."

"She'll explain."

In the second-floor office, overlooking Sacramento Street, Ruth encountered a young Chinese American woman seated behind an oak desk.

"Please have a seat. The director is out today. My name is Doreen. Can I help you?"

"I don't know where to start."

"Try starting at the beginning."

"I was here in 1942 with my fiancé and his Liberator crew. The young men were about to go overseas in a B-24."

Doreen waited patiently, not sure where the story was going. "My fiancé, Jerome, became very close to a young Chinese boy named Stan. Stan showed us around San Francisco and took us to Nob Hill. He showed us this building and told us the story of how his grandmother stayed here."

"Yes, how can I help you?"

"He said he met with Donaldina Cameron. Is she here today?"

"Miss Cameron passed away many years ago."

"They all died," Ruth blurted out, unsure of where this was going. She was surprised by the tears in her eyes.

"Why don't you show me the photo?" Doreen said, pointing at the photograph Ruth was clutching.

"It's all I have of Jerome," Ruth said, bringing the photograph into the light.

Doreen inspected the old photograph of the young airman. "Is this your fiancé?"

"Yes. In his letters, Jerome always talked about Stan. I wanted to visit this place for both of them."

"You said that Stan's grandmother stayed here?"

"Yes, Stan took us on a walking tour and showed me this home and told me about his grandmother."

"Well, thousands of young women came through this home, starting in 1874. This place is the birthplace of so many Chinese American families, including Stan's."

Doreen gave Ruth a tour of Cameron House and then asked, "Do you want to help us? We can always use volunteers. No money, but lots of good people."

"I used to volunteer in a school in Mexico City, where I lived."

"Go to the Jean Parker Elementary School at 840 Broadway. Tell them Doreen at Cameron House sent you. They'd love to have you as a volunteer. Here, let me write down the address."

Ruth looked at the name and address on the scrap of paper.

"You can't miss it. The school is right at the eastern end of the Broadway Tunnel. And thank you for sharing the photo of Jerome and your stories about your fiancé and Stan."

* * *

Ruth spent the next fifteen years volunteering at the Jean Parker Elementary School. She became a beloved fixture of the small school nicknamed "The Small and Mighty School."

Most of the students were Chinese. Ruth asked all the parents and teachers about Stanley Low, but no one knew of the Chinese boy from Salem, Oregon.

One day, she again asked a stranger, who listened intently. When she finished her story, he asked, "You said he died in the war, and he's Chinese?"

"Yes."

"Then go over to St. Mary's Square on California Street. There is a plaque with the names of Chinese American boys who died in the war."

That afternoon, Ruth walked the one mile to St. Mary's Square, where she found the memorial plaque. She scanned the names. In the first row, she touched the name Clifford S. Low.

This must be Jerome's friend. No wonder I haven't found anyone who knew him. He was Clifford Stanley Low.

Feeling the letters of his name as if reading braille, Ruth closed her eyes and remembered Stan's boyish face and shy smile. That afternoon on Nob Hill was forever etched into her memory. Ruth felt connected to her life in San Francisco and her work in Chinatown. She belonged here, and now she had finally brought Stan home.

* * *

One year later, suffering from abdominal pain, Ruth took Bus 6 up Market Street to UCSF Medical Center on Parnassus Avenue. In the radiology department, she presented the receptionist with a prescription for an ultrasound.

"Take a seat. The doctor will be out to see you shortly."

Fifteen minutes passed before the resident doctor greeted her and took Ruth into the ultrasound suite.

"Hello, Mrs. Hirshfield. My name is Dr.—"

Ruth had been staring at the doctor's name badge and blurted out, "You're Dr. Russell Low!"

"Yes, have we met? Are you here for an abdominal ultrasound?"

"No. I mean, yes, but first. Are you related to Clifford Stan Low?"

The resident dropped the clipboard.

"Yes, how did you know?"

"Well, do I have a story to tell you."

St. Mary's Square memorial plaque honoring the Chinese Americans who died in World War I and World War II. Old St. Mary's Cathedral is the same house of worship where Ah Ying, Gee Sung, and Billy hid from the Chinatown vigilante mob in 1892. Courtesy of Montgomery Hom.

CHAPTER 32

EPILOGUE

A fter the war in the Pacific ended, the journey home took many paths. Loren Low and Fred Kossow were honorably discharged in October 1945.

Fred Kossow returned to his hometown of Gridley, California, just north of Sacramento. He worked as a farmer, but his real passion was raising thoroughbred racehorses. His other joy was organizing reunions for the 804th Aviation Engineers. He knew all the men by name and serial number, and had located most of them, except for Loren Low. With his beloved wife, Bernie, Fred raised four children in Gridley.

Loren Low returned to Stockton, California, just a hundred miles from Fred Kossow in Gridley. In December 1945, he met the love of his life, Rose Fong. They were married in June 1947 and raised four children in Stockton. Loren spent his life working as a carpenter, but his real passions were traveling in his camper, running, and cycling. Throughout his life, he was a storyteller and a unique combination of John Wayne and Tarzan. As they say in our family, Loren wore the "white hat" and had the physique of Johnny Weissmuller.

Leonard Wollman spent years recuperating from the injuries he sustained on Saipan. The plane crash on Saipan crushed his lower legs, and doctors told him that he would never walk again. Leonard would have nothing to do with that way of thinking. He was determined

Leonard Wollman and June Wollman at the presentation of the Air Medal, December 11, 1944. Courtesy of the Wollman family.

to walk and underwent multiple operations. After infections set in, a double lower extremity amputation seemed like the only remaining option to save his life. Only the miracle of the new wonder drug, penicillin, altered the infection's course and prevented the surgeon's scalpel from taking his legs.

For his heroic actions on Saipan on June 17, 1944, Lt. Leonard Wollman was awarded an Air Medal at St. Albans Naval Hospital on December 11, 1944. Captain Lester L. Pratt, commanding officer of the hospital, made the presentation, which was witnessed by Leonard's wife, June Rick Wollman.

Leonard Wollman became a no-nonsense educator who was known as a problem solver. He taught physical education and chemistry and then spent decades as an elementary school principal in

Florida. For twelve years, he also co-owned and ran a Jewish summer camp called Camp Ocala. Throughout his life, Leonard Wollman was a stoic, strong-willed Marine, whom they called the Major, his final rank in the Marine Reserves. A lifelong learner, Leonard also had a passion for magic. He often delighted his students with spontaneous magic shows. When he retired, his school rented a hot-air balloon to take their beloved principal on one last flight.

Lt. James McMurria and seven of his crew members survived their Liberator's crash on January 20, 1943. They washed up on a small island off the coast of New Guinea after clinging to a life raft for three days. They lived with natives for several months, evading capture. In an attempt to get back to Port Moresby, they were taken from island to island in outrigger canoes by different groups of natives. They were, unfortunately, turned over to the Japanese after making it back to New Guinea.

In a remarkable tale of survival, Jim McMurria spent thirty-five months as a POW until the end of the war. He was one of only seven men, out of seventy-nine, to walk out of the Rabaul prison camp. In April 2002, Jim McMurria was eighty-four years old and living in Greenville, South Carolina, when he received a phone call from a young man in California seeking information about his uncle, Clifford S. Low. Our hour-long conversation shed light on the events in New Guinea during January 1943. He told an intriguing story. A couple of days after his Liberator crashed and the eight men washed up on Wageo Island, they spotted a solo American Liberator flying overhead and fired their only flare five hundred feet into the air. When the Liberator did not return, McMurria assumed that his signal had not been seen. In his mind, it was most certainly Regan's plane on January 22, 1943. Jim McMurria's book *Trial and Triumph* is a rare firsthand account of the Southwest Pacific War. In his own words, Jim McMurria felt "fantastically lucky to have survived."

Robert C. Chinn, the young man Stan met at Cameron House in June 1942, was deployed to French North Africa with the 30th Infantry Regiment. Operation Torch commenced on November 8,

PFC Lloyd Mills
(left) and Lt.
Robert Chinn
(in front), Sicily,
1943. Courtesy
of Sherry Smith.

1942, with Gen. George S. Patton's invasion at the beaches at Fedala in Morocco. Lt. Robert Chinn commanded a machine gun platoon that later took part in Tunisia and Sicily's battles.

A prolific writer, Bob sent letters to his wife, Janet, in which he proudly described his men during the Sicilian landing: "Our battalion was selected to land first and clear the beach of pillboxes, barbed wire, and defenses—we did a damn fine job. I am very proud of my platoon—they knocked out an enemy artillery piece and inflicted a number of casualties and took quite a few prisoners."

Stubborn German resistance along the northern coast of Sicily prompted Patton to order a risky amphibious assault. A small team was tasked with landing behind enemy lines to outflank and defeat the German and Italian forces. On the morning of November 8, 1943, Lt. Chinn and the small assault team landed near Santa Agata, surprising the German and Italian troops. In the ensuing battle, enemy gunfire mortally wounded twenty-three-year-old Lt. Robert C. Chinn. He carried his most treasured possessions in his pocket, a letter from his beloved Janet and a photograph of his three-month-old son, Robert Junior. To the end, Bob showed uncommon bravery and compassion, grasping the hand of an enemy and saying, "You are a good sport. You are all right."[1] PFC Lloyd Mills, who had stayed with the wounded Lt. Robert Chin to protect him and render aid, was captured by Germans. Mills survived eighteen months as a prisoner of war until he was liberated in May 1945.

The families of the other men, those who did not return, continued with their lives but never forgot the sons, brothers, and uncles they lost. The form their remembrances took was different and personal for each family.

My father, Loren Low, kept his kid brother's cherished wings and Air Medal in his sock drawer next to his Silver Star. While many World War II veterans had difficulty speaking about their wartime experience, Loren was full of stories. We all grew up hearing about Saipan, his last meeting with Stanley in Honolulu while going AWOL, and how he lost his little brother one month later when his B-24 was shot down in New Guinea. Loren's stories kept Stanley alive.

For decades, Stan's mother kept the postcards and newspaper articles that Stan proudly sent to her. Our family treasured the book Pat Robinson sent her, *The Fight for New Guinea*. I am looking at my grandmother's tattered copy with her ribbon marking page 146, describing her Stan as the "Chinese boy from Salem, Ore., the nose gunner in Regan's plane, who brought down one of the Zeros."

In November 1943, the United States Army returned to his mother a small box of Stan's possessions. The package included a photo album, one New Testament, two combat wings, two pairs of socks, a US Treasury check for $1.28, and the three Chinese coins Kay had given her son when he went overseas.

---

1   Bob Chinn, *The Other Side of Paradise*.

Emily Vinson was devastated by Paul's death. For the rest of her life, she refused to allow any mention of the war that took her Paul. Emily remarried but never forgot her first love. After her second husband, Charles, passed away in 1969, Emily chose to remember both men by mounting two diamonds in a single ring. Combining Paul's diamond from 1942 with the diamond from Charles, she created a symbol of both men's love. Emily wore the ring for the rest of her life, and it became a family heirloom passed on from generation to generation.

Scott Regan's mother, Frances, listed her son as missing in action in the *Los Angeles Times* on May 11, 1943. She died just three weeks later, on June 5, 1943, perhaps of a broken heart.

Many of the families named nephews after their lost aviator. Scott Luke Regan's sister, Peggy, named her son Scott Luke Borba. For his entire life, Scotty carried the memory of his uncle, the B-24 pilot lost in New Guinea. Scotty preserved the cherished photographs and stories of the uncle he lost in the war, and the portrait of his Uncle Scott hung prominently on the wall of his home. Stan's younger sister, Mei-Mei, named her first child after her brother and childhood best friend.

George Kerby's family maintained a close relationship with the *Charlotte Observer*, where George had worked before the war. George Kerby's aunt, Mrs. H. H. Holder, placed a missing in action notice in the *Observer* on March 6, 1942, the day after her sister Ruth received the telegram indicating her son had been missing since January 22, 1943. She related the details of George's most recent letter, describing their final volunteer reconnaissance mission before going on a week of leave. After an agonizing wait of three years, the family placed a killed in action notice in the same newspaper on January 25, 1946.

Jerome Lesser's family kept their grief private for several months. A notice in the sports section of the local newspaper finally appeared on July 17, 1943. In the *Brooklyn Daily Eagle*, an article headlined "Athletes in Uniform" by Ben Gould listed as missing in action Lt. Jerome Lesser, a former City College fencing champion, who was also an accomplished skater and skier.

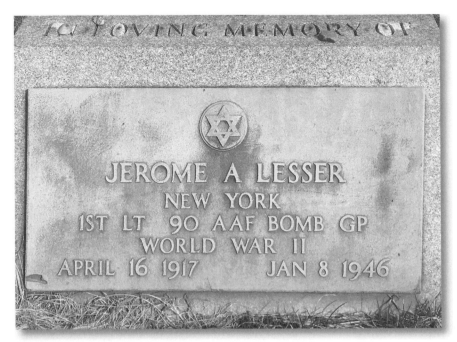

Memorial placed for Jerome A. Lesser by his father, Alfred Lesser, at the Hungarian Union Field Cemetery, now the Mount Carmel Cemetery, in Queens, New York. Courtesy of Barbara Rotenberg.

Jerome Lesser's family named nephews after the fallen bombardier. In 1950, Jerome's father, Alfred Lesser, placed a bronze marker at the Hungarian Union Field Cemetery in Brooklyn, remembering the son he lost. For almost eighty years, the family has continued to honor Jerome's memory at his yahrzeit, the day commemorating the anniversary of his death, lighting candles and reciting the Kaddish mourner's prayer in synagogue.

Grace Lesser, Jerome's younger sister, to whom he wrote so many wartime letters, was a brilliant young scholar. Her field, econometrics, involves applying statistical methods to economic data to give empirical content to economic relationships. Grace Lesser played an important role in the war, working on the Manhattan Project and the atomic bomb, which brought the war to an end in August 1945. Grace received a letter of commendation from President Harry Truman for this work. For a time, Grace also safeguarded the fencing foils that took Jerome to New York City championships in the 1930s.

When the B-29 *Enola Gay* flew its mission to Hiroshima on August 6, 1945, an observation B-29 Superfortress accompanied it. On board this second plane was a decorated American gunner from Brooklyn, Abraham Veroba. Veroba went on to become a beloved cantor as predicted by Jerome Lesser and Leonard Wollman in 1942.

The family of Earl Byrd, or Early Bird as the men knew him, received a visit by Army brass on March 5, 1944. On this solemn day in Addie, North Carolina, they presented his

Grace Lesser Rosenzweig. Courtesy of the Lesser family.

mother, Lewellen Nancy Byrd, with Earl's Air Medal with two Oak Clusters. The entire family gathered in the family home as Lewellen sadly shook the officer's hand and received Earl's medal.

The family of Floyd Eldon McCallum, or Eldie as the crew called him, continued to wait for Eldie to come walking out of the jungles of New Guinea. The old-timers, like Clifford Sparks, told the stories about young Eldie's prowess as a hunter and outdoorsman. After all, Eldie had written them about the maps showing the escape routes through the New Guinea jungle. For years, they insisted that Eldie was too tough to die in some crocodile-infested jungle halfway around the world.

Across the country, there are scattered World War II memorials listing the names of the ten men on Scott Regan's Liberator.

Clifford S. Low is included on a plaque that Ruth visited in St. Mary's Square in San Francisco's Chinatown, honoring the Chinese Americans who made the ultimate sacrifice for their country in World

Presentation of Earl Byrd's Air Medal with two Oak Clusters to his mother, Lewellen Byrd. The two Oak Clusters indicate that Earl Byrd was awarded the equivalent of three Air Medals. Courtesy of the Byrd family.

War I and World War II. Paul C. Vinson's name is present on World War II memorials in Shirley, Massachusetts. John Crane is memorialized on a plaque honoring over three hundred Notre Dame alumni who died in World War II. All ten men in Regan's Liberator crew are included in the Manila American Cemetery and Memorial. As with all memorials, the starkly carved names in cold stone and bronze do not do justice to the rich lives and loves of these young American heroes.

Regan's B-24 Liberator was never found. It is fitting that the final resting place of these ten men is in the hearts and minds of those who come to know something of their lives and loves through the pages of *The All-American Crew.*

Perhaps the words of Harry Truman, repeated 407,000 times across America, best express the gratitude of a nation and world that found life born out of the sacrifices of these many men: "They stand in an unbroken line of patriots who have dared to die that freedom might live, and grow, and increase its blessing. Freedom lives, and through it, they live in a way that humbles the undertakings of most men."

AFTERWORD AND ACKNOWLEDGMENTS

Researching and writing *The All-American Crew* was a collaborative journey that involved many families, who generously shared long-forgotten letters and faded photographs tucked away in old albums. We all grew up with some distant knowledge of these young men who became warriors halfway around the world. Some came home from the war, while others did not. Over time, our memories of them became blurred images of who they once were. Even those who returned from the war are now gone. Remarkably, after almost eighty years of silence, this project and book have brought them back to life as vibrant young men. They live, breathe, laugh, and love in the pages of *The All-American Crew*.

In several instances, nephews of the ten men on Regan's B-24 Liberator kept their memories alive. Three of us met online almost twenty years ago. Bob Byrd, the nephew of Earl "Early Bird" Byrd; George Eldon Corwin, the nephew of Floyd "Eldie" McCallum; and I independently searched for details about our uncles and their lost warplane. We exchanged a few emails and photographs, but the search seemed to come to a dead end. The lost crew's fate was apparent, but the details of their lives were lost to the ravages of time. A fourth nephew, Scott Borba, whose uncle Scott Regan was the pilot, could have joined our "club," but we never had the good fortune of connecting with him.

We each searched in vain for information about the pilot, Scott L. Regan. Scott had two sisters who changed their name after marrying, complicating the search. Finally, connecting with Cary Borba Perrin, a niece of Scott Regan, shed light on his life and family. The shared stories and photographs brought to life the pilot of *The All-American Crew*.

Virginia K. Anderson, Jean Bierschenk, and Sheila Jaffray provided valuable research for the officers, copilot George Kerby and navigator John Crane.

The enlisted men who served as the B-24 gunners were also well represented. Searching for Paul Vinson took me to his Find-a-Grave memorial. A message of tribute that I left connected me with Christy Rosenhahn and her mother, Joanne Davidson, the daughter of Emily Vinson Macintosh. Joanne's research, letters from Paul to Emily, and photographs recreated a long-forgotten romance. Emily never forgot her first love and kept Paul alive for her children and grandchildren. Kathy Ziegler, another relative of Paul Vinson, also provided insightful information about the Vinson family. For decades, Paul's Purple Heart, citations, and photographs were held in safekeeping by his nephew Robert Prescott, who generously shared this material for *The All-American Crew*.

The letters written home from the war were at the core of the research. Most were long forgotten and almost lost forever in the rubbish pile, to be discarded during spring cleaning. I discovered the postcards and letters sent by Stan to his mother at the bottom of an old cardboard box that no one wanted after Kay passed away in 1974. Fate sent the box my way. Inside were Kay's treasures, including the letters and newspaper clippings from the son she lost to the war. As far as I knew, my father, Loren, had never written a letter home from the war. However, in 2017, a box arrived from my cousin Candace. It included a packet of eighty wartime letters written by my father to his mother, who kept them neatly bundled with a red, white, and blue ribbon.

The remarkable letters shared by Barbara Rotenberg and Allen

Rosenzweig trace Jerome Lesser's journey from a young Army recruit at Maxwell Field through Bombardier School in Victorville, California, his training in Topeka, and his eventual deployment overseas in the southwest Pacific. These letters recreated his training timeline and Jerome's transformation from an aviation cadet to a Liberator bombardier and American warrior.

The story of Robert C. Chinn, whom Stan met during his pilgrimage to Cameron House in 1942, was brought to life by the photos and letters shared by his son Bob Chinn and niece Valerie Tawa. In addition, Sherry Smith provided remarkable photographs of her grandfather, Lloyd Mills, with Lt. Robert Chinn during WWII.

Reconnecting to the women of *The All-American Crew* was equally challenging and rewarding. In Jerome's letters, he mentions Ruth, whom he plans to marry and take on a honeymoon to Hawaii. We knew nothing else about this mysterious person. However, a photograph of Ruth kept by his sister Grace included her handwritten notation "Ruth Hirshfield, Jerome's fiancé." I searched on Ancestry.com for Ruth Hirshfield and found dozens of possible candidates. Needing to narrow down the search, we discovered that the photography studio for Ruth's portrait was located in Brooklyn. Searching for "Ruth Hirshfield from New York" still left several candidates. Using the photographs posted on Ancestry.com, I chose one of the Ruth Hirshfields and sent a message to the family tree owner. Donna Eschen graciously replied. We compared notes and photographs of her aunt Ruth and Jerome's Ruth, but the evidence did not convince us that it was the same person. Finally, Donna related the story of how Ruth had known a young airman in World War II and shared a 1940s photograph of him dressed as an aviator. The airman in the image looked like Jerome, but we were not confident until Barbara Rotenberg found the same photograph in the Lesser family album!

We had found Jerome's Ruth, whom I had met three decades before as a young resident doctor in San Francisco.

The Chinese nightclub scene in the 1940s at the Forbidden City was brought to life through the contributions of Shari Yee Matsuura, the daughter of Coby Yee; Cynthia Yee; David Gee, the son of Larry Ching; and Patricia Nishimoto. The generosity of their time and spirit help to preserve this colorful part of San Francisco Chinatown's history.

Leonard Wollman's family, including April Grant, Eric Wollman, and Richard Smith, graciously shared Leonard's life stories and photographs before, during, and after World War II. Leonard's determined, tough, can-do attitude came through clearly in their stories of the father and uncle whom they referred to as the Major.

Andy Winnegar flew as an ARM2/C in a TBM Avenger in Composite Squadron Four (VC-4) on the *USS White Plains* with pilot Ltjg. Walter P. Owens and Marine observer Capt. Grady Gatlin. Andy provided rich details about the flights and missions of these aircraft during the battles for control of Saipan in June 1944. Three of the VC-4 TBM Avengers flew with Marine spotters, including Lt. Leonard Wollman. The United States Navy awarded Winnegar a Distinguished Flying Cross and seven Air Medals for his service in the Pacific theater in 1944.

I had the pleasure of meeting Fred Kossow in 2008 after my father passed away. Numerous phone calls and in-person interviews with Fred in Gridley, California, provided wonderfully rich and often humorous details about the war in the Central Pacific. Fred's recollection of events that had occurred sixty years earlier with the 804th Aviation Engineers was remarkable. His descriptions of Loren Low brought to life a young man and first-class "catskinner" I had never known. Fred was a storyteller, and I am indebted to his enthusiasm and generosity of spirit. I recently connected with Fred's family, including his children Mike and Susan, who shared photos and more stories. As often happens, the person being interviewed ultimately became a character in the story.

Bob Livingstone provided extensive technical review, editing, numerous World War II photographs, and personal anecdotes about life in Queensland and the War in the Southwest Pacific. Bob J. Tupa reviewed the manuscript and contributed photographs and access to records of the 90th Bombardment Group and Col. Art Rogers's memoirs. Both men are world-class experts in World War II aviation and the B-24 Liberator, and I am deeply indebted to their generous contributions.

I am thankful for a lifetime of colorful war stories told by my father, Loren I. Low, the Saipan aviation engineer. Loren's descriptions of the war in the Pacific, the events leading to his Silver Star, and his brother, the B-24 gunner, kept this world vividly alive for my siblings and me.

Finally, I am thankful for the encouragement and generous support from all of the readers of my first novel, *Three Coins*. Because of you, the story continues on the pages of *The All-American Crew*.

Initially, it was the diversity of these men's backgrounds that I found most striking. But in the end, I realized it was their unwavering commitment to one another and to a belief in the ideals of freedom that should inspire us today. They were boys and young men who willingly fought and died in war thousands of miles from home to protect a world and a way of life that is so easily taken for granted.

ABOUT THE AUTHOR

Our connections to the past are not always obvious, yet those connections define not only where we come from but also who we are and where we may be going.

Russell Low was born into a family that is intimately associated with the history of the American West. However, growing up in Central California, his life was more connected to hamburgers and sports than Chinese American history.

Russell N Low. Photograph by Ken Fong.

His connection to the past was born out of a fascination with a treasure trove of old family photos. Many were from the early days of black-and-white photography. Uncovering the stories behind these photographs became a decades-long passion whose fruits became the series of *Three Coins* novels.

Russell used skills he had honed as a physician, researcher, and educator in the search for these stories. Applying these skills to historical research, he uncovered previously unknown dramas involving human trafficking, kidnappings, romance, hop farmers, laundrymen, and war heroes.

Low's storytelling takes us on a journey, beginning with a nine-year-old slave girl who struggled to find freedom and romance. The three Chinese coins she threw into the water on her trip to Gum Saan in 1880 touched off a string of events that changed her life. Across decades and multiple generations, these ripples continue to change the world in ways she could never have imagined.

The All-American Crew tells the story of Ah Ying's grandsons, Stanley and Loren, in the Pacific during World War II. The saga begins by reconnecting Stanley to his family's beginnings in America at the Presbyterian Mission Home in San Francisco. His transformation from a Chinese American boy not yet old enough to vote or drink beer into a B-24 Liberator nose gunner is set against the lives of nine other American men who are his crew members.

Along the way, Stanley experiences loneliness, his first beer, his first romance, and the horrors of war. His older brother, Loren, joins the Aviation Engineers and builds the runways that the Liberators and fighters will need to win the war in the Pacific. The connections between these brothers and the events and people of World War II form the foundation of this third novel in the Three Coins series.

There are other remarkable connections between the story of the All-American Crew and the very beginnings of the Three Coins saga. When Ruth Hirshfield returned to San Francisco, she was drawn to Grace Cathedral on Nob Hill, living right across the street. Grace Cathedral is only a few blocks from 933 Sacramento Street, where Stan's grandmother, Ah Ying, lived at the Occidental Home for Girls after being rescued from a life of child slavery in 1886. When Ah Ying and her children fled the earthquake and fire in 1906, they trudged through the same neighborhood of Nob Hill that eight decades later became Ruth's new home.

Grace Cathedral itself is connected to the story of *Three Coins*. Charles Crocker of "The Big Four" had accumulated a fortune from Chinese workers' labor on the Transcontinental Railroad. In 1874, desiring a home with the best views in San Francisco, Crocker bought up a whole city block near the exclusive Nob Hill summit. Crocker purchased the property for $25,500 and built his 12,000-foot mansion. After the 1906 earthquake, his son, William Crocker, donated the property to the Episcopal Church. It is fitting that this land purchased with the sweat and blood of sixteen thousand Chinese workers, men like Stan's grandfather, Hung Lai Wah, became a place of worship, Grace Cathedral. Ruth was not aware of this history, but the coincidences and connections across decades and generations are remarkable.

Russell lives in La Jolla, California, with his wife, artist Carolyn Hesse-Low. Their family celebrates art, creativity, and exploration of things past and present. You may learn more about the author of *Three Coins* and *The All-American Crew* at russlow.com.

BOB LIVINGSTONE
TECHNICAL ADVISOR

Born in Brisbane, Queensland, Australia, in 1948, Bob Livingstone is intimately familiar with the land, the men, and the planes featured in *The All-American Crew*. An acknowledged world-class aviation expert specializing in World War II and the B-24 Liberator, Bob's expertise grew out of a lifetime in aviation.

He spent his first paycheck, in 1966, on flying lessons at Archerfield—a key military airfield for the Royal Australian Air Force during World War II—and has never looked back. After service in Vietnam with the Australian Army in 1969–70, he joined the Department of Civil Aviation as an air traffic controller. Bob worked for twenty years at Australia's busiest control tower, Bankstown, near Sydney, where he became the senior air traffic control officer. He spent another ten years at Sydney Kingsford Smith International Airport.

Bob's passion for flying and historical research has made him a highly sought-after expert in World War II aviation. His interest in the B-24 Liberator is personal, as his father, Warrant Officer R. M. Livingstone, was a Royal navigator on Royal Australian Air Force Liberators in World War II.

Bob's decades-long research into the B-24 Liberator culminated in 2014 with his service as the technical advisor for Angelina Jolie's movie adaptation of the book *Unbroken: A World War II Story of Survival, Resilience*, and *Redemption*, by Laura Hillenbrand.

Bob Livingstone. Courtesy of Bob Livingstone.

Bob's credits include numerous articles about aviation and the book *Under the Southern Cross: The B-24 Liberator in the South Pacific.*

When asked how he came to possess the wealth of information at his fingertips, he replied: "Just put in a lifetime of interest in aviation, WWII, flying aircraft, reading everything published, being part of aviation museums and historical societies, making model airplanes, hanging around airports, working in the industry (air traffic control), mixing with veterans, researching and writing articles and books on all aspects of aviation—easy!"

Warrant Officer R. Murray Livingstone, 19, July 1943. Courtesy of the Livingstone family.

APPENDIX

In grateful memory of

Sergeant Paul C. Vinson

WHO DIED IN THE SERVICE OF HIS COUNTRY

in the Pacific Area.

HE STANDS IN THE UNBROKEN LINE OF PATRIOTS WHO HAVE DARED TO DIE

THAT FREEDOM MIGHT LIVE, AND GROW, AND INCREASE ITS BLESSINGS.

FREEDOM LIVES, AND THROUGH IT, HE LIVES—

IN A WAY THAT HUMBLES THE UNDERTAKINGS OF MOST MEN

Harry Truman

PRESIDENT OF THE UNITED STATES OF AMERICA

Letter of appreciation sent by President Harry Truman to the family of Sergeant Paul C Vinson, acknowledging his ultimate sacrifice for his country. Courtesy of Joanne Davidson.

CITATION   OF HONOR

UNITED STATES   ARMY AIR FORCES

Sergeant Paul C. Vinson

WHO GAVE HIS LIFE IN THE PERFORMANCE OF HIS DUTY

January 8, 1946

HE LIVED TO BEAR HIS COUNTRY'S ARMS. HE DIED TO SAVE ITS HONOR. HE WAS A SOLDIER . . . AND HE KNEW A SOLDIER'S DUTY. HIS SACRIFICE WILL HELP TO KEEP AGLOW THE FLAMING TORCH THAT LIGHTS OUR LIVES . . . THAT MILLIONS YET UNBORN MAY KNOW THE PRICELESS JOY OF LIBERTY. AND WE WHO PAY HIM HOMAGE, AND REVERE HIS MEMORY, IN SOLEMN PRIDE REDEDICATE OURSELVES TO A COMPLETE FULFILLMENT OF THE TASK FOR WHICH HE SO GALLANTLY HAS PLACED HIS LIFE UPON THE ALTAR OF MAN'S FREEDOM.

H. H. ARNOLD
General of the Army
Commanding General, Army Air Forces

Citation of Honor for Paul C. Vinson, 1946. Courtesy of Robert Prescott.

Silver Star awarded to Loren I. Low, Saipan, 1944. Courtesy of the Low family.

Aviator's Wings and Air Medal awarded to Clifford S. Low, New Guinea 1943. Courtesy of the Low family.

Purple Heart awarded to Paul C. Vinson in 1943. Courtesy of Robert Prescott.

Air Medal with two Oak Clusters awarded to Earl Byrd 1944. Courtesy of Bob Byrd.

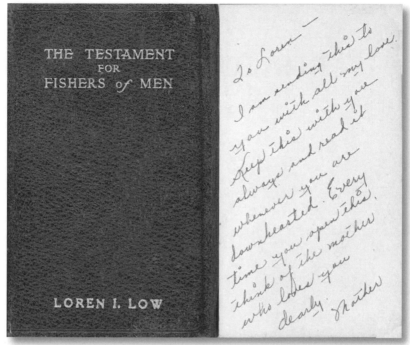

The messages in the New Testament Bibles sent to her sons in the Pacific
Theater show the love and concern of a mother sending her boys off to war.
Courtesy of Christopher Low, Patricia Gowland, and the Low family collection.

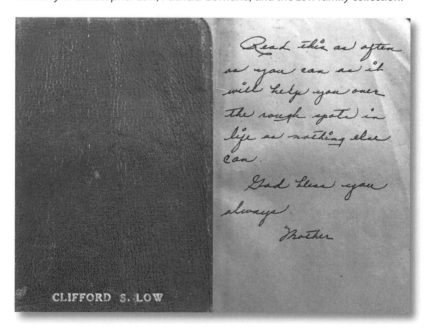

BIBLIOGRAPHY

Ambrose, Stephen E. *The Wild Blue: The Men and Boys Who Flew the B-24s Over Germany 1944–1945*. New York: Simon & Schuster, 2001.

Ashcroft, Bruce. Staff Historian, HQ AETC Office of History and Research. "We Wanted Wings: A History of the Aviation Cadet Program," 2005. https://media.defense.gov/2015/Sep/11/2001329827/-1/-1/0/AFD-150911-028.pdfhttps://media.defense.gov/2015/ Sep/11/2001329827/-1/-1/0/AFD-150911-028.pdf.

Callander, Bruce D. "The Aces that History Forgot." *Air Force* magazine, September 5, 2008.

Chen, William, ed. *Unsung Heroes: Recognizing and Honoring Chinese American World War II Veterans: Congressional Gold Medal Recipients*. Boston, MA: Chinese Historical Society of New England, 2020.

Chinn, Bob. *The Other Side of Paradise. Volume One*. Los Angeles, CA: Rare Bird Books, 2016.

Ciardi, John. *Saipan: The War Diary of John Ciardi*. Fayetteville: The University of Arkansas Press, 1968.

Engineering the Impossible. Brig Gen FO Carroll. Coral Nests for the Superforts. *Popular Mechanics*, April 1945.

Ennels, Jerome A., Robert B. Kane, and Silvano A. Wueschner. *Cradle of Airpower. An Illustrated history of Maxwell Air Force Base, 1918–2018*. Montgomery, AL: Air University Press, 2018. https://www.airuniversity.af.edu/Portals/10/AUPress/Books/B_0153_ Ennels_ Cradle_of_Airpower.pdf.

Faulkner, Tom. *Flying with the Fifteenth Air Force: A B-24 Pilot's Missions from Italy During WWII*. Denton: University of North Texas Press, 2018.

Gailey, Harry A. *MacArthur's Victory:. The War in New Guinea 1943–1944*.

New York: Presidio Press, 2004.

Gamble, Bruce. *Target: Rabaul: The Allied Siege of Japan's Most Infamous Stronghold, March 1943–August 1945*. Minneapolis, MN: Zenith Press, 2013.

Gerrish, Lt. Col. Ken. *The First Fighters in New Guinea 1942–1944*. 16mm color home movies. National Archives. Online: www.youtube.com/watch?v=F53Mo374edg

Goldberg, Harold J. *D-Day in the Pacific: The Battle of Saipan*. Bloomington: Indiana University Press, 2007.

Griggs, Alan L. *Flying Flak Alley: Personal Accounts of World War II Bomber Crew Combat*. Jefferson, NC: McFarland & Company Inc., 2008.

"History of the USS *White Plains* CVE-6." Compiled October 8, 1945. https://www.navsource.org/archives/03/066.htmhives/03/066. htm.

Howard, Clive, and Joe Whitley. *One Damned Island After Another: The Saga of the Seventh Air Force in World War II*. Chapel Hill: The University of North Carolina Press, 1946.

Kaiser, Fred. *A Teenager's View of World War II: The Adventures of a Young Airman in the Army Air Force 1942 to 1945*. New York: iUniverse, Inc., 2000.

Kaufman, Isidor. *American Jews in World War II*. New York: Dial Press, 1947.

Lambert, John W. *The Pineapple Air Force: Pearl Harbor to Tokyo*. Atglen, PA: Schiffer Publishing, 2006.

Leckie, Robert. *Strong Men Armed: The United States Marines vs. Japan*. New York: Da Capo Press, 1962.

Lefemine, James E. *Unit History of the 400th Bombardment Squadron "Jolly Rogers" Reprint: The Black Pirates of the 90th Heavy Bombardment Group*. CreateSpace, 2014.

Livingstone, Bob. *Under the Southern Cross: The B-24 Liberator in the South Pacific*. Nashville, TN: Turner Publishing, 1998.

McDonald Jr., Lt. J. M., Sgt. Earl V. Houck, and Cpt. Henry C. Holliday. Unit History. 90th Bombardment Group. December 19, 1945. Declassified IAW EO12958.

McMurria James. A. *Trial and Triumph*. 1992.

Newton, Wesley P. *Montgomery in the Good War. Portrait of a Southern City 1939–-1946*. Tuscaloosa: University of Alabama Press, 2000.

O'Brien, Francis A. *Battling for Saipan*. New York: Ballantine Books, 2003.

Pierce, Marlyn R. "Earning Their Wings: Accidents and Fatalities in the United States Army Air Forces During Flight Training in World War Two." PhD diss., Kansas State University, 2013. Online: https://core. ac.uk/download/pdf/18529342.pdf.

Preflight Class of 43-J. US Army Air Forces Corps of Aviation Cadets. Pre- flight Sschool for Pilots. Aviation Maxwell Field. Montgomery, AL: Cadet Social Fund, Maxwell Field, 1943.

Ralph, Barry. *The Crash of Little Eva: The Ultimate World War II Survivor Story.* New York: Pelican Publishing, 2006.

Robinson, Pat. *The Fight for New Guinea.* New York: Random House, 1943.

Rogers, Arthur H. *Jolly Rogers: The 90th Bomb Group in WWII.* February 1944.

Rottman, Gordon L. *Saipan & Tinian 1944: Piercing the Japanese Empire.* Oxford, UK: Osprey Publishing, 2004.

Rust, Kenn C. *Seventh Air Force Story.* Historical Aviation Album, 1979.

Scearce, Phil. *Finish Forty and Home: The Untold World War II Story of B-24s in the Pacific.* Denton: University of North Texas Press, 2012.

The Jolly Rogers: The 90th Bombardment Group in the Southwest Pacific 1942– 1944 (Schiffer Military History). Atglen, PA: Schiffer Publishing Ltd., 1997.

Winnegar, Andy. "66 Missions with VC-4." *Market Street Geezers: Who and What We Remember* (blog). March 19, 2019. https:// marketstreetgeezers.com/andy-winnegar/

Woods Jr., Wiley O. Jr. *Legacy of the 90th Bombardment Group: The Jolly Rogers.* Nashville, TN: Turner Publishing, 1994.

Wright, J. L. *The Search That Never Was: The Untold Truth about the 1948–49 Search for World War II American Personnel Missing in Action in the South Pacific.* Houston, TX: Strategic Book Publishing, 2013.

Wrinn, Daniel. *Operation Forager: 1944 Battle for Saipan, Invasion Tinian, and Recapture of Guam* (WW2 Pacific Military History Series). Independently published, 2021.

INDEX

C

BOOKS IN THE THREE COINS SERIES

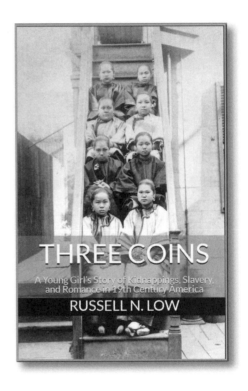

Three Coins: A Young Girl's Story of Kidnappings, Slavery, and Romance in 19th-Century America by Russell N. Low

Ah Ying is only nine years old when she awakens in the hold of a ship bound for America. Sold by her family for a few Chinese yuan, she is beaten and burned as a child slave in San Francisco's Chinatown. Her defiant survival allows Ah Ying to take control of her life, as she finds romance, is rescued by missionaries, and is given a new life at the Mission Home. Life is good until her rescuers become her captors and she is again forced to flee to be with her beloved Gee Sung. What ensues is a race between her love for Gee Sung, the Tong highbinders who want to enslave her, and the Presbyterian missionaries who want to save her soul. *Three Coins* is based on a true story that touches upon the themes of human trafficking, immigration, cultural and racial discrimination, violence, and romance that are as relevant today as they were 140 years ago.

Available on Amazon: www.amazon.com/dp/1796601349.